BEST of the BEST from
Louisiana
COOKBOOK III

Selected Recipes from Louisiana's
FAVORITE COOKBOOKS

Louisiana's majestic trees with hanging moss

BEST of the BEST from
Louisiana
COOKBOOK III

Selected Recipes from Louisiana's
FAVORITE COOKBOOKS

Edited by
Gwen McKee and Barbara Moseley

QUAIL RIDGE PRESS
Preserving America's Food Heritage

Recipe Collection ©2014 Quail Ridge Press, Inc.

Recipes reprinted with permission and all rights reserved under the name of the cookbooks, organizations, or individuals listed in the "Contributing Cookbooks" section. No part of this book may be reproduced or utilized in any form without written permission from the publisher.

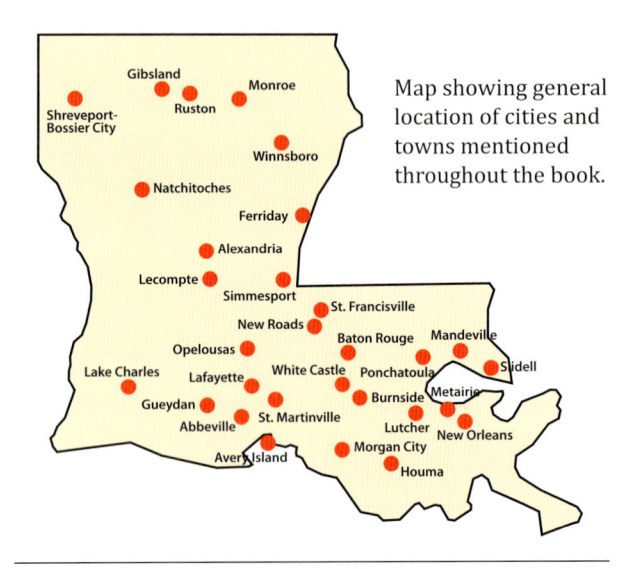

Map showing general location of cities and towns mentioned throughout the book.

Library of Congress Cataloging-in-Publication Data

Best of the best from Louisiana cookbook III: selected recipes from Louisiana's favorite cookbooks / edited by Gwen McKee and Barbara Moseley .
  p. cm. — (Best of the best state cookbook series)
    Includes index.
    ISBN 978-1-934193-97-6
  1. Cooking, American—Louisiana style. I. McKee, Gwen, editor of compilation. II. Moseley, Barbara, editor of compilation. III. Title: Selected recipes from Louisiana's favorite cookbooks.
       TX715.2.L68B472 2013
       641.59763--dc23   2013023269
                                                            CIP

ISBN-13: 978-1-934193-97-6
First printing, October 2014 • Second, September 2015
Printed in the United States of America

Front cover: St. Louis Cathedral

Food photos and styling by Christian and Elise Stella

QUAIL RIDGE PRESS
P. O. Box 123 • Brandon, MS 39043 • 1-800-343-1783
info@quailridge.com • www.quailridge.com
www.facebook.com/cookbookladies

Contents

Preface 6

Beverages & Appetizers 9

Bread & Breakfast 35

Soups, Stews & Chilis 55

Salads 75

Vegetables 89

Pasta, Rice, Etc. 107

Poultry 125

Meats 141

Seafood 163

Cakes 191

Cookies & Candies 211

Pies & Other Desserts 227

Contributing Cookbooks 248

Index of Recipes 261

The Quest for the Best 267

Preface

*I*n 1983, Barbara Moseley and I traveled all over Louisiana in search of really good cookbooks containing those special recipes that have made Louisiana famous for its cooking. We happily sampled our way around the state, and in 1984, proudly introduced *Best of the Best from Louisiana* at the World's Fair in New Orleans. It was a hit from the start, and continues to be the best-selling cookbook in our BEST OF THE BEST STATE COOKBOOK SERIES.

By 1998, so many new Louisiana cookbooks had been published, that we once again set out to capture the expanding wealth of great cooking in the Pelican State. *Best of the Best from Louisiana II* was introduced to rave reviews with another collection of serious-good recipes. It has also become one of the best-selling cookbooks in our state cookbook series. (This series now includes all fifty states. A brief history on how this series was developed is included on page 267.)

After sixteen years, it's time for *Best of the Best from Louisiana III*. In this third edition, my co-editor Barbara Moseley and I wanted to continue the tradition of collecting those incredible Louisiana recipes from the many new cookbooks we discovered. We have added full-color food photographs, as well as historical facts and cultural trivia that capture the unique features of Louisiana, such as the historical town of Natchitoches, the oldest city of the Louisiana Purchase, founded in 1814 and celebrating its Tri-Centennial.

Read the tribute to *River Road Recipes*, the best-selling community cookbook series of all time. First published in 1959, this cookbook helped me as a young bride to bring my Baton Rouge heritage with me all the way to Chicago—where I had to take two buses

PREFACE

and an L-train to find frozen okra to make gumbo, but well worth the effort. Our parents and dear friends sent us pecans, and when I made pralines, it astounded everybody who tasted one. One of my bosses wanted to set me up in a business—Gwen's Candies. After about my twentieth batch, I decided maybe it would be best to just share my recipe and let others make their own . . . and I've been sharing recipes ever since. (Try Pat's Pralines and Creole Pralines on page 223.) I've always been proud of my Louisiana heritage . . . and I always will be.

Most recipes begin in someone's kitchen, and the best ones that get passed around literally by word of mouth may end up in a cookbook, and we do our best to find them for all to enjoy. Thanks to all the lovely people who allowed us to share a few of their favorite recipes (see "Contributing Cookbooks" section on page 248).

For the third time, it has been a joy to gather more favorite Louisiana recipes from seasoned Louisiana cooks, and to share with you fascinating facts, historical data, unique places to visit, and things to see and do in the Pelican State. You'll get to know a lot of Louisianians in the process—and I predict you will love it all.

Don't wait for Mardi Gras, or a Saints game; use any of the thousands of other excuses Louisianians come up with to gather together for good times with good friends, always over good food. As the Cajun French say, "Laissez les bon temps rouler." Let the good times roll. Or simply say, "Come on, y'all . . . let's eat!"

Gwen McKee

P.S. There are so many beautiful people, places, and events in Louisiana, and we were able to just touch on them in our photos and captions—there is so much more. We invite you to come see and explore and taste for yourself. Louisiana is fun—and delicious!

Street car, New Orleans

8

Beverages & Appetizers

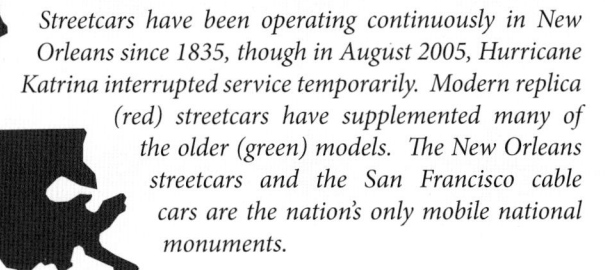

Minted Ice Tea 10	Jalapeño Cheese Squares ..20
Almond Tea........................10	Spinach Cheese Squares ...20
Red Rooster 11	Baked Brie..........................21
NOLA Hot Buttered Rum..11	Checkerboard Cheese........22
New Orleans Milk Punch..11	Atchafalaya Cheese Straws 23
Coffee KEDM......................12	
Café au Lait Punch............12	Baked Cheese Petits Fours 24
Andouille Cheese Dip........13	Lirette's Pesto....................24
Hot Bacon and Swiss Dip..13	Shrimp-Boursin Mousse Canapés with Fresh Thyme.............................25
Hot Spinach and Oyster Dip..................................14	
Cool As a Cucumber Dip...15	Crawfish Saganaki 26
Shrimp Dip 15	Cajun Hot Bites..................27
Rosalie's Tangy Shrimp Dip 16	Muffuletta Croquettes.......28
	Cajun Stuffed Mushrooms30
Holiday Pecan Dip 17	Spicy Catfish Puffs 31
Chocolate Chip Cream Cheese Ball....................17	Alligator Balls.....................32
	Artichoke Toast..................32
Onion Soufflé.....................18	Marlyn's Trash...................33
Sweet Potato Cheese Pâté..18	

Streetcars have been operating continuously in New Orleans since 1835, though in August 2005, Hurricane Katrina interrupted service temporarily. Modern replica (red) streetcars have supplemented many of the older (green) models. The New Orleans streetcars and the San Francisco cable cars are the nation's only mobile national monuments.

BEVERAGES & APPETIZERS

Minted Ice Tea

2 quarts water
4 family-size tea bags
10 mint leaves
1½ cups sugar
1 (6-ounce) can frozen
   lemonade
Cold water
Fresh mint sprigs for garnish

Bring 2 quarts water to boil in saucepan. Remove from heat and add tea bags. Let steep 15 minutes. Remove tea bags and discard. Stir in mint leaves, sugar, and lemonade. Pour into a 1-gallon container, and add enough cold water to make 1 gallon. Serve over ice and garnish with mint. Makes 1 gallon.

Crescent City Collection

Almond Tea

2 cups boiling water
3 tea bags
6 tablespoons lemon juice
   concentrate
1 cup sugar
1½ teaspoons almond extract
1 teaspoon vanilla extract
6 cups cold water

Pour boiling water over tea bags in large drink container. Steep to desired strength. Remove tea bags. Add lemon juice concentrate, sugar, almond extract, and vanilla. Stir till sugar dissolves. Add cold water. Refrigerate till chilled. Serve over ice. Makes 2 quarts.

Secret Ingredients

BEVERAGES & APPETIZERS

Red Rooster

3 cups orange juice
3 cups cranberry juice
3 cups vodka

Combine all ingredients in large shallow freezer container. Freeze 24 hours, or till slushy. Serve as a slush. Serves 10.

Something to Talk About

NOLA Hot Buttered Rum

1 stick real unsalted butter, softened
2 cups brown sugar
1 teaspoon ground cinnamon
½ teaspoon nutmeg
Pinch of ground cloves
Captain Morgan's Spiced Rum
Boiling water

In bowl, cream butter, sugar, cinnamon, nutmeg, and cloves. Refrigerate till firm. Spoon 2½ tablespoons butter mixture into each mug. Pour 3 ounces rum into each mug (filling halfway). Top with boiling water, stir well, and serve immediately.

A Confederacy of Scrumptious

New Orleans Milk Punch

1½ cups milk
1½ cups half-and-half
½ cup white crème de cacao
½ cup bourbon
2 tablespoons confectioners' sugar
2 egg whites
Cinnamon to taste

Combine all ingredients, except cinnamon, in blender container. Process till frothy. Pour over cracked ice in 4 drink glasses. Sprinkle with cinnamon. Serves 4.

Secret Ingredients

BEVERAGES & APPETIZERS

Coffee KEDM

1 tablespoon hazelnut liqueur
1 tablespoon chocolate liqueur
1 tablespoon coffee liqueur
2 tablespoons Irish cream liqueur
1 tablespoon brandy (optional)
1–1½ cups freshly brewed dark roast coffee
Whipped cream

Divide liqueurs into 2 large coffee cups or mugs. Add hot coffee. Top with plenty of whipped cream. Serves 2.

Variations & Improvisations

Editor's Extra: KEDM is a public radio station in Monroe.

Café au Lait Punch

A favorite for ladies' luncheons. Coffee extract may be substituted for the strong coffee when making this a mid-morning treat.

1 cup sugar
1 cup dark roast coffee or coffee extract, room temperature
1 liter ginger ale, room temperature
1 liter club soda, room temperature
2 cups half-and-half
½ gallon vanilla ice cream, softened

Combine sugar, coffee, ginger ale, club soda, and half-and-half in large punch bowl; mix well. Fold in ice cream, and stir to combine. Makes 12–14 (2-cup) servings.

Warm Welcomes (River Road Recipes IV)

BEVERAGES & APPETIZERS

Andouille Cheese Dip

1 pound andouille sausage, chopped
1 small onion, chopped
1 (10¾-ounce) can cream of mushroom soup
1 (1-pound) box Velveeta cheese, cubed

In saucepan, sauté andouille and onion. Add soup and cheese. Heat on low heat till cheese is melted, stirring often. Serve in heated chafing dish or small crockpot with tortilla chips or Ritz Crackers. Serves 10.

Hey, Good Lookin', What's Cooking?

Hot Bacon and Swiss Dip

1 (8-ounce) package cream cheese, softened
1 cup mayonnaise
1 cup shredded Swiss cheese
4 green onions, chopped
½ teaspoon Tabasco
8 slices bacon, crisp-cooked, crumbled
1 cup butter cracker crumbs
Paprika to taste
Chopped fresh parsley to taste

Combine cream cheese, mayonnaise, Swiss cheese, green onions, and Tabasco in mixing bowl, and beat till combined, scraping bowl occasionally. Spread cream cheese mixture in a 2½-cup baking dish or 9-inch round baking dish, and sprinkle with bacon and cracker crumbs.

Bake at 350° for 15–20 minutes, or till bubbly. Sprinkle lightly with paprika and parsley, and serve with assorted party crackers. Serves 10–12.

Mardi Gras to Mistletoe

BEVERAGES & APPETIZERS

Hot Spinach and Oyster Dip

2 tablespoons olive oil
½ cup finely chopped onion
½ cup minced celery
2 tablespoons minced garlic
1 (10-ounce) package frozen chopped spinach, cooked, drained
1 (8-ounce) package cream cheese, softened
¼ cup skim milk
1 pint oysters, coarsely chopped with their liquor
Salt, pepper, and hot sauce to taste

Heat olive oil in a nonstick skillet. Add onion, celery, and garlic, and sauté till soft, but not browned. Place mixture in a blender or food processor along with spinach, cream cheese, and milk. Process until smooth. Pour into a saucepan. Cook over medium heat till heated through, stirring constantly. Add oysters and their liquor. Cook 10 minutes, or till oysters are cooked through, stirring constantly. Season with salt, pepper, and hot sauce. Spoon into a heated serving dish. Surround with toasted slices of French bread or crackers. Serves 20–30.

Crescent City Collection

In Louisiana, early French settlers were reported to have harvested oysters. As oysters rose in popularity, their collection, sale, and distribution also expanded. Louisiana is the largest producer of oysters in the United States. Louisiana oysters vary considerably in salt content. In months of high rainfall, oysters may be less salty in taste, especially in spring. Oysters are largest during the cooler months—the oyster builds up an insulating blanket that yields a larger oyster. Oysters are available year-round in Louisiana, so you will never have to go without.

BEVERAGES & APPETIZERS

Cool As a Cucumber Dip

1 (8-ounce) package cream cheese, softened
1 cup mayonnaise
¾ cup sour cream
1 tablespoon Worcestershire
1 tablespoon dill weed
¼ cup chopped green onions
Salt and pepper to taste
3–4 cucumbers, peeled, seeded, chopped

Combine cream cheese, mayonnaise, sour cream, Worcestershire, dill weed, and green onions in a bowl; mix well. Season with salt and pepper. Fold in cucumbers. Chill, covered, for 1 day before serving. Serves 16.

Marshes to Mansions

Shrimp Dip

1 (8-ounce) package cream cheese, softened
¾ cup mayonnaise
2 tablespoons French salad dressing
2 tablespoons lemon juice
3 cloves garlic, finely chopped
2 ribs celery, finely chopped
1 teaspoon black pepper
1 pound boiled shrimp, seasoned
½ green bell pepper, finely chopped
½ onion, finely chopped

Combine cream cheese and mayonnaise, mixing well. Blend in next 5 ingredients. Chop shrimp, bell pepper, and onion in food processor to desired consistency. Add to cream cheese mixture, blending well. Refrigerate overnight for best results. Serve with chips or crackers of choice. Makes 3 cups.

Down the Bayou . . . and Back Again

BEVERAGES & APPETIZERS

Rosalie's Tangy Shrimp Dip

2 quarts water
1 tablespoon liquid crab boil
3 tablespoons salt
1 medium onion, chopped
1½ lemons
1 pound whole medium shrimp
1 (8-ounce) package cream cheese, softened
1 tablespoon horseradish

Place water, crab boil, salt, onion, and unsqueezed lemon halves in large saucepan. Bring water to a boil; add shrimp. Boil 15 minutes. If shrimp are small, boil 5 minutes less; if large, 5 minutes longer. Turn off heat; let stand 5 minutes. Drain all water, except ¼ cup. Peel cooled shrimp and chop finely. Combine cream cheese, shrimp, and pulp from inside boiled lemons. Add horseradish and reserved ¼ cup shrimp water. Blend and refrigerate. Serve cold with chips, raw vegetables, or as filling for stuffed tomatoes and jalapeño peppers.

Pots, Pans, and Pioneers III

Kisatchie National Forest

With some 604,000 acres of public land, more than half of which is vital longleaf pine and flatwoods vegetation, Kisatchie National Forest is one of the largest pieces of natural landscape in Louisiana. Located in the forested piney hills and hardwood bottoms of seven central and northern parishes, it supports many rare plant and animal species. The forest has more than 40 developed recreation sites, numerous campsites, and over 100 miles of trails for hiking, mountain biking, and horseback riding.

BEVERAGES & APPETIZERS

Holiday Pecan Dip

1½ cups chopped pecans
2 cups finely shredded Cheddar cheese
6 green onions, chopped with stems
½ cup mayonnaise (or more)
½ cup red pepper jelly
½ teaspoon MSG seasoning
½ teaspoon ground red pepper

Roast chopped pecans briefly in skillet on medium heat to bring out flavor; cool. In a medium bowl, mix pecans, Cheddar cheese, and green onions. Add approximately ½ cup mayonnaise or enough to hold mixture together. Mix well, and pat into 8x10-inch shallow serving dish; refrigerate. Before serving, cover top of dip with red pepper jelly. Sprinkle seasoning and red pepper over top. Serve with crackers.

Steel Magnolias in the Kitchen

Chocolate Chip Cream Cheese Ball

1 stick butter, softened
1 (8-ounce) package cream cheese, softened
¼ teaspoon vanilla
¾ cup confectioners' sugar
2 tablespoons packed brown sugar
¾ cup miniature semisweet chocolate chips
¾ cup finely chopped pecans

Cream butter, cream cheese, and vanilla in mixing bowl till light and fluffy. Add confectioners' sugar and brown sugar gradually, beating just till smooth. Stir in chocolate chips. Chill, covered 2 hours. Shape into a ball on a large piece of plastic wrap. Cover with plastic wrap and chill 1 hour longer. Roll ball in chopped pecans just before serving. Serve with regular or chocolate-flavored graham crackers. Serves 15–20.

Something to Talk About

BEVERAGES & APPETIZERS

Onion Soufflé

24 ounces cream cheese, softened
½ cup mayonnaise
1 (12-ounce) package frozen chopped onions, thawed, drained
2 cups grated Parmesan cheese
½ cup chopped artichoke hearts, drained (optional)
Dash of Creole seasoning or cayenne pepper (optional)

Combine cream cheese and mayonnaise in bowl; mix till smooth. Add onions, Parmesan cheese, artichokes, and seasoning; mix well. Spoon into greased 8-inch baking dish. Bake at 400° for 10–15 minutes, or till bubbly. Serve with corn chips. Serves 12–15.

Secret Ingredients

Sweet Potato Cheese Pâté

1 (8-ounce) package cream cheese, softened
2 cups cold mashed sweet potatoes
¼ cup finely chopped onion
2 tablespoons finely chopped jalapeño chile
1 garlic clove, minced
1 teaspoon seasoned salt
1 teaspoon Worcestershire
2 teaspoons Louisiana hot sauce
¼ cup chopped pecans

Beat cream cheese and sweet potatoes in a mixing bowl till smooth. Add onion, jalapeño, garlic, seasoned salt, Worcestershire, hot sauce, and pecans; mix well. Chill, covered, 4 hours, or until easy to handle. Shape into a ball. Chill, covered, 4 hours, or till firm. Serve with assorted crackers, breadsticks, or vegetables for dipping. Makes about 3 cups.

Roux To Do

BEVERAGES & APPETIZERS

Onion Soufflé

BEVERAGES & APPETIZERS

Jalapeño Cheese Squares

4 cups shredded Cheddar cheese
4 eggs, beaten
1 teaspoon minced onion
4 whole jalapeño chiles, sliced, patted dry

Combine cheese, eggs, onion, and jalapeños in a bowl, and mix well. Pour into an 8x8-inch baking pan. Bake at 350° for 30 minutes. Cut into small squares, and serve at room temperature. Makes 50 squares.

Crescent City Collection

Spinach Cheese Squares

3 cups shredded Monterey Jack cheese
2½ cups shredded sharp Cheddar cheese
20 ounces frozen chopped spinach, thawed and squeezed dry
6 eggs
Cajun or Creole seasoning to taste

Preheat oven to 350°. Combine Monterey Jack cheese and Cheddar cheese in bowl. Stir in spinach. Add eggs and seasoning; mix well. Pour into greased 9x13-inch baking pan. Bake 40 minutes. Let cool; cut into desired-size servings. Serves 8.

Something to Talk About

BEVERAGES & APPETIZERS

Baked Brie

1 Pillsbury Refrigerated Pie Crust
1 jar raspberry preserves, divided
1 cup broken pecans, divided
1 cup brown sugar, divided
1 (8-ounce) round Brie cheese
2 tablespoons butter, melted

Preheat oven to 350°. Unroll pie shell and place in pie plate. Put a heaping tablespoon or more of raspberry preserves on pie shell. Layer ½ cup pecans and ½ cup brown sugar over preserves. Place Brie on top of mixture. Bring up all sides of pie shell to cover contents. Turn over and brush melted butter on top of pie shell, to brown it. Repeat raspberry preserves, ½ cup brown sugar, and ½ cup pecans and place on top of shell. Put Brie in oven and wait till it starts to melt, usually 20–30 minutes. If not browned enough at end, put under broiler for a minute or so.

Vedros Family Recipes

Bonnie & Clyde

Clyde Barrow and Bonnie Parker were part of the notorious fugitive Barrow Gang, which went on a two-year crime spree in Texas and several midwestern states. In May 1934, they were finally ambushed by a posse on Highway 154 between Sailes and Gibsland in Bienville Parish, east of Shreveport. Every May, Gibsland holds the Bonnie and Clyde Festival to commemorate the event. The 1967 movie *Bonnie & Clyde* starring Warren Beatty and Faye Dunaway was a romanticized account of their sprees. It was nominated for eight Oscars and won two.

BEVERAGES & APPETIZERS

Checkerboard Cheese

½ cup extra virgin olive oil
½ cup white wine vinegar
1 (2-ounce) jar diced pimento, drained
¼ cup chopped parsley
3 tablespoons minced green onions
3 garlic cloves, minced
1 teaspoon sugar
1 teaspoon dried basil
½ teaspoon salt
½ teaspoon freshly ground pepper
8 ounces sharp Cheddar cheese, chilled
8 ounces cream cheese, chilled
8 ounces Monterey Jack cheese, chilled

Combine olive oil, vinegar, pimento, parsley, green onions, garlic, sugar, basil, salt, and pepper in a jar with a tight-fitting lid. Secure lid to jar, and shake to mix well.

Cut Cheddar cheese into halves lengthwise. Cut each half into slices ¼ inch thick. Repeat with cream cheese and Monterey Jack cheese. Arrange Cheddar cheese, cream cheese, and Monterey Jack cheese alternately on edge in a shallow baking dish or lipped serving tray to form a checkerboard pattern. Shake marinade, and pour over cheese arrangement. Marinate, covered, in refrigerator at least 8 hours before serving. Serves 24.

Roux To Do

BEVERAGES & APPETIZERS

Atchafalaya Cheese Straws

1¼ cups shredded Cheddar cheese
¾ cup all-purpose flour
½ stick unsalted butter, softened
1 large egg yolk, beaten
½ teaspoon cayenne
Creole or Cajun seasoning to taste

Preheat oven to 325°. Mix together cheese and flour with your hands. Work the butter in with your hands. Add egg yolk and seasonings, and work in with your hands. Knead the dough for a few minutes till it is a nice shiny ball. Roll out to a ¼-inch thickness. Cut into 2-inch strips, and place on ungreased cookie sheet. Bake 15–20 minutes, or till golden orange. Let cool. Store any remaining cheese straws in an airtight container.

Note: Also good with Gruyère, Comté, or Beaufort cheese.

Good Gumbo Weather

Battle of New Orleans

The War of 1812 was a 32-month military conflict between the United States and Great Britain, along with its remaining North American colonies and its Indian allies. The outcome resolved many issues that remained from the American War of Independence. The United States declared war against Great Britain in 1812 for several reasons, including trade restrictions, the impressments of American merchant sailors into the Royal Navy, British support of American Indian tribes against American expansion, along with other issues.

A British invasion force sailed to Louisiana, and was met and defeated with heavy British losses at the Battle of New Orleans. The victory, under the leadership of General Andrew Jackson, boosted the confidence of the new nation and helped to propel Jackson into the White House where he served two terms. The anniversary of the battle (January 8th) was celebrated as a national holiday for many years, and continues to be commemorated in south Louisiana.

BEVERAGES & APPETIZERS

Baked Cheese Petits Fours

2 (6-ounce) jars Old English sharp cheese spread, softened
2 sticks butter, softened
1 tablespoon Tabasco
1 tablespoon Worcestershire
2 tablespoons dill weed
½ teaspoon onion juice
½ teaspoon onion salt
2 loaves sliced white bread, crusts trimmed

Preheat oven to 350°. Beat cheese spread and butter together in mixing bowl till smooth. Add Tabasco, Worcestershire, dill weed, onion juice, and onion salt, and beat till smooth. Spread a thin layer of cheese filling on 3 slices of bread. Stack slices on top of each other. Cut stack into 4 quarters. Spread cheese filling over sides of each quarter. Repeat procedure with remaining filling and bread. Freeze squares on a baking sheet for 1 hour. Bake 15–20 minutes, or till light brown. Serve hot. Serves 15.

Something to Talk About

Lirette's Pesto

1 cup firmly packed fresh parsley
½ cup firmly packed fresh basil
2 cloves garlic
¼ teaspoon salt
¼ cup chopped walnuts or pecans
½ cup grated Parmesan cheese
⅓ cup extra virgin olive oil

Place parsley, basil, garlic and salt in food processor. Cover and process till blended. Add nuts and process again. Add Parmesan cheese and process shortly. Drizzle oil through hole in cover while processing. If necessary, add a little more oil to get a pasty consistency. Spread on baguettes and heat in 350° oven till toasty, or mix with your favorite pasta.

Pots, Pans, and Pioneers V

BEVERAGES & APPETIZERS

Shrimp-Boursin Mousse Canapés with Fresh Thyme

- 2 teaspoons canola oil
- 4 ounces shrimp, peeled, deveined
- Pinch of kosher salt, or to taste
- Pinch of pepper, or to taste
- ½ teaspoon minced shallot
- ⅛ teaspoon minced garlic
- ½ (5-ounce) package Boursin cheese
- ⅛ teaspoon thyme leaves
- 24 Canapé Bases
- ¼ teaspoon thyme leaves for garnish

Heat 10-inch sauté pan over medium-high heat till hot, and add canola oil. Heat till oil is hot. Add shrimp, and season with a pinch of salt and pepper. Cook 3–4 minutes. Stir in shallot and garlic and cook for 1 minute, or just till shrimp are cooked through, stirring constantly. Combine shrimp mixture, cheese, and ⅛ teaspoon thyme to a food processor. Process till smooth, scraping side of bowl as needed. Season to taste with salt and pepper. Spread the tops of the Canapé Bases evenly with mousse and arrange on a serving platter. Garnish with ¼ teaspoon thyme and serve immediately. Makes ½ cup plus 2 tablespoons mousse.

CANAPÉ BASES:

- 4 slices bread, crusts trimmed
- 2 tablespoons olive oil
- Kosher salt and pepper to taste

Place oven rack in middle position, and then preheat oven to 325°. Cut bread slices into 16 rounds using a 1½-inch round cutter. Arrange rounds in a single layer on baking sheet; do not allow edges to touch. Brush tops with olive oil and sprinkle lightly with salt and pepper. Bake 10 minutes. Rotate baking sheet and bake 10 minutes longer, or till golden brown. Remove to wire rack to cool. Makes 16.

Cooking with a Private Chef

BEVERAGES & APPETIZERS

Crawfish Saganaki

½ cup olive oil
1 large onion, finely chopped
1 medium green bell pepper, finely chopped
2–3 large cloves garlic, minced
2 large tomatoes, peeled, seeded, finely chopped
½ cup finely chopped fresh parsley
1 teaspoon red pepper flakes (optional)
2 pounds peeled Louisiana crawfish tails
2 tablespoons lemon juice
Salt and black pepper to taste
1 cup crumbled feta cheese
2 baguettes, sliced ½ inch thick

Heat olive oil in a large, deep skillet or Dutch oven. Add onion and green pepper; sauté over medium-low heat till very soft, about 15 minutes. Add garlic and sauté 1 minute longer. Add chopped tomatoes and sauté 5 minutes, stirring frequently. Mix in parsley and red pepper flakes, if desired.

Put crawfish tails along with their juices into tomato mixture. Stir well and sauté on medium-high about 5 minutes, stirring frequently, till crawfish tails are fully cooked. Add lemon juice, and season to taste. Just before serving, add feta cheese; stir well.

Transfer to chafing dish or heated ceramic casserole. Surround with sliced baguettes; spoon hot crawfish mixture onto bread rounds. Serves 20.

Variations & Improvisations

Louisiana's Products

Louisiana's chief agricultural products are seafood, soybeans, cotton, cattle, sugarcane, poultry and eggs, dairy products, and rice. It is the biggest producer of crawfish in the world, supplying approximately ninety percent. Its industry consists of chemical products, petroleum and coal products, processed foods, transportation equipment, and paper products. Tourism is a big element in the economy, especially in the New Orleans area.

BEVERAGES & APPETIZERS

Cajun Hot Bites

Eat the chicken and chew the cane!

60 (1-ounce) chicken tenderloins
4 large eggs
4 tablespoons water
4 tablespoons Tabasco
8 cups all-purpose flour
6 tablespoons salt
6 tablespoons black pepper
2 tablespoons cayenne pepper
1 gallon oil
60 (5-inch) sugarcane skewers

Marinate chicken tenderloins in the egg, water, and Tabasco mixture 30 minutes. Cut skewers from meat of sugarcane stick. Skewer tenderloins on cane sticks in an in-and-out crochet fashion. Mix together flour, salt, pepper, and cayenne. Bread chicken kabobs in seasoned flour mixture and deep-fry at 360° till golden brown and crispy. Drain on paper towels.

GLAZE:
6 tablespoons butter
3 ounces cane syrup
16 ounces Tabasco pepper jelly
6 tablespoons chipotle pepper sauce
8 tablespoons water

Combine all ingredients in a skillet and simmer 3–4 minutes till of glaze consistency. Toss sugarcane skewered fried tenderloins in the hot Glaze, and serve by crossing the cane skewers in the center of service dish with cane leaves as garnish. Serves 12.

Editor's Extra: Sugarcane is not easy to come by, so use any skewers. This restaurant-sized recipe makes a lot. Easy to quarter or eighth.

Recipe provided by Fremin's, Thibodaux
Louisiana's Best Restaurant Recipes

BEVERAGES & APPETIZERS

Muffuletta Croquettes

BREAD CRUMBS:

14 (½-inch-thick) slices white or sourdough bread

Preheat oven to 325°. Trim crusts from bread slices. Arrange in single layer on baking sheet; do not allow edges to touch. Toast 10 minutes and then turn slices. Toast 10–12 minutes longer or till slices are dry. Remove to wire rack to cool. Process in food processor till finely ground. Place in a small bowl, and set aside.

MUFFULETTA CROQUETTES:

2½ ounces Provolone cheese, thinly sliced
1½ ounces salami, thinly sliced
1½ ounces mortadella (Italian sausage), thinly sliced
8–10 large green olives, pitted
1 cup all-purpose flour
1 egg
¼ cup milk
2 cups canola oil
Curly endive for garnish

Finely chop cheese, salami, and mortadella. Process in food processor just till mixture begins to adhere. Coarsely chop olives and add to cheese mixture. Pulse 6–8 times to combine.

Place flour in a small bowl. Whisk egg and milk in another small bowl till blended. Heat canola oil in a small saucepan over medium heat to 375°, monitoring temperature with a fry thermometer. Shape cheese mixture into 1-inch balls. Coat croquettes with flour, shaking off any excess. Dip in egg wash, allowing excess to drain. Gently coat croquettes again in flour and then again in egg wash. Finally coat with bread crumbs. Be sure croquettes are completely covered with bread crumbs. The breading process should be carried out slowly and carefully to produce the best results.

Fry croquettes in hot oil 30–45 seconds or till golden brown and beginning to sizzle. Drain on paper towels on platter. Arrange on endive-lined serving platter. Makes 18–20 croquettes.

Cooking with a Private Chef

BEVERAGES & APPETIZERS

Muffuletta Croquettes

BEVERAGES & APPETIZERS

Cajun Stuffed Mushrooms

½ pound bulk Cajun pork sausage
1 cup chopped onion
¼ cup chopped green bell pepper
24 large stuffing mushrooms, cut stems and save
½ teaspoon salt
½ teaspoon garlic powder
½ teaspoon cayenne pepper
1 cup water
¾ cup quick rice
¼ cup chopped parsley
2 cups mayonnaise
1½ cups grated Parmesan cheese

Brown sausage, onion, bell pepper, and mushroom stems. Add salt, garlic powder, and cayenne pepper. Add water, and bring to a boil. Add quick rice and parsley. Cover and remove from heat. Let stand 15 minutes. Meanwhile, blend mayonnaise and cheese. Combine half the mayonnaise mixture with all the cooked sausage-rice. Stuff mushrooms with this, and spoon remaining mayonnaise-cheese mixture on top of mushrooms. Place in 9x12-inch baking dish and bake at 350° for 35 minutes. Mushrooms will appear puffy and golden when done.

Tell Me More

Cajun Music

Cajun music is played predominantly at Louisiana festivals and dance halls, and in many weddings in Acadiana. Born from ballads, it is also dance music, with or without words. The music was originally played for small get-togethers on the front porch, but also enjoyed at all-night dance houses called "bal de maison," or at a fais do-do in a public dance hall.

Variations of Cajun dance are a Cajun one-step, also called a Cajun jig, a Cajun two-step or related Cajun jitterbug, and a Cajun waltz. In mild contrast, zydeco dancing is a syncopated two-step or jitterbug. A Cajun dancer covers the dance floor, while the zydeco dancer dances in a smaller area.

Spicy Catfish Puffs

These little puffs are a great starter course or dinner party hors d'oeuvre. —Chef John Folse

Vegetable oil, divided
½ cup all-purpose flour
¾ teaspoon baking powder
Salt and cayenne pepper to taste
2 eggs, separated
¼ cup milk
¼ teaspoon Louisiana hot sauce
1 cup cooked, flaked catfish
½ cup shredded jalapeño cheese
1½ cups cooked white rice
¼ cup minced onion
¼ cup minced celery
¼ cup minced green bell pepper

In a large skillet over medium heat, heat 2 inches vegetable oil for deep-frying to 350°. In a bowl, sift together flour, baking powder, salt, and cayenne, then set aside. In a second bowl, beat together egg yolks, milk, 1 tablespoon oil, and hot sauce. Add milk mixture to dry ingredients and mix till just blended. Fold in catfish, cheese, rice, onion, celery, and bell pepper, then set aside.

Using an electric mixer, beat egg whites till stiff peaks form. Gently fold whites into batter till uniform. Working in batches, drop batter by tablespoonfuls into hot oil (keep oil temperature at 350° at all times), and fry till golden brown and puffs float. Do not overcrowd skillet. Using tongs or a slotted spoon, remove catfish puffs from oil and place on paper towels to drain. Serve immediately with Louisiana Seafood Cocktail Sauce or Louisiana Tartar Sauce. Serves 6.

Hooks, Lies & Alibis

BEVERAGES & APPETIZERS

Alligator Balls

1 pound chopped alligator
   meat
1 egg
1 tablespoon finely chopped
   onion
1 tablespoon finely chopped
   celery
¼ cup bread crumbs

1 tablespoon finely chopped
   parsley
3 tablespoons finely chopped
   shallots
2 tablespoons lemon pepper
½ teaspoon salt
1 cup cooking oil
Flour to dredge

Combine all ingredients, except oil and flour; form balls one inch in diameter. Allow to set one hour. Dredge in flour, and fry in oil till brown. Serve hot.

deBellevue Williams Cochon de Lait

Artichoke Toast

Simple, simple, simple—and so delectable!

1 (6-ounce) jar marinated
   artichoke hearts, chopped
6 ounces grated Parmesan
   cheese, preferably fresh
½ cup chopped green onion
   tops

1 cup Hellmann's mayonnaise
Dash of Tabasco to taste
Cayenne pepper to taste
1 package cocktail-size
   sourdough bread

Mix all ingredients together, except bread. Blend well. Spread liberally on bread rounds. (Can be placed on cookie sheets and frozen at this point. Drop in plastic bags and return to freezer till ready to bake.) Place desired amount of toasts on cookie sheet, and bake in 375° oven for 10–15 minutes, till bread is crisp and topping is hot and bubbly. Serves 50.

So Good . . . Make You Slap Your Mama!

BEVERAGES & APPETIZERS

Marlyn's Trash

There's no set recipe for making this wonderful snack—no magic involved. If there's a secret, it's in the seasoned butter, and you can make that as bland or as zesty as your taste buds dictate. It is important to roast trash slowly, and toss or stir often, tasting as you go. This is my downfall—overtasting! You may cut this recipe down, for it will feed the multitudes. I bag it in cellophane, tie it with a pretty ribbon, and give it to my favorite people just to say "you're special."

—Marlyn Monette

SEASONED BUTTER:
- 4–5 sticks butter
- Tabasco, to taste
- Crushed garlic, to taste
- 1 tablespoon Worcestershire
- Red pepper, to taste
- Creole or Cajun seasoning
- Pinch of sugar

Melt butter in heavy saucepan; add remaining ingredients, tasting for flavor. It may require a little more Worcestershire or Tabasco. Using 2 turkey roaster pans, pour scant amount of butter mixture in the bottom of each pan.

MIX:
- 1½ pounds pecan halves
- 1 pound walnuts halves
- 1 pound whole almonds
- 1 large can whole cashews
- 1 large bag Gardetto's Snack Mix
- 2 large bags Chex Mix
- 2 (10-ounce) boxes Goldfish crackers
- 1 (9-ounce) box Wheat Thins
- 1 (13-ounce) box Cheez-Its

Divide ingredients between the 2 roasters and toss. Drizzle more Seasoned Butter over mixture as you toss, looking for dry spots.

Bake in a 275°–300° oven for about 1½ hours, stirring or tossing every 15 minutes. As you toss, more garlic powder and other dry seasonings may be added, but go lightly on the salt.

Let cool completely before storing in containers.

So Good . . . Make You Slap Your Mama! II

Louisiana State Capitol in Baton Rouge

Bread & Breakfast

Crawfish Cornbread 36
Ursula's Cornbread Dressing.........................37
Trosclair's Cornbread and Andouille Sausage Stuffing..........................38
All Saints Day Oyster Dressing.........................39
Confetti French Bread.......40
French Bread 40
Olive It! Muffuletta Frittata..........................42
Captain John's Cathead Biscuits 43
Ollie's Biscuits 45

Sausage Biscuit Bites 45
Sweet Potato Biscuits.........46
Creole Beignets...................46
Hot Beignets.......................47
Faubourg Coconut Shrimp Beignets with Pepper Jelly Sauce 48
Breakfast Rice 49
Aunt Pitty Pat's Blintz Casserole 50
Stuffed French Toast 52
Pain Perdu..........................52
Magnificent Morning Breakfast Pie..................53

The 34-story Louisiana State Capitol in Baton Rouge is the tallest capitol in the United States. It was completed in a little over a year at a cost of five million dollars, and was dedicated on May 16, 1932. Visitors can walk up the 49 granite steps to the main entrance, each engraved with a state's name and year of statehood. Alaska and Hawaii, which were admitted after the completion of the capitol, are both on the last step along with the phrase "E pluribus unum (Out of many, one)." Inside, the enormous foyer is a simply breathtaking room of marble, brass, statues, paintings, etc. A ride up two elevators to the observation deck affords grand views of the Mississippi River and bridges, the huge ExxonMobil refinery, the old capitol, downtown Baton Rouge, LSU, and beyond ... amazing in all directions.

BREAD & BREAKFAST

Crawfish Cornbread

1 cup chopped onion
½ cup chopped green bell pepper
½ cup chopped celery
¼ cup oil
1 pound crawfish tails
1 teaspoon salt
1 teaspoon baking powder
1 cup cornmeal
1 (16-ounce) can cream-style corn
1 cup grated cheese (Cheddar)
¼ cup chopped jalapeños
2 eggs

Sauté chopped vegetables in oil till tender. Mix all ingredients. Pour into greased 9x13-inch casserole dish. Bake at 375° for 30–40 minutes. Serve hot.

Recipes from the Heart

The Old State Capitol

In 1847, the city of Baton Rouge donated a plot of land situated on a bluff overlooking the Mississippi River to the state for the construction of the state capitol. When completed, the castle-like building was considered the best example of Gothic Revival architecture in the South.

During the Civil War, the government was moved in 1862 to Opelousas, then Shreveport in 1864, then to New Orleans. After having been gutted by an accidental fire, the old building was restored in 1880 to its classic beauty, adding its famous spiral staircase and stained glass dome, as well as a fourth floor. The state legislature returned there on May 8, 1882, until moving to the new capitol in 1932.

BREAD & BREAKFAST

Ursula's Cornbread Dressing

This cornbread dressing has been a dinner staple on our table for as long as I can remember. Ursula Beaugh was my neighbor, and this is a family heritage recipe. I cannot imagine a holiday meal without this dressing. However, I do not use it just at holiday time. The dressing enhances Sunday dinner, whether it's baked chicken or a roast. Seasoned ground meat is added to the cooked cornbread. —Corinne Cook

CORNBREAD:
- 2½ cups yellow cornmeal
- ¾ cup all-purpose flour
- 1½ teaspoons salt
- 3 teaspoons baking powder
- 1 tablespoon sugar
- 3 tablespoons oil
- 3 eggs
- 3 cups milk

Mix all ingredients together. Pour into a greased 11-inch, ovenproof heavy skillet, and bake at 425° for 30–35 minutes.

MEAT MIXTURE:
- 2 pounds lean ground beef
- 2 onions, chopped
- 1 green bell pepper, chopped
- 3 cloves garlic, chopped
- 1 cup chopped celery
- Salt, black pepper, and cayenne pepper to taste
- 1 (14-ounce) can beef broth
- 2 (10¾-ounce) cans cream of mushroom soup
- 1 teaspoon Kitchen Bouquet
- ¼ cup chopped fresh parsley
- ¼ cup chopped green onions
- 3 eggs, lightly beaten

In a large skillet, brown beef; drain. Add onions, bell pepper, garlic, and celery. Season to taste. This should be relatively spicy, because you will be mixing it with cornbread. Add beef broth and cook slowly, about 45 minutes, covered.

Add cream of mushroom soup, Kitchen Bouquet, parsley, and green onions. Crumble cornbread, and add it to the meat mixture. Check seasoning. Stir in eggs. Spoon into a large baking dish sprayed with nonstick coating. Bake at 350° for 30–45 minutes, or till bubbly. Serves 12–14.

Extra! Extra! Read More About It!

BREAD & BREAKFAST

Trosclair's Cornbread and Andouille Sausage Stuffing

4 tablespoons unsalted butter
1 cup finely diced andouille sausage
1 cup finely diced red onion
1 cup finely diced green bell pepper
½ cup finely diced celery
2 tablespoons minced fresh garlic
1 tablespoon chopped fresh thyme leaves
1 tablespoon Creole seasoning
4 cups crumbled leftover cornbread
½–1 cup chicken stock
1 cup finely sliced green onions
1 egg

Melt butter in a large cast-iron skillet over medium-high heat; add andouille; cook till it starts to render. Add onion, bell pepper, celery, garlic, thyme, and Creole seasoning. Reduce heat to medium. Sweat the vegetable mixture till tender, stirring often.

Add cornbread, and stir well to coat with andouille and vegetable mixture. Reduce heat to medium low. Gradually add stock till the mixture is moist. Stir in green onions. Place stuffing in a greased dish and cool in refrigerator. Once cool, add the egg and mix well. Bake in 350° oven 30 minutes.

Good Gumbo Weather

Editor's Extra: To sweat ingredients, put the lid on, and gently cook until soft and translucent. No browning or frying here—this method lets the aromatic flavors blend together with plenty of moisture.

BREAD & BREAKFAST

All Saints Day Oyster Dressing

1 stick butter
2 large onions, chopped
⅓ cup chopped celery
4 slices bread
Water
1 egg, beaten
2 teaspoons chopped parsley
1 pint oysters, drained
Salt and pepper to taste
Pinch of basil, sage, thyme, and marjoram
Bread crumbs
Dots of butter

Melt butter in a 10-inch skillet. Sauté onions and celery till transparent. Soak bread in water; drain and squeeze water out. Tear into small pieces. Add to onion mixture. Add egg, parsley, and oysters; season with seasonings to taste. Simmer till oysters begin to curl. If mixture is soggy, add bread crumbs; it should be very moist, but there should be no excess liquid. Turn into a greased 2-quart casserole. Dot with butter. Bake at 350° about 30 minutes. Serves 6–8.

Who Dat Cookin'

Superdome

With a roof area is 9.7 acres, the Mercedes-Benz Superdome in New Orleans is the largest fixed dome structure in the world. Dedication ceremonies were held on August 3, 1975. It is the home stadium of the NFL's New Orleans Saints. The team regularly draws capacity crowds of 73,000+. The Superdome has hosted seven Super Bowls—more than any other stadium.

BREAD & BREAKFAST

Confetti French Bread

1 stick butter, softened
½ cup mayonnaise
1 cup chopped pitted black olives
2 garlic cloves, chopped
6 green onions, chopped
2 cups shredded mozzarella cheese
1 large loaf French bread, cut in half horizontally

Beat butter and mayonnaise in a bowl till light and fluffy. Add olives, garlic, green onions, and cheese; mix well. Spread over cut sides of bread and place on a baking sheet, cut side up. Bake in 350° oven 15–20 minutes, or till cheese is melted. Serves 10–12.

Marshes to Mansions

French Bread

Bakeries in New Orleans bake a lot more than bread. They are, in fact, incredible places—a feast for the senses. Put cholesterol and diet and all that stuff completely out of your mind before entering one and let your nose lead the way. Petits Fours, Brioche, Strawberry Shortcakes, Neopolitan Squares, Cream Puffs, Wine Cakes, Pecan Pies, Rum Balls, Éclairs, Dobache Cakes—you don't have to know the name . . . just point to it and say, "I want one of those," and go ahead and indulge. One bite assures that you'll have a little bit of heaven right here on earth. —Gwen McKee

So much a part of New Orleans cuisine is this all-important bread that it deserves its own special place in a New Orleans cookbook—but I do not give a recipe because I have rarely made it. Nobody makes it—my grandmothers didn't even make it. What they did, however, was make things with it: garlic bread, po-boys, bread puddings, French toast, all kinds of stuffings and dressings—nary a crumb was wasted. It's such a necessary part of the enjoyment of gumbo and étouffée and jambalaya and on and on and on. My favorite recipe is—go to the bakery and buy it!

The Little New Orleans Cookbook

BREAD & BREAKFAST

Confetti French Bread

BREAD & BREAKFAST

Olive It! Muffuletta Frittata

This dish was inspired by New Orleans's famous muffuletta sandwiches. The saltiness of the olive salad adds a flavorful touch to this distinctive meat-and-cheese oven-cooked, omelet-like egg dish.

—Todd-Michael St. Pierre

6 large eggs
2 tablespoons sour cream
¼ teaspoon salt
¼ teaspoon freshly ground pepper
½ green onion, coarsely chopped
½ teaspoon minced fresh oregano
1 cup cubed wheat bread
2 thin slices ham, coarsely chopped
3 thin slices Genoa salami, coarsely chopped
2 thin slices Provolone cheese, coarsely chopped
1 tablespoon unsalted butter
⅓ cup Italian-style deli olives, pitted, chopped
1 tablespoon pickled pepperoncini, coarsely chopped
Dash of Louisiana hot sauce

In a medium bowl, beat eggs, sour cream, salt, and pepper with electric mixer on medium speed till well blended, 2–3 minutes. Or, whisk till well blended. Mix in green onion, oregano, and bread cubes. Let stand 20 minutes, or covered in refrigerator overnight.

Preheat oven to 350°. Mix ham, salami, and Provolone cheese into egg mixture. Melt butter in 8- or 9-inch oven-proof skillet over medium heat, then add egg mixture. Bake till egg is fluffy and cooked, about 12 minutes.

While the frittata bakes, mix the olives, pepperoncini, and hot sauce in small bowl to make a quick Italian-style olive salad. When frittata is done, slice into 4 wedges; garnish each slice with olive salad, and serve immediately. Serves 4.

Taste of Tremé

BREAD & BREAKFAST

Captain John's Cathead Biscuits

It must have been someone with a great sense of humor who first called these biscuits cathead. I think I first heard the term mentioned by Miss Emily Bruno of the Emily House on Lake Bruin in St. Joseph, Louisiana. Boy, could she make a cathead biscuit! What I like most about this recipe is the number of variations that can come about by adding other ingredients such as crackling, cheese, herbs, or whatever else comes to mind. —Chef John Folse

2 cups all-purpose flour
1 tablespoon baking powder
½ teaspoon baking soda
½ teaspoon salt
⅓ cup shortening
1 tablespoon plus 1 teaspoon butter
⅔ cup buttermilk
2 tablespoons butter, melted

Preheat oven to 450°. In mixing bowl, sift flour, baking powder, baking soda, and salt. Blend well, then cut in the shortening and butter using a pastry cutter. The particles should remain pea-size or that of coarse cornmeal. Add buttermilk, and using a large cooking spoon, stir just enough to blend the buttermilk into the flour mixture.

Sprinkle the work surface with flour and turn dough out onto work surface. Knead just till dough comes together. Do not overwork the dough, as the less you handle it, the flakier your biscuits will be. Break dough into 8 equal portions and pat approximately ½ inch thick onto baking sheet. The biscuits should be irregular in shape, but no more that ½-inch high and 1 inch apart. Bake biscuits till golden brown, 10–15 minutes. Remove from oven and brush with melted butter. Serves 8.

__Hot Beignets & Warm Boudoirs__

Plantations Along the River Road

Destrehan Plantation is most associated with Jean-Noël Destréhan, first U.S. senator from Louisiana and influential in the transition of the territory to statehood. The house, listed on the National Register of Historic Places, outlived the oil refinery that had been built around it. In 1971, American Oil donated it to the River Road Historical Society. Tours daily.

San Francisco Plantation House, located upriver from Reserve on Louisiana Highway 44, was declared a National Historic Landmark in 1974. The house has been restored to its 1850s appearance, and is open for tours daily. It is also available for rental for special occasions.

Laura Plantation is a restored National Register of Historic Places Louisiana Creole plantation on the west bank of the Mississippi River near Vacherie. Surviving outbuildings include six slave quarters. It is one of only fifteen plantation complexes in Louisiana with this degree of complete structures. Guided tours.

Evergreen Plantation on Highway 18 near Wallace, was constructed in 1790. The plantation includes 37 contributing buildings, making it one of the most complete plantation complexes in the South. The complex was declared a National Historic Landmark in 1992. It is still a working sugar cane plantation today. Tours, except Sunday.

BREAD & BREAKFAST

Ollie's Biscuits

4 cups Pioneer buttermilk
   biscuit mix
1 cup sour cream
1 cup diet 7-UP

Pinch of baking powder
2 tablespoons sugar
1 stick butter, melted

Combine all ingredients except melted butter. Roll out dough and cut with biscuit cutter. Place biscuits on a baking sheet and drizzle with melted butter. Bake at 375° for 20–25 minutes. Makes a dozen or more biscuits.

Classic Cajun Deux

Sausage Biscuit Bites

These biscuits are delicious, so easy to make, and they freeze beautifully.

¾ pound Jimmie Dean sausage,
   mild or hot
2¼ cups Bisquick baking mix

⅔ cup milk
¼ cup butter, melted

Cook sausage till browned, stirring to crumble; drain well; set aside. Blend Bisquick, drained sausage, and milk only till mixture is moistened—do not overbeat. Place on lightly floured surface and knead 4–5 times. Roll dough to ½-inch thickness, and cut with a 1½-inch biscuit cutter. Place biscuits on ungreased baking sheet, and brush tops with melted butter; bake in 450° oven 10–12 minutes, or till golden brown. Makes 12–14 biscuits.

So Good . . . Make You Slap Your Mama!

BREAD & BREAKFAST

Sweet Potato Biscuits

½ cup shortening
2 cups all-purpose flour
⅔ cup sugar
2 tablespoons baking powder
1 teaspoon salt
2 cups cooked, mashed sweet potatoes
¼ cup milk

Cut shortening into dry ingredients till coarse texture. Add sweet potatoes, and mix well. Add milk gradually to form a soft dough. Place on floured board, and knead lightly about 10 minutes. Roll or pat to ½-inch thickness. Cut with biscuit cutter. Place on greased cookie sheet, and bake in preheated 475° oven 10–12 minutes. Serve with plenty of butter.

Pots, Pans, and Pioneers V

Creole Beignets

½ cup granulated sugar
2 eggs
1 cup milk
2 teaspoons baking powder
2½ cups all-purpose flour
Pinch of salt
Oil for frying
Confectioners' sugar

Thoroughly mix together all ingredients except oil and confectioners' sugar. Drop by teaspoonfuls in hot oil, and fry till lightly brown. Roll in confectioners' sugar. Makes about 2 dozen.

Down the Bayou . . . and Back Again

BREAD & BREAKFAST

Hot Beignets

¾ cup sugar
½ teaspoon salt
¾ cup shortening
⅔ cup milk, scalded
1 package active dry yeast
¾ cup water, very warm (115°)

1 egg
3 cups sifted all-purpose flour, divided (or more)
Granulated or powdered sugar

Stir sugar, salt, and shortening into hot milk; cool to lukewarm. Sprinkle yeast into very warm water; stir till dissolved. Add lukewarm milk mixture, egg, and ½ the flour; beat well with mixer or spoon for 1 minute. Add remaining flour (and more, if needed, to make soft dough). Turn onto lightly floured surface; knead till smooth and elastic. Place in greased bowl; cover and let rise in warm place, free from draft, till doubled, about 1 hour. Punch down; let rise again about ½ hour. Roll out into a ½-inch-thick square; cut into 2½- to 3-inch squares. Place on greased baking sheet; let rise till light. Fry in deep, hot fat. Let cook about 2 minutes, or till brown on each side. Drain on absorbent paper. Serve piping hot, sprinkled with granulated or powdered sugar. Makes 2 dozen.

Pots, Pans, and Pioneers III

Beignets were brought to Louisiana in the 18th century by French colonists, and became a large part of home-style Creole cooking. The French-style deep-fried pastry may be savory as well as sweet. Sweet beignets are customarily served topped with powdered sugar and enjoyed with coffee and chicory or café au lait. Today, Café du Monde and Morning Call in New Orleans, and Coffee Call in Baton Rouge are popular food destinations specializing in sweet beignets. Beignets were declared the official state doughnut of Louisiana in 1986.

BREAD & BREAKFAST

Faubourg Coconut Shrimp Beignets with Pepper Jelly Sauce

PEPPER JELLY SAUCE:

1 tablespoon oil
1 small jalapeño pepper, seeded, finely chopped
1 cup apple jelly
2 tablespoons cider vinegar
2 tablespoons whole-grain mustard
1 teaspoon Slap Ya Mama Hot Sauce

In a small saucepan, heat oil over medium heat. Add jalapeño and cook, stirring occasionally, for 5 minutes. Add remaining ingredients; cook till jelly is melted. Pour into serving dish. Can be made in advance; warm briefly in microwave before serving.

BEIGNETS:

Oil for frying
¾ pound shrimp, peeled, deveined, cut into ½-inch pieces
Salt and pepper to taste
2 cups all-purpose flour
1 tablespoon baking powder
1 cup shredded sweetened coconut
¼ cup finely chopped scallions
1 teaspoon salt
1 (12-ounce) bottle Abita Amber beer
¼ cup water

In a large skillet, heat 2 tablespoons oil over high heat. Add shrimp, season with salt and pepper, and cook till pink, 1–2 minutes. Transfer to paper-towel-lined plate; let cool. Fill a heavy, medium saucepan halfway with oil, and heat over medium-high heat till oil registers 360° on a deep-fat thermometer.

In a large bowl, toss together flour, baking powder, coconut, scallions, and salt. Whisk in beer and water. Stir shrimp into batter. Scoop some shrimp and batter into a soup spoon, then with other spoon, scrape the batter into the hot oil. Fry 6 Beignets at a time, turning once, till puffy and light brown, 1 minute on each side. Drain on paper towels; season with salt. Serve with the Pepper Jelly Sauce.

A Confederacy of Scrumptious

BREAD & BREAKFAST

Breakfast Rice

1 pound Jimmy Dean Sausage (Sage or Hot)
1 cup chopped onion
1 cup chopped celery
½ cup chopped red bell pepper
½ cup chopped yellow bell pepper
2 cloves garlic, chopped
2 (10¾-ounce) cans cream of mushroom soup
1 (10¾-ounce) can cream of chicken soup
1 cup raw rice
¼ teaspoon salt
¼ teaspoon pepper
Louisiana hot sauce top taste (optional)

Brown sausage in skillet. Drain grease, remove sausage and return grease to skillet. (If sausage is too lean, it may be necessary to add 1 tablespoon cooking oil to sauté the vegetables). Add chopped onion, celery, peppers, and garlic; sauté well. Add cooked sausage and soups. Heat thoroughly, making sure all ingredients are mixed well. Add rice and seasonings. Mix. Pour into casserole sprayed with nonstick spray. Cover and bake at 350° for 1 hour. Serves 4–6.

Classic Cajun

Louisiana does NOT have counties.

It has parishes. All the other states have counties except Alaska, which has boroughs and census areas. Formed from French and Spanish colonies that were both officially Roman Catholic, Louisiana's local government was based upon parishes as the local ecclesiastical division. Following the Louisiana Purchase in 1803, the Territorial Legislative Council divided the Territory of Orleans (the predecessor of Louisiana state) into 12 counties. The borders of these counties were poorly defined, but they roughly coincided with the colonial parishes, and hence used the same names.

BREAD & BREAKFAST

Aunt Pitty Pat's Blintz Casserole

BATTER:

2 sticks butter, softened	1 tablespoon baking powder
½ cup sugar	½ cup milk
4 eggs	1 teaspoon vanilla extract
2 cups all-purpose flour	1 pinch of salt

Combine all ingredients in bowl; mix well. The batter will be thin. Pour half of the batter into a 9x13-inch baking dish.

FILLING:

32 ounces farmer cheese, or 16 ounces cream cheese or cottage cheese	¼ cup sugar
	1 pinch of salt
2 eggs	Juice of 1 lemon

Combine all ingredients in bowl; mix well. Pour Filling over Batter. Top with remaining Batter. Bake at 325° for 45 minutes. Serve hot, topped with sour cream, fresh strawberry syrup, or pie filling. Serves 12.

Note: This dish can be made in advance and frozen. If you do this, cook for 30 minutes; then cool, cover with foil, and freeze. Defrost, and cook 15 minutes before serving.

Da Cajn Critter

Editor's Extra: This can be a divine dessert as well as a fancy brunch dish.

BREAD & BREAKFAST

Aunt Pitty Pat's Blintz Casserole

BREAD & BREAKFAST

Stuffed French Toast

6 (1-inch-thick) French bread slices
¾ cup peach preserves
6 tablespoons cream cheese, softened
6 eggs
½ cup milk
1 tablespoon flour
½ cup fresh white bread crumbs
½ cup packed brown sugar
1 tablespoon cinnamon
2 tablespoons (about) vegetable oil

Slit top of each slice of bread to within 1 inch of edge, making a pocket. Spoon 2 tablespoons of preserves and 1 tablespoon of cream cheese into each pocket. Combine eggs, milk, and flour in a bowl; whisk till smooth. Mix bread crumbs, brown sugar, and cinnamon in separate bowl.

Heat a large nonstick skillet over medium heat, and brush with some oil. Dip bread slices in egg mixture, and then into bread crumb mixture, coating completely. Cook in skillet 2 minutes per side or till golden brown, brushing the skillet with additional oil as needed. Serve with maple syrup. Serves 6.

Secret Ingredients

Pain Perdu
(Lost Bread)

3 eggs
½ cup sugar
½ teaspoon vanilla
1 cup milk
8 or more slices day-old bread
½ cup oil

In a bowl, beat eggs with a fork. Add sugar, vanilla, and milk; mix together. Pass bread in mixture until it is fully covered. Put ½ cup oil in a skillet and heat on medium. Fry bread down on both sides. Serve warm.

Amy's Cajun Recipes

BREAD & BREAKFAST

Magnificent Morning Breakfast Pie

1 pound uncooked shrimp, peeled, deveined, chopped
2 tablespoons butter
1½ cups shredded Swiss cheese
1 unbaked (10-inch) deep-dish pie shell
4 eggs
1 cup light cream
2 teaspoons chopped onion
¼ cup each: chopped red, green, and yellow (optional) bell pepper

Sauté shrimp in butter in skillet for 2 minutes. Remove shrimp to a bowl with a slotted spoon. Add cheese, and toss to mix well. Prick pie shell with a fork. Spoon shrimp mixture into pie shell. In a bowl, beat eggs and cream; mix in onion and bell peppers. Pour over shrimp mixture. Bake at 375° for 40–45 minutes, or till set. Serves 6–8.

Roux To Do

Huey P. Long

Huey Pierce Long, Jr., nicknamed "The Kingfish," was the 40th governor of Louisiana from 1928 to 1932, and a U.S. senator from 1932 until his assassination in 1935. A Democrat, he was an outspoken populist who denounced the rich and the banks, and is best known for his "Share Our Wealth" program, created in 1934 under the motto "Every Man a King."

Long was assassinated by Dr. Carl Weiss in 1935 in the state capitol he built; Long was 42. In 1938, the state legislature appropriated $50,000 to replace Long's original simple grave marker with a more monumental one; two years later, a marble pedestal surmounted by a bronze statue of Long (facing the capitol) was erected on the capitol grounds. Long remains a controversial figure in Louisiana history, with critics and supporters debating whether he was a dictator, demagogue, or populist.

PAUL LOWRY

Cathedral-Basilica of Saint Louis, a.k.a. St. Louis Cathedral, New Orleans

Soups, Stews & Chilis

Fresh Corn Soup 56
Shrimp and Corn Soup.....56
Crawfish and Corn Soup...58
Vedros Family's Crawfish Bisque 59
She-Crab Soup 60
Turtle Soup 61
Cream of Artichoke Soup with Bleu Cheese 62
Beef Vegetable Soup 64
Broccoli Soup.....................64
Basic Roux 65

K's Cajun Seasoning 66
The Tail of the Turkey Gumbo..........................67
Chicken and Sausage Gumbo..........................68
Red Bean Gumbo 70
Cup O' Crab Gumbo..........71
Breaux Bridge Crawfish Stew...............................72
Beef Stew Crockpot............73
Deer Chili 73

The Cathedral-Basilica of Saint Louis, King of France, is the seat of the Roman Catholic Archdiocese of New Orleans. The first church on the site was built in 1718, and the third, built in 1789, was raised to cathedral rank in 1793. It was expanded and largely rebuilt in 1850. The St. Louis Cathedral has the distinction of being the oldest continuously operating cathedral in the United States. Overlooking Jackson Square, it is New Orleans' most visited and photographed landmark.

SOUPS, STEWS & CHILIS

Fresh Corn Soup

½ pound salt pork, cut into pieces
2 tablespoons fat (or shortening)
2 tablespoons chopped green bell pepper
1 medium onion, chopped
1 clove garlic, minced
2 quarts water
1 cup canned whole tomatoes
2 cups fresh corn
Salt and pepper to taste

Boil salt pork in water to remove excess salt; discard water and set meat aside. Heat fat in large soup pot; add bell pepper, onion, and garlic. Cook 20 minutes on low heat. Add meat and water. Simmer till meat is tender. Add tomatoes and corn; cook about 45 minutes longer. Season to taste. Serve hot with croutons or French bread. Serves 8.

Note: Two cans cream-style corn may be substituted for fresh corn.

Down the Bayou

Shrimp and Corn Soup

2 pounds peeled shrimp
Salt and black pepper to taste
¼ cup oil
¼ cup all-purpose flour
1 cup chopped onion
½ cup chopped celery
1 (11-ounce) can shoepeg corn
2 (16-ounce) cans cream-style corn
½ lemon, sliced
2 tablespoons ketchup
1 gallon water
¼ cup chopped green onion tops

Season shrimp and set aside. Make roux of oil and flour. Add onion and celery to roux, and cook till onions are wilted, stirring occasionally. Add corn, sliced lemon, ketchup, and water; cook about 25 minutes. Add shrimp, and cook another 15 minutes; season to taste. Add onion tops. Let set a few minutes before serving in soup bowls. Serves 6–10.

Hey, Good Lookin', What's Cooking?

SOUPS, STEWS & CHILIS

Fresh Corn Soup

SOUPS, STEWS & CHILIS

Crawfish and Corn Soup

On a busy night, use this quick version of a rich, velvety, popular soup made with basic ingredients. —Holly Clegg

½ cup chopped onion
½ pound sliced mushrooms
1 (8-ounce) package reduced-fat cream cheese
1 (10¾-ounce) can cream of potato soup
2 cups skim milk
2 cups frozen corn
1 (16-ounce) bag crawfish tails, rinsed, drained
Dash of cayenne
½ cup chopped green onions

In nonstick pot coated with nonstick cooking spray, sauté onion and mushrooms for 5 minutes, or till tender. Add cream cheese and potato soup, mixing till combined. Gradually add milk and corn, and cook over low heat till thoroughly heated. Add remaining ingredients, cooking for about 10 minutes, or till heated. Serves 8.

Gulf Coast Favorites

On August 29, 2005, Hurricane Katrina's storm surge caused 53 different levee failures in greater New Orleans, causing two-thirds of the flooding, which submerged 80% of the city. It was the costliest natural disaster, as well as one of the five deadliest hurricanes in the history of the United States. At least 1,833 people died in the hurricane and subsequent floods. Total property damage was estimated at $81 billion, nearly triple the damage brought by Hurricane Andrew in 1992.

SOUPS, STEWS & CHILIS

Vedros Family's Crawfish Bisque

When eating Crawfish Bisque, always place your empty shells around the rim of your soup bowl!

STUFFED CRAWFISH HEADS:

½ loaf stale French bread
3 pounds crawfish tails
6 stalks celery
4 large onions
1 bunch green onions
2 cloves garlic
6 eggs, beaten

Parsley to taste
Salt, red pepper, and black pepper to taste
1 stick butter
Approximately 125 cleaned crawfish heads
Flour (for rolling heads)

Soak bread in water and squeeze dry. Grind together crawfish tails, (reserve some for Bisque, if desired) celery, onions, green onions, garlic, and bread. Mix well. Add beaten eggs and parsley; season well. Add additional bread crumbs, if too soupy. Fry mixture in butter 15 minutes. Let cool. Stuff cleaned crawfish heads with mixture, reserving 1 cup of mixture for Bisque. Brown in 350° oven 15 minutes. (Heads also can be fried in oil). Stuffs about 125 heads.

BISQUE:

1 cup oil
1 cup all-purpose flour
1 large onion, chopped
2 cloves garlic, chopped
3 pieces celery, chopped
4 quarts warm water

1 cup reserved crawfish stuffing mixture
1 tablespoon Worcestershire
Salt and pepper to taste
½ cup chopped green onions
Crawfish claws, if available

In large pot, make a roux with oil and flour. Stir constantly till dark brown. Add onion, garlic, and celery. Sauté till tender. Add water, stuffing mixture, Worcestershire, salt and pepper to taste. Bring to a boil; simmer 1 hour. Add stuffed heads and green onions. Simmer another 30 minutes. Add claws and reserved crawfish tails, if desired. Serve over cooked rice. Enjoy! Serves 8–10.

Vedros Family Recipes

SOUPS, STEWS & CHILIS

She-Crab Soup

It is easy to distinguish between a male crab and a female crab by looking at their underside. An easier and safer way to differentiate the two without getting pinched is to look at the color of the claws. Female crabs have red tips on their pinchers, which make them look like their fingernails are painted. —Chef John Folse

- 1 pound jumbo lump crabmeat
- ½ cup crab roe
- ¼ cup butter
- ½ cup minced onion
- ¼ cup minced celery
- ¼ cup minced red bell pepper
- 1 tablespoon minced garlic
- 2 tablespoons flour
- 3 cups milk
- 2 cups heavy whipping cream
- ½ teaspoon mace
- 1 teaspoon grated lemon peel
- Salt and pepper to taste
- Granulated garlic to taste
- ¼ cup dry sherry
- 1 teaspoon paprika
- 2 tablespoons chopped parsley

Gently pick through crabmeat and discard any shells or cartilage, taking care not to break lumps. Set aside. Chop roe, and set aside. In a Dutch oven, melt butter over medium-high heat. Add onion, celery, bell pepper, and minced garlic. Sauté 3–5 minutes, or till vegetables are wilted. Sprinkle in flour, blending well into vegetable mixture. Add milk and whipping cream, then season with mace, lemon peel, salt, pepper, and granulated garlic. Bring to a low boil, reduce to simmer, and add half of crabmeat. Cook 10–15 minutes, stirring occasionally, then adjust seasonings, if necessary. Add roe, remaining crabmeat, and sherry. Return to a low boil and heat crabmeat thoroughly. Ladle into warmed soup bowls, garnish with a pinch of paprika and parsley, and serve hot. Serves 6.

Note: If buying whole crabs, you will need 8 or 9 females to get enough meat for 6 people.

Hooks, Lies & Alibis

SOUPS, STEWS & CHILIS

Cream of Artichoke Soup with Bleu Cheese

1 medium onion, chopped
3 tablespoons butter
¼ cup all-purpose flour
1½ cups chicken stock
½ cup dry vermouth
2 (14-ounce) cans artichoke hearts, drained, rinsed, divided
2 tablespoons finely chopped parsley
1¼ cups half-and-half
Salt and pepper to taste
4 ounces crumbled bleu cheese

Sauté onion in butter in large saucepan till tender. Add flour; cook 2 minutes, stirring constantly. Remove from heat. Whisk in stock and vermouth. Stir in 1 can artichoke hearts and parsley. Cook over medium heat 5 minutes, stirring constantly.

Pour into a blender container. Process till puréed. Return to saucepan. Add half-and-half, remaining can artichoke hearts, chopped, and salt and pepper. Cook over medium heat till heated through. Ladle into soup bowls. Sprinkle the bleu cheese over soup. Serves 4–6.

Secret Ingredients

Frogmore Plantation in Ferriday across the Mississippi River from Natchez, Mississippi, shows the contrast of an 1800s cotton plantation and the computerized 900-bales-per-day plantation operating today. It is the only tour of its kind in the South, and was selected by Rand McNally as a "Must See Site" in the South/Southeast.

SOUPS, STEWS & CHILIS

Turtle Soup

2½ sticks (1¼ cups) unsalted butter, divided
¾ cup all-purpose flour
1 pound turtle meat, cut into ½-inch cubes
1 cup minced celery
1¼ cups minced onions
1½ teaspoons minced garlic
3 bay leaves
1 teaspoon dried oregano
½ teaspoon dried thyme
½ teaspoon freshly ground black pepper
1½ cups tomato purée
1 quart beef stock or broth
Salt and freshly ground pepper to taste
½ cup lemon juice
5 hard-cooked eggs, finely chopped
1 tablespoon minced parsley
6 teaspoons dry sherry

Melt 1 cup butter in a heavy saucepan. Add flour and cook over medium heat till roux is a light brown color, stirring constantly; set aside. Melt remaining ¼ cup butter in a 5-quart saucepan. Add turtle meat and sauté till browned. Add celery, onions, garlic, bay leaves, oregano, thyme, and pepper. Cook till vegetables are translucent. Add tomato purée; reduce heat and simmer 10 minutes. Add beef stock. Simmer 30 minutes.

Add roux and cook over low heat till soup is smooth and thickened, stirring constantly. Season with salt and pepper. Stir in lemon juice, eggs, and parsley. Remove bay leaves. Spoon into 6 bowls. Top each with 1 teaspoon sherry. Serves 6.

Recipe provided by Jamie Shannon, Commander's Palace
Crescent City Collection

Longfellow-Evangeline

In 1847, American poet Henry Wadsworth Longfellow published an epic narrative poem about the expulsion of the Acadians (1755–1764) called "Evangeline, A Tale of Acadie." The poem follows an Acadian girl named Evangeline and her search for her lost love Gabriel, set during the time of the expulsion of the Acadians from Nova Scotia. The Evangeline Oak, on the banks of Bayou Teche in St. Martinville, is the legendary meeting place of the two lovers. In 1929, a statue of Evangeline—posed for by silent Mexican film star Dolores del Río, who starred in the 1929 film *Evangeline*—was donated to the town of St. Martinville by the film's cast and crew. There, in 1934, the Longfellow-Evangeline State Historic Site became the first state park in Louisiana. A popular tourist attraction, tours are given daily.

SOUPS, STEWS & CHILIS

Beef Vegetable Soup

6 beef soup bones with meat around them
3 medium carrots, sliced (optional)
4 medium potatoes, peeled, cut into chunks
1 large onion, chopped or sliced
2 stalks celery, cut into chunks
1 large green bell pepper, julienned
2 medium tomatoes, peeled, chopped
Salt and pepper to taste
Louisiana red pepper sauce to taste
Water
Cooked rice

Combine all ingredients in large stockpot. Add enough water to cover all. Bring to a boil over medium heat. Cook 2 hours, or till meat is tender. Serve over rice. Serves 6.

Classic Cajun Deux

Broccoli Soup

¾ cup chopped celery with leaves
¼ cup chopped onion
2 tablespoons butter
2 cups beef broth
1 bunch broccoli (about 1½ pounds), cut in small pieces
½ teaspoon salt
¼ teaspoon pepper
1 cup milk

Sauté celery and onion in butter till wilted; add broth, broccoli, salt, and pepper. Bring to a boil, cover, and cook over medium heat till broccoli is tender, about 20 minutes. Purée ingredients in electric blender, food mill, or mixer. Stir in milk and reheat. If too thick, add additional broth or milk, and adjust the seasoning, if necessary. Makes about 1 quart.

Pots, Pans, and Pioneers II

SOUPS, STEWS & CHILIS

Basic Roux

A heavy pot is a must to make a pretty roux. The heavier the pot, the easier your job will be. Before you start your roux, start heating water in kettle, the amount depending on whether your are making a gumbo or a stew. You must always add HOT water to a roux. It is very important not to change the temperature of the roux by adding cold water to it. The measurements given make a roux large enough for a stew with 1 hen, or a gumbo with 2 pounds shrimp.

⅔ cup all-purpose flour   ¾ cup oil

Mix the flour and oil in a heavy iron pot until it is thoroughly mixed before you turn on the fire under the pot. After it is mixed, turn the fire on medium to low, stirring constantly. Stir all over the bottom of the pot to be sure that no particles stick to the bottom. As you stir, the roux browns slowly. Don't cook your roux fast, because as it reaches the done point, it will be too hot, and burn. When your roux is a rich dark brown, turn off the heat immediately, continuing to stir. Add hot water to lower the temperature slightly so the roux will stop browning. Or, you can add chopped onions and/or bell peppers to lower temperature. Continue stirring, return to heat, and add the remainder of the ingredients for your stew or gumbo.

Tell Me More

Kent Plantation House in Alexandria is central Louisiana's oldest standing structure. Listed on the National Register of Historic Places, it is a representation of plantation life between 1795 and 1855. Besides the main structure, the bousillage Creole house, milk house, slave cabin, and blacksmith shop are restored period outbuildings now used as a showcase for tourists.

SOUPS, STEWS & CHILIS

K's Cajun Seasoning

Quick to fix; eliminates search for numerous cans and jars of spices—they are all mixed here in one spicy blend for a quick, tasty seasoning.

- 1 (26-ounce) box salt
- 3 tablespoons black pepper
- 2 tablespoons garlic powder
- 1 teaspoon onion powder
- 2 tablespoons dried parsley flakes
- 1 teaspoon nutmeg
- 4 tablespoons cayenne pepper
- 2 tablespoons chili powder
- 2 tablespoons Ac'cent (optional)

Mix all in large bowl. Fill a shaker for daily use; store remainder in tightly covered container.

Quickie Tip: Brang some o' dis K's Cajun Seasoning to your frans, Cher; d'ell ahpreeciate dat a' planty!

The Little Gumbo Book

How do you pronounce New Orleans?

Most locals say Noo-Awlinz, accent on Aw, and cringe at New-Or-Lee-Ans, accent on Lee. You will also hear New-Or-Leenz and Noo-All-Yunz. The shorthand is N'Awlins, which seems to be used a lot in print, and when people try to capture the accent. The French said it La-Nouvelle-Or-Lay-Ahn. However you say it, do it like Satchmo—with a big smile, a nose wrinkle, and showing lots of teeth.

How do you pronounce Louisiana?

It was originally named La Louisiane for King Louis XIV of France. Louisiana is mostly said like two ladies' names with an "e" in between—Louise-e-Anna (five syllables). You'll hear shortened versions like Loo-zee-anna (four), and Luz-anna (three), and sometimes just two syllables, what some like to call their home state—"Sweet Lou."

SOUPS, STEWS & CHILIS

The Tail of the Turkey Gumbo

This story has a very happy ending.

Turkey bones (with 1–2 pounds meat left on)
Water to cover
2 teaspoons K's Cajun Seasoning (see page 66), or salt and pepper
¾ cup all-purpose flour
1¾ cups oil (with some portion bacon drippings, if desired)
2 onions, chopped
1 bell pepper, chopped
3 stalks celery, chopped
1½ teaspoons minced garlic
2 quarts reserved turkey stock
1 (1-pound) can chopped tomatoes
½ teaspoon ground bay leaves
½ teaspoon dried basil
¼ teaspoon red pepper
1 pound ham, diced
Cooked rice

Place turkey carcass in stock pot with water to cover, sprinkle seasoning on top, stir, and let boil about 1½ hours. Remove carcass and meat; reserve broth. Cut turkey into bite-size pieces.

Brown flour in oil to make a dark roux. Add onions, bell pepper, celery, and garlic, and stir till soft. Stir in a cup or so of hot stock, then pour roux into stock pot with reserved broth. Cook ½ hour, then add tomatoes, turkey, seasonings, and ham, and cook another ½ hour. Serve with rice. Offer filé and Tabasco. Serves 8–10.

Note: This is such a perfect thing to do with the carcass of the Thanksgiving turkey . . . so good it's often looked forward to as much as the Thanksgiving meal itself! Is this an Easter turkey? Then you may want to put some peeled Easter eggs (leave whole) in the gumbo pot right before serving, one for each bowl. Voilà. Easter Bunny Gumbo! —*Gwen McKee*

The Little Gumbo Book

SOUPS, STEWS & CHILIS

Chicken and Sausage Gumbo

A Louisiana favorite, Chicken and Sausage Gumbo can be prepared easily and conveniently. Roux, the secret of good gumbo, gives it that nutty flavor and color without the fat. I use browned flour to create my roux. Serve over rice. —Holly Clegg

½ cup all-purpose flour
1 pound reduced-fat sausage, sliced in ¼-inch pieces
2 pounds boneless, skinless chicken breasts, cut into pieces
1 onion, chopped
1 teaspoon minced garlic
1 green bell pepper, cored and chopped
2 stalks celery, chopped
8 cups fat-free chicken broth
1 (16-ounce) package frozen cut okra, or freshly cut okra
1 teaspoon dried thyme leaves
¼ teaspoon cayenne
Salt and pepper to taste
1 bunch green onions, chopped
Cooked rice

Preheat oven to 400°. Place flour on a baking sheet and bake 20 minutes, stirring every 7–10 minutes till a dark nutty brown color develops. Set aside.

In large nonstick pot coated with nonstick cooking spray, stir-fry sausage over medium heat till crispy brown; set aside. Remove any excess fat, and recoat with nonstick cooking spray. Add chicken, and cook, stirring, just till starting to brown. Add onion, garlic, green pepper, and celery, cooking till tender. Add browned flour, and stir continuously. Gradually add remaining ingredients, except sausage and green onions. Bring to a boil, reduce heat, and simmer 30 minutes, or till chicken is tender. Add sausage and green onions, cooking about 5 minutes more. Serve over rice. Serves 14.

Gulf Coast Favorites

SOUPS, STEWS & CHILIS

Chicken and Sausage Gumbo

SOUPS, STEWS & CHILIS

Red Bean Gumbo

1 cup all-purpose flour
1 cup oil
5 medium onions, chopped
2 green bell peppers, chopped
1 teaspoon salt
½ teaspoon garlic powder
½ teaspoon minced garlic
½ teaspoon black pepper
½ tablespoon chopped parsley
¼ teaspoon cayenne
1 (10¾-ounce) can golden mushroom soup
1 (10-ounce) can Ro-Tel tomatoes
4 dashes Tabasco
½ teaspoon liquid smoke
1 pound smoked sausage, cubed
½ pound tasso, cubed
1½ pounds andouille, cubed
1 (16-ounce) can Blue Runner Red Beans, pureéd
1 bean can of water
1 bunch green onions, chopped
1 dozen eggs
Cooked rice

Make a roux with flour and oil. Add chopped onions, bell peppers, and salt. Cook till tender. Add all dry seasonings. Mix well. Add mushroom soup, Ro-Tel, Tabasco, and liquid smoke. Add cubed sausage, tasso, and andouille. Add puréed beans to pot. Fill bean can with water, and add to pot. Bring to a boil then simmer 45 minutes. Add green onions. Carefully crack and add eggs, one at a time, to gumbo (poach them in the gumbo); don't stir for 15 minutes. Turn off heat and carefully stir. Place lid back on and let stand 15–20 minutes before serving over rice. Serves a bunch.

Vedros Family Recipes

SOUPS, STEWS & CHILIS

Cup O' Crab Gumbo

Easy enough for a beginner—exquisite enough for a king!

- 1 cup chopped green onions
- 1 cup chopped celery
- 1 stick real butter
- 3 tablespoons flour
- 1 cup finely cut okra (optional)
- 1 (1-pound) can cream-style corn
- 3 cloves garlic, minced
- ¼ teaspoon nutmeg
- 1 teaspoon honey (or sugar)
- 1½ teaspoons salt
- ½ teaspoon white pepper
- 1 quart water
- 1 pound fresh lump crabmeat
- Fresh snipped parsley
- Cooked rice, if desired

In Dutch oven, sauté onions and celery in butter till soft. Mix in flour and stir till barely brown. Stir in okra, cooking till soft, about 10 minutes. Add remaining ingredients except crabmeat and parsley. Bring to a boil, lower heat, cover, and simmer 10 minutes. Add crabmeat; stir and cook another 15 minutes, then turn heat off. Serve over hot rice, if desired, with a sprinkle of snipped parsley. Superb on its own with toast points or dainty crackers. Serves 6–10.

Note: This elegant gumbo can be prepared in about a half hour and served right away. You won't think it possible, but it is even more delectable after it has had a day of rest in the refrigerator (or a fortnight in the freezer!). It is so simple and so simply good! Curry powder or mace can be substituted for the nutmeg for equally delicious variations. Fun to serve in crockery custard cups, but definitely deserving of your bone china. Be sure to use real butter for maximum flavor. You may have to add a bit more water if serving over rice, as this is creamy and thick...and delightfully delicate. —*Gwen McKee*

The Little Gumbo Book

SOUPS, STEWS & CHILIS

Breaux Bridge Crawfish Stew

1 cup vegetable oil
1 cup all-purpose flour
2 cups chopped onions
1 cup chopped celery
1 cup chopped bell pepper
2 tablespoons minced garlic
2 pounds cleaned crawfish tails
¼ cup tomato sauce
3 quarts crawfish stock or water
1 cup chopped green onions
1 cup chopped parsley
Salt and cayenne pepper to taste
A dash or 2 of Tabasco

In a 2-gallon pot, heat oil over medium-high heat. Add flour; using a wire whisk, stir constantly till dark brown roux is achieved. When brown, add onions, celery, bell pepper, and garlic; sauté till vegetables are wilted, 3–5 minutes. Add crawfish tails, and cook till meat is pink and slightly curled.

Stir in tomato sauce, and slowly add crawfish stock, stirring constantly till all is incorporated. Bring to a low boil, reduce to simmer, and cook 30 minutes, stirring occasionally. Add green onions and parsley, and season to taste using salt and pepper. When done, serve over white rice with a few dashes of Tabasco.

Good Gumbo Weather

The Capitol Park Museum in Baton Rouge displays the history, industry, and culture of Louisiana that should be a must-see for tourists. From Sportsman's Paradise to the Louisiana Purchase to Mardi Gras . . . you can even hear Huey Long giving a speech. Artifacts include a Civil War submarine, a 48-foot wooden shrimp trawler, a record-breaking marlin, a New Orleans Lucky Dog cart, and musical artifacts from Fats Domino, Buddy Guy, Clarence Gatemouth Brown, Aaron Neville and much more. It is across the way from, and with a beautiful view of, the impressive state capitol.

SOUPS, STEWS & CHILIS

Beef Stew Crockpot

2 tablespoons vegetable oil
2 pounds beef stew meat, cut into 1-inch cubes
¼ cup all-purpose flour
Salt to taste
½ teaspoon black pepper
1 teaspoon Worcestershire
1 bay leaf
3 potatoes, diced, uncooked
1 stalk celery, chopped
1 teaspoon paprika
2 onions, chopped
2 teaspoons Kitchen Bouquet

In a crockpot, place vegetable oil, meat, flour, salt, and pepper; stir to coat meat. Cook on LOW till meat and flour brown. Add remaining ingredients, and stir till well mixed. Cover and cook on LOW about 10 hours or on HIGH for 4–6 hours. Serves 4–6.

The Landing Restaurant, Natchitoches
Louisiana's Best Restaurant Recipes

Deer Chili

1 pound ground deer meat
1 pound ground beef
½ pound ground pork
¼ cup cooking oil
2 large onions, chopped
3 ribs celery, chopped
1 large green bell pepper, chopped
4 large cloves garlic, chopped
2 (8-ounce) cans tomato sauce
2 (16-ounce) cans refried beans
2 ounces chili powder
Salt and pepper to taste
¼ cup dry sherry
Grated Cheddar cheese

Brown meats in oil. Add onions, celery, bell pepper, and garlic; cook till tender. Add tomato sauce, beans, and chili powder. Cook about 1 hour on low fire. Season, and add wine. Cook 10 minutes. Serve with grated cheese on top. Serves 8–10.

Classic Cajun Deux

LSU Tiger Stadium, Baton Rouge

Salads

Mixed Greens with Green
  Goddess Dressing 76
Grape Salad 77
Shoepeg Corn Salad...........77
Eunice and Steve's Strawberry
  Festival Salad 78
Orange and Onion
  Salad 80
Oriental Chicken Salad 81
Curried Chicken and Dried
  Cherry Salad 81

Shrimp and Pasta Boscolli
  Salad 82
Green Shrimp Salad 82
Orzo and Shrimp Salad.....85
Bow Tie Pasta Salad with
  Pesto 86
Old-Fashioned Wilted
  Salad 87
Ollie's Hot Potato Salad.....87

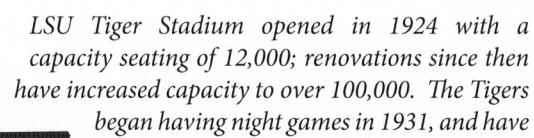

LSU Tiger Stadium opened in 1924 with a capacity seating of 12,000; renovations since then have increased capacity to over 100,000. The Tigers began having night games in 1931, and have an amazing win record there at night.

It is known as Death Valley (a.k.a Deaf Valley), and has been ranked the loudest stadium in all of college football by the NCAA in 2013. Former Alabama head coach Bear Bryant said, "It's like being inside a drum." Former Arkansas Governor Mike Huckabee stated, "Unfair is playing LSU on a Saturday night in Baton Rouge."

LSU beat Auburn 7–6 at Tiger Stadium in the legendary "Earthquake Game" in 1988 when the crowd reaction registered as a legitimate earthquake on the seismograph in the Louisiana Geological Survey office on campus.

SALADS

Mixed Greens with Green Goddess Dressing

GREEN GODDESS DRESSING:

2 cups sour cream
2 cups mayonnaise
1 (2-ounce) tube anchovy paste
1 tablespoon lemon juice
2–3 tablespoons tarragon vinegar
1½ bunches parsley, finely chopped

2–3 garlic cloves, finely chopped
2 bunches green onions, white part and a small amount of green part, finely chopped
Freshly ground pepper to taste

Blend sour cream and mayonnaise in a bowl. Add anchovy paste, lemon juice, and vinegar; mix well. Add parsley, garlic, and green onions; mix well. Season with pepper. Chill in the refrigerator. Makes 1 quart dressing.

SALAD:

1 (14-ounce) can hearts of palm, sliced

Mixed lettuces
Croutons

Add hearts of palm to lettuce in salad bowl. Pour dressing over salad and toss to coat. Top with croutons.

Da Cajn Critter

SALADS

Grape Salad

Pretty in stemware.

1 (8-ounce) package cream cheese, softened
1 (8-ounce) carton sour cream
⅓–½ cup sugar
1 teaspoon vanilla
4 cups green and red grapes
1 cup brown sugar
Chopped pecans

Mix together cream cheese, sour cream, sugar, and vanilla; add grapes. Stir, coating well.

Mix brown sugar and chopped pecans. Sprinkle on top of coated grapes. Serve chilled. Serves 8–10.

Hey, Good Lookin', What's Cooking?

Shoepeg Corn Salad

2 (12-ounce) cans shoepeg corn, drained
1 (14-ounce) can French-style green beans, drained
1 (8-ounce) can small green beans, drained
1 bunch green onions, chopped
¼ cup chopped green bell pepper
½ cup finely chopped celery
¾ cup sugar
¾ cup white vinegar
½ cup oil
1 teaspoon pepper
1 teaspoon celery salt

Combine veggies; set aside. Mix remaining ingredients in saucepan, and bring to a boil. Cool; pour over vegetables. Best to marinate overnight. Serves 6–8.

Mane Ingredients III

SALADS

Eunice and Steve's Strawberry Festival Salad

1 bunch romaine lettuce (washed, tough ends removed, coarsely cut)
½ medium red onion, sliced
1 pint fresh Louisiana strawberries, washed, stemmed, halved

Combine all ingredients in large bowl.

SUGARED ALMONDS:

2 tablespoons butter
½ cup slivered almonds
⅓ cup granulated sugar

In saucepan over medium heat, melt butter; stir in almonds and sugar. Sauté till golden brown.

POPPY SEED DRESSING:

¾ cup light mayonnaise
¼ cup milk
2 tablespoons poppy seeds
2 tablespoons raspberry vinegar
⅓ cup granulated sugar

Combine all ingredients in small mixing bowl; toss with salad and Sugared Almonds; chill briefly and serve. Serves 4–6.

A Street Car Named Delicious

The town of Ponchatoula puts on the state's largest free festival the second weekend of April each year in honor of the beloved strawberry. There's a parade, bands, floats with throws, contests, midway rides, lots of nonprofit booths, and strawberries galore . . . fried strawberries, chocolate-covered strawberries, strawberry beignets, and even strawberry snowballs and ice cream. Yum!

SALADS

Eunice and Steve's Strawberry Festival Salad

SALADS

Orange and Onion Salad

This salad is refreshing, colorful, and delicious with oriental cuisine—or any cuisine!

- 2 tablespoons red wine vinegar
- 1 teaspoon Dijon mustard
- ½ teaspoon salt
- Pinch of cayenne pepper
- Pinch of coarsely ground black pepper
- 1 tablespoon honey
- 6 tablespoons vegetable oil
- 1½ teaspoons poppy seeds
- 1 small head iceberg lettuce
- 1 (11-ounce) can Mandarin oranges, drained
- ½ small red onion, thinly sliced
- ½ cup sliced almonds, roasted

Combine first 8 ingredients; blend well; chill. Place torn iceberg lettuce, well-drained Mandarin oranges, onion slices, and almonds in a salad bowl. Toss with dressing, and serve immediately. Serves 4–6.

So Good . . . Make You Slap Your Mama!

"The Causeway" is composed of two 24-mile-long parallel bridges crossing Lake Pontchartrain from Metairie to Mandeville. The bridges are supported by 9,500 concrete pilings. From 1969 till 2011, it was listed by Guinness World Records as the longest bridge over water in the world. In 2011, in response to the opening of the allegedly longer Jiaozhou Bay Bridge in China, Guinness created two categories for bridges over water: Lake Pontchartrain Causeway then became the longest bridge over water (continuous), while Jiaozhou Bay Bridge became the longest bridge over water (aggregate).

SALADS

Oriental Chicken Salad

- 1 cup mayonnaise
- ¼ cup honey
- 2 tablespoons soy sauce
- 1 baked, smoked or boiled chicken, deboned, chopped
- ½ cup dried cranberries
- ½ cup toasted almonds
- ¼ cup chopped green onions
- ½ cup dry chow mein noodles

Combine mayonnaise, honey, and soy sauce in large bowl; mix well. Fold in chicken, cranberries, and almonds. Fold in green onions. Chill till serving time. Top with chow mein noodles. Serve on a bed of lettuce, or in avocado halves with crackers or rolls. Serves 6–8.

Something to Talk About

Curried Chicken and Dried Cherry Salad

- ½ cup mayonnaise
- ½ teaspoon turmeric
- ½ teaspoon ground cumin
- ½ teaspoon ground coriander
- ½ teaspoon ground clove
- 3 ounces (about ⅔ cup) dried cherries
- 2 cups diced, cooked chicken breasts

Mix spices into mayonnaise in a medium bowl. Stir in cherries, and allow to stand 5 minutes. Mix in chicken, and chill.

Serve over lettuce for a meal. For an appetizer, serve in a shallow bowl with toast points or toasted baguette slices. Serves 4.

Note: One tablespoon curry powder can replace the spices. Spices can be doubled for a bolder flavor, and mayonnaise can be doubled for a creamier dish.

Variations & Improvisations

SALADS

Shrimp and Pasta Boscolli Salad

½–1 pound fresh medium to large shrimp
Olive oil
Fresh lemon and lime juice to taste
1 clove garlic, crushed
1 tablespoon traditional basil pesto
1 (16-ounce) package seashell or rigatoni pasta
1 (14-ounce) can chopped hearts of palm, drained
1 (6-ounce) jar marinated artichoke hearts, partially drained, cut in half
1 (16-ounce) jar olive salad mix

Sauté shrimp in olive oil, lemon and lime juice, garlic, and pesto till pink and tender. Boil pasta till tender with 1 teaspoon olive oil. Drain pasta dry, and put into large serving bowl. Add hearts of palm, marinated artichoke hearts, and olive salad mix. Toss with shrimp, chill, and serve. Serves 6–8.

Steel Magnolias in the Kitchen

Green Shrimp Salad

1 pound peeled small shrimp
3 cups mayonnaise
2 tablespoons lemon juice
2 ripe avocados
1 bunch celery, chopped
2 bunches green onions, chopped

Sauté shrimp in saucepan with desired seasonings. Cool down shrimp with ice. Mix mayonnaise, lemon juice, and avocados in a blender till creamy. Finally, mix in shrimp, celery, and green onions. Serves 4.

The Magnolia Room, Bunkie
Louisiana's Best Restaurant Recipes

SALADS

Shrimp and Pasta Boscolli Salad

SALADS

Atchafalaya Basin

The Atchafalaya Basin, or Atchafalaya Swamp, is the largest wetland and swamp in the United States. Located in south central Louisiana, it is a combination of wetlands and river delta area where the Atchafalaya River and the Gulf of Mexico converge. The river stretches from near Simmesport in the north through parts of eight parishes to the Morgan City area in the south. The Atchafalaya is unique among Louisiana basins because it has a growing delta system with nearly stable wetlands.

Atchafalaya Video Tour: www.atchafalaya.org

SALADS

Orzo and Shrimp Salad

24 ounces orzo
Salt to taste
1½ bunches green onions, trimmed, chopped
12 ounces feta cheese, crumbled
¾ cup chopped fresh dill weed
7 tablespoons fresh lemon juice
6 tablespoons olive oil
3 pounds shrimp, peeled, deveined
Pepper to taste
2 English hothouse cucumbers, divided
2 baskets cherry tomatoes, cut into halves, divided
1 cup pine nuts (optional)
2 sprigs dill weed

Cook pasta in boiling salted water in saucepan 10 minutes, or just till tender; drain. Rinse with cold water till cool; drain again. Combine pasta, green onions, cheese, chopped dill weed, lemon juice, and olive oil in a bowl, and mix well.

Cook shrimp in boiling salted water in stockpot 2 minutes, or till shrimp turn pink; drain. Rinse with cold water to cool; drain again. Add to pasta mixture. Season with salt and pepper. Chill, covered, for up to 8 hours.

Cut 1½ cucumbers lengthwise into quarters, and cut crosswise into ¼-inch pieces. Add cucumber pieces, ¾ of the tomatoes, and the pine nuts to pasta mixture; mix well. Spoon salad into a large serving bowl, and arrange remaining tomatoes and cucumber rounds around the edge of the bowl. Garnish with sprigs of dill weed. Serves 20.

Mardi Gras to Mistletoe

SALADS

Bow Tie Pasta Salad with Pesto

¾ cup pine nuts
16 cups water
2 unpeeled garlic cloves
2 tablespoons salt, divided
Pepper to taste
1 pound bow tie pasta (farfelle)
1 tablespoon plus ¼ cup extra virgin olive oil, divided
3 cups packed fresh basil
1 cup packed baby spinach
2 tablespoons fresh lemon juice
¾ cup grated Parmesan cheese
6 tablespoons mayonnaise
1 pint cherry tomatoes, cut into quarters

Cook pine nuts in a small skillet over medium heat 4–5 minutes, or till toasted, shaking the pan occasionally. Bring water to a rolling boil in a large saucepan. Add garlic and boil 1 minute. Remove garlic with a slotted spoon and rinse with cold water to cool. Peel the garlic, and mince or press with a garlic press. Add 1 tablespoon salt, and pepper to taste to the boiling water. Add pasta, and cook till tender. Drain pasta, reserving ¼ cup cooking liquid. Toss pasta with 1 tablespoon olive oil. Spread in a single layer on a rimmed baking sheet. Let cool for 30 minutes.

Process ¼ cup of the pine nuts, the garlic, basil, spinach, lemon juice, ¼ cup olive oil, 1 tablespoon salt, and ½ teaspoon pepper in a food processor till smooth. Add Parmesan cheese and mayonnaise; mix till smooth. Spoon into a large bowl. Chill, covered, in the refrigerator.

To serve, toss cooled pasta with the pesto, adding 1 tablespoon of the reserved water at a time. Fold in remaining pine nuts and tomatoes. Serves 4–6.

Cooking in High Cotton

SALADS

Old-Fashioned Wilted Salad

2 tablespoons oil
4 teaspoons cider vinegar
2 teaspoons sugar
4 cups shredded leaf lettuce
1 cup chopped green onions
2 slices bacon, fried crisp, crumbled
2 hard-boiled eggs, peeled, sliced

Heat oil, vinegar, and sugar till very hot and sugar dissolves. Combine lettuce and green onions in a bowl. Pour heated mixture over lettuce and onions, and toss lightly. Top with bacon and sliced eggs. Serves 4.

Classic Cajun Deux

Ollie's Hot Potato Salad

½ pound bacon, cooked crisp, drippings reserved
⅓ cup vinegar, plus water to make ½ cup
1 egg, slightly beaten
1 teaspoon sugar
1 teaspoon salt
Black pepper to taste
½ cup chopped green onions
1 tablespoon Dijon mustard
5 cups peeled and diced cooked potatoes

Crumble bacon when cool; set aside. Combine ⅓ cup reserved bacon drippings with vinegar mixture, egg, sugar, salt, pepper, and green onions. Heat slowly over medium heat, and stir till thickened. Add mustard. Pour hot dressing over potatoes while potatoes are still hot. Add bacon and stir. Serve immediately. Serves 4.

Classic Cajun Culture & Cooking

World War II Museum, New Orleans

Vegetables

Creole String Beans 90	Stuffed Bell Peppers 99
Green Beans and Artichokes Romano 90	Ham, Okra, and Tomatoes 99
Eggplant Ritz Casserole 92	Mardi Gras Sweet Potatoes 100
Eggplant Casserole 93	Pickled Okra......................102
Shrimp-Stuffed Mirliton ...94	Fried Okra 102
Mirliton Casserole..............95	Jalapeño Corn Soufflé 103
Squash Fritters 97	Corn Casserole..................103
Aline's Squash Casserole...97	Spinach Madeleine 104
Squash Pecan 98	Spinach Casserole 105
Yellow Squash and Bacon 98	Nonnon Yeagley's Turnips.......................105

The National World War II Museum focuses on the contribution made by the United States to victory by the Allies in World War II, and the Battle of Normandy in particular. The museum originally opened as the D-Day Museum on June 6, 2000, the 56th anniversary of D-Day, focusing initially on the amphibious invasions of Normandy and the Pacific War. The Higgins Boats vital to D-Day operations were designed, built, and tested in New Orleans by Higgins Industries, so New Orleans was the natural home for such a project. Furthermore, New Orleans was the home of historian Stephen Ambrose, who spearheaded the effort to build the museum.

Creole String Beans

3 strips bacon, cut up
2 cups ham pieces, and ham bone
1 large onion, chopped
4 cloves garlic, minced
1 (15-ounce) can tomatoes
3 (16-ounce) cans string beans, drained
6 new potatoes, scrubbed, peeled or unpeeled
Salt and pepper to taste

Cook all ingredients, except potatoes, in large covered pot for 20 minutes. Add potatoes and salt and pepper. Cook till tender. Serves 6–8.

Note: May use fresh string beans instead of canned.

Down the Bayou

Green Beans and Artichokes Romano

This is an easy casserole that can also be prepared with broccoli.

½ cup chopped onion
1 clove garlic, minced
¼ cup olive oil
½ cup Italian bread crumbs
1 (14-ounce) can artichoke hearts, drained, quartered
½ cup sliced canned mushrooms, divided
1 (10-ounce) package frozen green beans, cooked, drained
½ cup freshly grated Romano cheese
Salt, pepper, and cayenne pepper to taste

Sauté onion and garlic in olive oil till onion is tender. Stir in bread crumbs, mixing till oil is absorbed. Remove from heat. Add artichoke hearts, mushrooms, green beans, and cheese. Season to taste. Put in greased casserole dish and bake at 350° for 20 minutes to soften cheese. Serves 4.

Extra! Extra! Read More About It!

VEGETABLES

Creole String Beans

VEGETABLES

Eggplant Ritz Casserole

1 pound ground beef
1 medium onion, chopped
1 small green bell pepper, chopped
2 ribs celery, chopped
2 cloves garlic, chopped, or 1 teaspoon garlic powder
3 medium eggplants, peeled and diced
1 (10¾-ounce) can cream of mushroom soup
1 (8-ounce) box Ritz Crackers, crushed (reserve one cup for topping)
Parsley
Salt and pepper to taste
Butter to dot topping
Paprika for garnish

Brown ground beef with onion, bell pepper, and celery. Add garlic, eggplants, and small amount of water (about ⅛ cup). Simmer till eggplant is very tender. Add soup, crushed crackers, and parsley. Season to taste. Place in casserole dish, and top with reserved crushed crackers. Top crackers with dots of butter and paprika. Bake at 350° for 30 minutes. Serves 6–8.

Note: Mirliton or squash may be substituted for eggplant.

Come to the Table

The New Orleans dialect is practically a language of its own. Some say it sounds sort of "Southern Bronx." Besides the language, there are lots of things unique to New Orleanians.

- You make groceries.
- You call a median in the middle of a boulevard the neutral ground.
- Your burial plot is six feet over—not under.
- When you hear magazine, you don't think of something to read—it's a street.
- You know how to pronounce Tchoupitoulas (Chop-a-TOO-las).
- You don't realize that Mardi Gras is not a national holiday till you're grown.
- You go out to dinner and talk about nothing but other good places to eat.
- No matter where you eat away from home, you are disappointed in the food.
- Your question to any caller is, "Where y'at?"
- You love the Saints forever, win or lose.

VEGETABLES

Eggplant Casserole

2 or 3 medium eggplants
Water
1 teaspoon salt
1 small onion, chopped
1 (2-ounce) jar chopped pimento

½ stick butter
½ cup whipping cream
4 eggs
1 cup cracker crumbs
¾ cup grated cheese

Boil peeled and cut-up eggplants in water in which salt has been added. Boil till tender; drain. Add onion, pimento, butter, and cream. Beat eggs in small bowl, and fold into eggplant mixture. Put in greased casserole, and top with crumbs and grated cheese. Heat in oven till hot and bubbly. Serves 8–10.

Pots, Pans, and Pioneers I

The Audubon Aquarium of the Americas is recognized as one of the leading aquariums in the United States. Run by the Audubon Institute, which also supervises the Audubon Zoo and Audubon Park, it is picturesquely located by the edge of the French Quarter along the banks of the Mississippi River. You can walk through a clear tunnel surrounded by 132,000 gallons of water to see the Caribbean Exhibit. And you can feel the humid greenhouse climate in the glass structure of the Amazon Exhibit. Opened in 1990, the exhibits now include 10,000 North and South American animals representing 530 species.

VEGETABLES

Shrimp-Stuffed Mirliton

4 (8-ounce) mirliton squash
½ pound uncooked shrimp, peeled
½ pound coarsely chopped cooked smoked ham
1 medium-size onion, chopped
2 garlic cloves, minced
¼ cup finely chopped fresh parsley
¼ teaspoon ground thyme
¼ teaspoon ground hot red pepper
¼ teaspoon Tony Chachere's seasoning
Salt to taste
11 tablespoons butter, cut into ½-inch bits, divided
1 cup soft, fresh bread crumbs (made from fresh French bread)

Drop mirlitons into enough boiling water to immerse completely. Cook briskly, uncovered, about 45 minutes, or till they show no resistance when pierced with the point of a knife. Drain; when cool, cut lengthwise into halves. Remove seeds, and hollow out each half with a spoon to make boat-like shells about ¼ inch thick. Reserve pulp. Invert shells on paper towels to drain.

Pureé pulp. Transfer pulp to a heavy ungreased skillet and, stirring constantly, cook over moderate heat till all liquid evaporates. Add 8 tablespoons butter bits to pureé and when it melts, stir in shrimp, ham, onion, and garlic; continue cooking till shrimp are pink and onion is soft. Add parsley, thyme, red pepper, Tony Chachere's, and salt. Taste for seasoning.

Spoon shrimp/squash stuffing into reserved mirliton shells, dividing it equally among them, mounding tops slightly. Sprinkle bread crumbs and remaining 3 tablespoons butter bits over mirlitons. Arrange shells in buttered dish, and bake at 350° in middle of oven for 30 minutes, or till tops are brown. Serve at once. Serves 8.

Tell Me More

VEGETABLES

Mirliton Casserole

6 mirlitons
1 pound ground beef
3 tablespoons butter
3 ribs celery, chopped
1 large onion, chopped
½ green bell pepper, chopped
2 pods garlic, minced
4 green onion tops, chopped
1 tablespoon chopped parsley
Salt and pepper to taste
Seasoned bread crumbs
Parmesan cheese

Cut mirlitons in half and boil in lightly salted water (to cover mirlitons completely) till tender; drain, cool. Remove seeds and center strings, and gently scrape out the pulp; set aside. Brown ground beef in butter; add celery, onion, bell pepper, and garlic. Cook till soft. Add mirliton pulp, and mash together. Cook about 15 minutes.

Add green onion tops and parsley, and season to taste. Pour into greased casserole dish, top with bread crumbs, and bake in 350° oven 30 minutes, till bubbly. Sprinkle with Parmesan cheese when serving. Freezes well. Serves 6–8.

Note: May substitute shrimp for beef, but add after cooking vegetables.

Vedros Family Recipes

In Louisiana Creole and Cajun cuisine, chayote is known as mirliton. It is a green pear-shaped squash that resembles cucumber in flavor.

Natchitoches

Natchitoches (Nack-A-Tish) is Louisiana's oldest town.

The quaint little town in the movie *Steel Magnolias* is real! Named after the Natchitoches Indian tribe, it was established in 1714 by Louis Juchereau de St. Denis as part of French Louisiana. It is the oldest permanent settlement in the Louisiana Purchase. Natchitoches is also recognized as the Bed & Breakfast Capital of Louisiana, and home to the Cane River Creole National Historical Park. The National Trust named it one of the 2005 "Dozen Distinctive Destinations" for Historic Preservation.

Since 1926, Natchitoches has been known for its popular Christmas Festival of Lights, which begins the first Saturday in December, and continues to brighten Cane River Lake until after New Year's Day.

Several motion pictures have been filmed in Natchitoches, including *Steel Magnolias*, *The Man in the Moon*, *The Horse Soldiers*, NBC's *The Year Without a Santa Claus*, *The American Standard*, as well as a Lifetime Television series, *Scarlett*.

The famous Natchitoches Meat Pie is one of the official state foods of Louisiana.

Squash Fritters

1–1½ teaspoons salt
1 medium onion, chopped fine
3 cups grated raw yellow squash
½ cup all-purpose flour
½ teaspoon baking powder
1 tablespoon sugar
2 eggs, beaten
2 tablespoons cooking oil

In bowl, add salt and onion to grated squash. Let stand 1 hour or more. Using a large strainer, squeeze a small amount of mixture through at a time, removing as much liquid as possible. Add remaining ingredients; if not thick enough to hold together, add more flour. Drop by heaping tablespoonfuls, well apart, in oil heated in skillet, and spread each fritter so it is about 3 or 4 inches in diameter. Fry till golden brown on both sides; drain on paper towels. Keep warm, and serve immediately.

Pots, Pans, and Pioneers II

Aline's Squash Casserole

2 pounds yellow squash
1 cup chopped onion
1 cup chopped green bell pepper
1 (8-ounce) can sliced water chestnuts
1 cup grated cheese
Salt and pepper to taste
1 cup mayonnaise
1 teaspoon sugar
1 egg, beaten
Bread crumbs
1 stick butter

Preheat oven to 350°. Cut and boil squash in salted water; drain well. Add onion and bell pepper to squash. Add remaining ingredients, except bread crumbs and butter. Spoon in casserole dish. Cover with bread crumbs, then with pats of butter. Bake 15 minutes at 350°.

Pots, Pans, and Pioneers V

VEGETABLES

Squash Pecan

3 pounds yellow squash
½ cup butter, melted
2 teaspoons sugar
2 eggs, beaten
¾ cup grated mild Cheddar cheese
1 cup mayonnaise
Salt and pepper to taste
1 cup broken or chopped pecans
½ cup buttered bread crumbs

Trim ends, and cut squash into thick slices. Boil till very tender; drain thoroughly. In a large bowl, mix butter, sugar, eggs, cheese, mayonnaise, salt and pepper. Add squash and mash everything together with a potato masher, or pulse a few times in food processor. Leave squash rather chunky.

Pour mixture into a buttered 10x13-inch glass baking dish. Top with pecans and bread crumbs. Bake 20 minutes at 400°. Serves 12–16.

Variations & Improvisations

Yellow Squash and Bacon

2 large strips bacon
5 medium squash (about 6 inches long)
1 small onion, chopped
Salt and black pepper to taste
A little sugar (optional)

Fry bacon till crisp; set aside. Slice squash crosswise (do not pare) about ⅛ inch thick; add to bacon drippings. Add chopped onion. Turn to low heat, and let cook slowly, covered. Will cook in own juice. Stir occasionally, chopping up squash with spoon each time till it is all broken up and tender. Add seasonings. Crumble up bacon and add to squash. A little sugar can be added, if desired.

Pots, Pans, and Pioneers I

Stuffed Bell Peppers

11 large green bell peppers, divided
1 pound ground beef
¼ cup oil
1 large onion, chopped
Salt and pepper to taste
¼ cup chopped green onion tops
2 cups cooked and cooled rice

Cut off and reserve the tops of 10 bell peppers; remove stems and seeds. Brown beef in oil in skillet. Chop remaining green bell pepper; add to beef with onion and cook about 10 minutes; season with salt and pepper. Add green onions and mix thoroughly. Mix in rice. Stuff mixture into 10 bell peppers and replace tops. Place stuffed peppers into a shallow baking pan and add a small amount of water to bottom of pan. Bake at 350° for 30 minutes. Serves 10.

Classic Cajun Deux

Ham, Okra, and Tomatoes

2 tablespoons cooking oil
1 pound sliced fresh okra (or frozen)
1 medium onion, chopped
3 or 4 tomatoes, cut up
1 pound diced ham
1 teaspoon salt
½ teaspoon pepper

Heat cooking oil; add okra, and smother down. Add onion and tomatoes; simmer 10 minutes. Add remaining ingredients, and continue to simmer about 30 minutes. Serves 4.

Pots, Pans, and Pioneers II

VEGETABLES

Mardi Gras Sweet Potatoes

3 pounds Oak Grove sweet potatoes
3 Granny Smith apples
¼ cup lemon juice
1¼ cups chopped pecans
1 stick butter

½ cup packed brown sugar
½ cup honey
2 tablespoons dark rum (optional)
½ teaspoon cinnamon

Preheat oven to 425°. Scrub potatoes and place in single layer in baking pan. Bake 40 minutes, or till tender. Remove from oven. Reduce oven temperature to 300°. Peel sweet potatoes and cut into wedges. Peel apples and cut into wedges. Toss apples in lemon juice in a bowl. Alternate layers of sweet potatoes and apples in a 9x13-inch baking dish sprayed with nonstick cooking spray. Sprinkle with pecans. Combine butter, brown sugar, honey, rum, and cinnamon in a saucepan. Bring to a simmer. Simmer till slightly thickened, stirring constantly. Pour over top. Bake 15 minutes, or till heated through. Serves 9.

Cooking in High Cotton

Mardi Gras Beads

Inexpensive strings of beads and toys have been thrown from Mardi Gras floats to parade-goers since at least the late 19th century. Until the 1960s, the multicolored beads were glass. These were supplanted by less expensive beads so more could be thrown. Doubloons and other things, including coconuts, were also thrown. In the 1990s, many people lost interest in small, cheap beads, often leaving them on the ground. With the advent of the 21st century, Krewes started to produce limited edition beads and plush toys unique to their krewe. Fiber-optic beads and lit-up LED-powered prizes are now among the most sought-after items. In a retro-inspired twist, glass beads have returned to parades, now one of the most valuable throws.

VEGETABLES

Mardi Gras Sweet Potatoes

Pickled Okra

4 pounds small okra
1 cup water
¾ cup plain salt
8 cups vinegar
10 pods red or hot pepper
2 tablespoons whole pickling spice
10 cloves garlic

Wash okra; leave small stems. Pack in hot sterile jars. Heat water, salt, and vinegar together, and bring to a boil; add seasonings, and simmer 10 minutes. Pour over okra in jars. Seal tightly, and let stand 8 weeks before using. Place in refrigerator, and chill before opening.

Pots, Pans, and Pioneers I

Fried Okra

1 pound fresh okra
2 eggs
¼ cup buttermilk
1 cup self-rising flour
1 cup self-rising cornmeal
Vegetable oil

Wash and slice okra. Pat dry with paper towel. Combine eggs and buttermilk. Add okra, and let stand 10 minutes. Combine flour and cornmeal. Drain okra, using a slotted spoon. Dredge okra in flour and cornmeal mixture. Fry in hot vegetable oil till golden brown. Serves 4–6.

Pots, Pans, and Pioneers IV

Jalapeño Corn Soufflé

1 cup yellow cornmeal
1 tablespoon sugar
1½ teaspoons baking powder
1 teaspoon salt
2 eggs, beaten
1 (16-ounce) can cream-style corn
1 large onion, diced
½ cup bacon drippings
3 cups shredded Cheddar cheese
2 jalapeño peppers, seeded, minced
4–5 garlic cloves, pressed
1 tablespoon Tabasco

Combine cornmeal, sugar, baking powder, and salt in a large bowl; mix well. Add eggs, corn, onion, bacon drippings, cheese, jalapeños, garlic, and Tabasco; mix well. Spoon into a greased 9x12-inch baking dish. Bake in preheated 400° oven for 40 minutes. Serves 12.

Marshes to Mansions

Corn Casserole

1 (16-ounce) can cream-style corn
1 (16-ounce) can whole-kernel corn, drained
½ cup chopped green bell pepper
1 (2-ounce) bottle chopped pimento
½ cup chopped onion
1 cup grated sharp Cheddar cheese
1 cup cracker crumbs
1 egg, beaten
⅔ cup milk
¼ cup margarine, melted
2 tablespoons sugar

Mix all ingredients together; stir well. Bake in greased 9x13-inch baking dish in 350° oven 45–50 minutes. Serves 6–8.

Mane Ingredients III

VEGETABLES

Spinach Madeleine

2 (10-ounce) packages frozen chopped spinach
4 tablespoons butter
2 tablespoons all-purpose flour
2 tablespoons chopped onion
½ cup evaporated milk
½ cup reserved vegetable liquor
½ teaspoon black pepper
¾ teaspoon celery salt
¾ teaspoon garlic salt
Salt to taste
1 teaspoon Worcestershire
Red pepper to taste
⅓ (1-pound) box Mexican Velveeta, cubed

Cook spinach according to package directions. Drain and reserve pot liquor. Melt butter in saucepan over low heat. Add flour, stirring till blended and smooth, but not brown. Add onion and cook till soft. Add liquids slowly, stirring constantly to avoid lumps. Cook till smooth and thick; continue stirring. Add seasonings and Velveeta. Stir till melted. Combine with cooked spinach. Serve immediately. Serves 5–6.

Note: The flavor improves if refrigerated overnight in a covered casserole dish. Top with buttered bread crumbs, and bake at 350° for 30 minutes. This may also be frozen.

River Road Recipes I

Saint Louis Cemetery, first opened in 1789, is actually three separate Roman Catholic cemeteries (No. 1 and No. 2 are near the Quarter; No. 3 is a couple of miles distant) in New Orleans. Historical and ghost tours are given daily to visit the graves of notable figures, including pirate Jean Lafitte and the famous voodoo queen, Marie Laveau. The custom of above-ground burial is a mixture of folklore and fact, due more to the French and Spanish tradition than to water table problems. Heavily flooded during the aftermath of Hurricane Katrina in 2005, the tombs escaped relatively unscathed.

VEGETABLES

Spinach Casserole

1 (10-ounce) box frozen cut spinach, thawed
1 (8-ounce) carton Kraft French Onion Dip
1 cup seasoned bread crumbs, divided
Tabasco sauce to taste

Cook spinach according to package directions. Drain, squeezing all water out. Mix with dip and ½ cup bread crumbs. Season with Tabasco. Pour into buttered casserole dish. Top with remaining ½ cup bread crumbs. Bake at 350° for 30–45 minutes.

Pots, Pans, and Pioneers II

Nonnon Yeagley's Turnips

My husband's grandmother was reputed to be one of the best cooks in Shreveport. These turnips will attest to that! —Marlyn Monette

6–8 medium fresh turnips, peeled
1–2 quarts water
1½ teaspoons sugar
Salt to taste
½ cup half-and-half
Pepper to taste
½ cup grated sharp Cheddar cheese

Cut turnips into 2-inch chunks and place in heavy saucepan with water, sugar, and salt. Boil turnips till tender, 20–30 minutes. Drain turnips and place in a 2-quart casserole. Toss with half-and-half and pepper; sprinkle with cheese. Keep warm till ready to serve. Serves 4–6.

So Good . . . Make You Slap Your Mama!

Louisiana wetlands

Pasta, Rice, Etc.

Chicken Tetrazzini...........108
Peggy's Shrimp Fettuccine....................109
Angel Hair Pasta with Crawfish Tails.............110
Meat-and-Spinach-Stuffed Pasta Shells 112
Pasta Primavera................113
Shrimp and Scallop Lasagna.......................114
Lasagna.............................115
Southern Baked Macaroni and Cheese..................116

Rice–Fluff Method 116
Dirty Rice Dressing..........117
Crawfish Rice.....................117
C'est Bon Jambalaya........118
Pork Chop Jambalaya......118
Baked Cabbage Jambalaya....................120
Spinach & Lump Crabmeat Quiche 121
Muffuletta 122

Louisiana is associated with swamps and wetlands more than any other state. The swamps are seemingly resilient to hurricane damage, as well as man's efforts to control the wetlands. On her many waterways, whether to fish or sightsee, it's a great way to pass a good time with friends. You can paddle a canoe, rev up a motor boat, catch a party boat, or venture out solo on a jet ski. Or take one of the many interesting swamp tours available, including the Honey Island Swamp Tour, departing from Slidell, which gives visitors an idea of how the wetlands have shaped the history of southern Louisiana. Among the cypress, tupelos, and river birch trees, alligators, herons, kingfishers, and nutria, you never know what lies around the next bend.

PASTA, RICE, ETC.

Chicken Tetrazzini

1 (4-pound) chicken, quartered
1 carrot, diced
1 medium onion, chopped
2 stalks celery, coarsely chopped
Salt and pepper to taste
3 tablespoons butter or chicken fat
3 tablespoons all-purpose flour
2 cups chicken broth
1 cup half-and-half
½ pound mushrooms, sautéed in butter
2 tablespoons sherry
½ pound spaghetti
¼ pound grated Parmesan or Cheddar cheese
½ cup buttered bread crumbs

Boil chicken with carrot, onion, celery, salt, and pepper in water to cover till tender. Allow chicken to cool in broth, then remove and cut into bite-size pieces. Strain broth and reserve.

Make a medium sauce with butter or chicken fat, flour, 2 cups chicken broth, and half-and-half. Add mushrooms and sherry.

Boil spaghetti according to package directions in reserved chicken broth. Combine sauce, mushrooms, chicken, and spaghetti in greased baking dish. Sprinkle with grated cheese and bread crumbs, and bake in 375° oven till heated thoroughly and lightly browned. Serves 8–10.

River Road Recipes II

PASTA, RICE, ETC.

Peggy's Shrimp Fettuccine

1 onion, chopped
½ green bell pepper, chopped
1 stick margarine or butter
2 pounds peeled, deveined shrimp
1 (10¾-ounce) can cream of mushroom soup
1 (14½-ounce) can evaporated milk
¼ cup all-purpose flour
1 cup water
Red pepper, black pepper, and salt to taste
1 (14-ounce) can sliced mushrooms, drained
4 ounces cheese (American or Swiss), shredded
¼ cup finely chopped green onion tops
¼ cup finely chopped parsley
1 package fettuccine noodles, cooked

In large saucepan, sauté onion and bell pepper in margarine. Add shrimp, soup, and milk; cook for a few minutes. Blend flour into water, and add to mixture. Season to taste, and add mushrooms, cheese, onion tops, and parsley. Cook over low heat about 25 minutes, or till thickened, and flavors blend. Serve over fettuccine. Serves 8.

Note: Try this mixture in tart shells, or serve on croissants. Crawfish may be substituted for shrimp.

Down the Bayou . . . and Back Again

Nicknames for New Orleans:
- **Crescent City** alludes to the course of the Lower Mississippi River around and through the city.
- **The Big Easy** was possibly a reference by musicians in the early 20th century to the relative ease of finding work there. It also may have originated in the Prohibition era, when the city was considered one big speak-easy, due to the inability of the federal government to control alcohol sales.
- **NOLA** is an abbreviation of New Orleans, Louisiana.
- **The City That Care Forgot** refers to the easy-going carefree nature of many residents.
- **Nawlins** is just New Orleans for short.

PASTA, RICE, ETC.

Angel Hair Pasta with Crawfish Tails

1 pound angel hair pasta
¼ cup olive oil
1 tablespoon freshly minced garlic
1 pound peeled crawfish tails
1 medium tomato wedge
1 cup chopped fresh yellow squash
1 cup chopped fresh zucchini
Pinch of oregano
6 basil leaves
¼ cup chopped fresh parsley
Dash of lemon pepper
Squeeze of lemon juice
Romano cheese for topping

Cook pasta; drain and set aside. Pour olive oil in a large skillet. Add garlic, crawfish tails, tomato, squash, zucchini, oregano, basil, and parsley; sauté about 8 minutes. While sautéing, add lemon pepper and lemon juice. Stir gently. Put individual servings of pasta on plates and top with sauté mixture. Sprinkle with Romano cheese. Serve hot. Makes 6 servings.

Dominic's Italian Restaurant, Natchitoches
Louisiana's Best Restaurant Recipes

Louisiana on Film

Louisiana's thriving film industry exists in New Orleans, Shreveport, and Baton Rouge. State financial incentives since 2002 and aggressive promotion have given Louisiana the nickname "Hollywood South." Some of the movies and TV productions filmed here over the years are: *Tarzan of the Apes* (1918), *A Streetcar Named Desire* (1951), *Steel Magnolias* (1989), *Interview With the Vampire* (1994), *Easy Rider* (1969), *The Big Easy* (1986), *The Curious Case of Benjamin Button* (2008), *Duck Dynasty* (2012–current, A&E Network), *True Blood* (2008–2014, HBO), *Tremé* (2010–current, HBO), *Swamp People* (2010–current, History Channel), and many more. There are places tourists can go where they can relive scenes from these movies and TV shows.
See www.louisianatravel.com/articles/famous-movies-filmed-louisiana

PASTA, RICE, ETC.

Angel Hair Pasta with Crawfish Tails

PASTA, RICE, ETC.

Meat-and-Spinach-Stuffed Pasta Shells

1 tablespoon olive oil
2 pounds lean ground beef, or a mix of beef and turkey
1 medium onion, chopped
2 cloves garlic, chopped
½ green bell pepper, chopped
1 or 2 ribs celery, chopped
Salt, black pepper, and cayenne pepper to taste
Pinch of dried oregano
2 tablespoons chopped fresh basil or parsley
1 (10-ounce) package frozen chopped spinach
1 (12- to 16-ounce) package jumbo pasta shells
¾ cup grated Romano cheese
1 cup plain bread crumbs
2 eggs, slightly beaten
1 quart marinara sauce, either homemade or purchased
½ cup grated mozzarella or Romano cheese for top

In a large skillet, heat olive oil, and brown meat. Pour off fat; add onion, garlic, bell pepper, and celery. Season with salt, peppers, and oregano. Cook till vegetables are tender; remove from heat. Add parsley or basil, and set aside. Meanwhile, cook spinach according to package directions, then squeeze dry. Set aside.

Cook pasta shells according to package directions; drain and set aside. Add drained spinach, Romano cheese, bread crumbs, and beaten eggs to the meat mixture, and stir. Spoon about 1½ tablespoons of filling into each pasta shell. Pour 2 cups of marinara sauce in bottom of a 9x13-inch baking dish sprayed with nonstick coating. Place stuffed shells in single layer over sauce. Pour remaining sauce over top of shells, and top with mozzarella or Romano cheese. Bake in preheated 350° oven for 20–30 minutes, or till bubbly. Serves 8.

Note: Stuffed shells can be made ahead and frozen. When ready to use, pour 2 cups sauce in bottom of baking dish, and place unthawed shells over sauce. Cover with foil, and bake 40 minutes at 350°. Uncover, sprinkle with cheese, and bake an additional 15–20 minutes, or till bubbly.

Extra! Extra! Read More About It!

PASTA, RICE, ETC.

Pasta Primavera

1 pound fresh asparagus
2 cups fresh broccoli flowerets
1 medium onion, chopped
1 large clove garlic, chopped
1 tablespoon olive oil
1 large carrot, scraped, diagonally sliced
1 medium-size sweet red bell pepper, coarsely chopped
1 medium-size sweet yellow bell pepper, coarsely chopped
1 cup whipping cream
½ cup chicken broth
3 green onions, chopped
2 tablespoons chopped fresh basil, or 2 teaspoons dried
½ teaspoon salt
8 ounces uncooked linguine, broken
½ pound fresh mushrooms, sliced
1 cup freshly grated Parmesan cheese
¼ teaspoon freshly ground pepper

Snap off tough ends of asparagus. Remove scales with a vegetable peeler or knife, if desired. Cut diagonally into 1½-inch pieces. Place asparagus pieces and broccoli flowerets in a vegetable steamer over boiling water; cover and steam 6–8 minutes, or till vegetables are crisp-tender. Remove from heat; set aside.

Sauté onion and garlic in oil in a large skillet till tender. Add carrot and bell peppers to onion mixture; sauté till crisp-tender. Remove from heat; drain.

Combine cream, broth, green onions, basil, and salt in a medium skillet. Cook over medium-high heat for 6 minutes, stirring occasionally.

Cook linguine according to package directions. Drain well; place in a large serving bowl. Add reserved vegetables, whipping cream mixture, and sliced mushrooms; toss gently. Sprinkle with Parmesan cheese and pepper; toss gently. Serve immediately. Serves 8.

Pots, Pans, and Pioneers IV

PASTA, RICE, ETC.

Shrimp and Scallop Lasagna

9 lasagna noodles
Salt to taste
3 tablespoons unsalted butter
1 small onion, chopped
1 green bell pepper, chopped
½ cup chopped celery
1 garlic clove, minced
3 tablespoons all-purpose flour
2½ cups half-and-half
1 cup freshly grated Romano cheese
2 green onions, chopped
½ teaspoon salt
¼ teaspoon pepper
1 pound large sea scallops
1 pound medium shrimp, peeled, deveined
½ cup freshly grated Parmesan cheese

Cook lasagna noodles in boiling salted water in a saucepan for 8 minutes, or till al dente; drain; set aside.

Melt butter in a large heavy skillet. Add onion, bell pepper, and celery. Cook over low heat 5 minutes, or till vegetables are soft. Add garlic. Cook 1 minute. Increase heat to medium-low, and whisk in flour. Gradually add half-and-half, allowing sauce to thicken slightly after each addition. Cook till sauce has thickened to about the consistency of whipping cream. Stir in Romano cheese and green onions. Stir in ½ teaspoon salt and pepper. Add scallops, and cook 3–4 minutes. Add shrimp, and cook 1–2 minutes, or till shrimp turn pink. Turn off heat.

Preheat oven to 375°. Spoon about 2 tablespoons of sauce into a 9x13-inch dish sprayed with nonstick cooking spray. Arrange 3 of the noodles side by side in the sauce. Spoon a third of the remaining sauce over the noodles. Top evenly with half the seafood. Continue layering with half of remaining noodles, half of remaining sauce, the remaining seafood, and remaining noodles. Top with remaining sauce, tucking in the edges of the noodles so they are coated with sauce. Sprinkle with Parmesan cheese. Bake, uncovered 20–25 minutes, or till bubbly. Remove from oven, and let stand 10 minutes before serving. Serves 6.

Cooking in High Cotton

PASTA, RICE, ETC.

Lasagna

1 pound ground beef
1 (16-ounce) can diced
 tomatoes
1 (12-ounce) can tomato paste
1 tablespoon crushed dried
 basil
2½ teaspoons salt, divided
1 garlic clove, minced
1 (10-ounce) package lasagna
 noodles
3 cups ricotta cheese or
 cottage cheese
½ cup grated Parmesan cheese
2 tablespoons parsley flakes
2 eggs, beaten
½ teaspoon pepper
16 ounces mozzarella cheese,
 shredded

Brown ground beef in saucepan, stirring till crumbly; drain. Stir in tomatoes, tomato paste, basil, 1½ teaspoons salt, and garlic. Simmer 30 minutes, stirring occasionally.

Cook pasta according to package directions. Drain and rinse.

Combine ricotta cheese, Parmesan cheese, parsley flakes, eggs, remaining 1 teaspoon salt, and the pepper in a bowl; mix well.

Layer pasta, ricotta cheese mixture, mozzarella cheese, and meat sauce one-half at a time in the order listed in a 9x13-inch baking dish. Bake in preheated 375° oven 30 minutes. Let stand 10 minutes before serving. Serves 6–8.

Crescent City Moons / Dishes and Spoons

Sean Payton, head coach of the New Orleans Saints, ranks among the most successful head coaches in franchise history. He is the only coach to lead the Saints to a Super Bowl championship (2009) and was a unanimous choice for NFL Coach of the Year. He has been the architect of an offense (along with Drew Brees) that has rewritten the record books, and has instilled a winning culture for the Saints.

PASTA, RICE, ETC.

Southern Baked Macaroni and Cheese

3 cups macaroni, uncooked
1½ cups milk
½ cup heavy cream
1 cup grated sharp Cheddar cheese
1 cup shredded Colby and Monterey Jack cheese blend
6–8 ounces Velveeta cheese, cubed
Salt and pepper to taste
Paprika
2 eggs, beaten
1 cup shredded smoked Cheddar cheese

Preheat oven to 350°. Cook macaroni; drain, and set aside. In large bowl, add milk, cream, and all cheeses except smoked Cheddar. Stir, and add salt, pepper, and paprika. Add eggs; mix well. Butter a 9x9-inch pan; add macaroni and cheese mix to pan. Top with smoked Cheddar. Bake 35–40 minutes. Serves 6.

Recipes from the Heart

Rice–Fluff Method

2 cups water
1 teaspoon salt
1 teaspoon butter
2 teaspoons vinegar
1 cup white rice

Bring water, salt, butter, and vinegar to a boil. Add rice, and let it return to a hard boil; lower flame to simmer. Cover tightly; do not stir or peek. Cook 35 minutes. Do not rinse. Remove cover 5 minutes before serving. Lift rice into dish with large serving fork. A heavy pot is best for this method, or use a trivet underneath.

Pots, Pans, and Pioneers I

PASTA, RICE, ETC.

Dirty Rice Dressing

1 pound chicken gizzards, ground
1 pound ground beef or pork
1 cup oil
½ cup chopped green bell pepper
1 cup chopped onion
¼ cup chopped celery
Salt and pepper to taste
4 cups cooked rice
¼ cup chopped green onion tops

Brown ground meats in oil in heavy pot. When browned well, add bell pepper, onion, and celery. Season to taste. Cook together on medium heat for 20 minutes. Add rice and onion tops. Mix well, cover, and simmer 10 minutes. Serves 6–8.

Classic Cajun

Crawfish Rice

2 cups frozen seasoning blend (onions, celery, peppers)
1 stick butter
2 packages crawfish tails (or imitation crabmeat, shrimp, or crawfish and crab)
2 packages frozen broccoli, defrosted (optional)
1 (10¾-ounce) can cream of mushroom soup
1 (4-ounce) can mushrooms
1 (16-ounce) jar Cheez Whiz
2½ cups cooked rice
Tony Cachere's Creole Seasoning or hot sauce to taste

Sauté frozen seasoning blend in butter. Add next 5 ingredients to seasoning blend. Season rice with Tony's or hot sauce. Mix all together, and bake at 350° for 20–30 minutes in a buttered 9x13-inch baking pan. Good to make the day before. Serves 8–10.

Hey, Good Lookin', What's Cooking?

PASTA, RICE, ETC.

C'est Bon Jambalaya

2 cups sausage rings (sliced sausage)
2 cups diced ham
2 cups chopped onions
½ cup chopped celery
6 toes garlic, chopped
½ cup chopped parsley
1 (10-ounce) can Ro-Tel tomatoes
4 tablespoons tomato paste
4 cups water
1 teaspoon chili powder
1 teaspoon salt
½ teaspoon pepper
½ teaspoon cayenne
½ bunch green onions, chopped
1½ cups raw rice, cooked

Mix all ingredients except green onions and rice in a large pot, and simmer, about 30 minutes. Add green onions. Cook rice, and stir into mixture. Ready to serve. Serves 8.

deBellevue Williams Cochon de Lait

Pork Chop Jambalaya

¼ inch oil in bottom of pot
2 pounds pork chops
Salt and pepper to taste
1 cup chopped onion
¾ cup chopped green bell pepper
¼ cup chopped celery
1 cup water
4 cups cooked rice
1½ cups chopped green onion tops

Add oil to a large skillet; brown pork chops that have been seasoned to taste. Remove chops from skillet. Sauté onion, bell pepper, and celery in oil that chops were browned in. Remove as much oil from pot as you can, and add a small amount of water to form a gravy. Put chops back into the pot. Cook on medium heat about 20 minutes. Add cooked rice and onion tops; stir well. Cover and simmer 10 minutes. Serves 4.

Classic Cajun

PASTA, RICE, ETC.

C'est Bon Jambalaya

PASTA, RICE, ETC.

Baked Cabbage Jambalaya

1 pound ground beef
1 large onion, chopped
2 ribs celery, minced
2 garlic cloves, minced
1 pound smoked sausage, cut into bite-size pieces
1 head cabbage, chopped

1 cup uncooked rice
1 (10-ounce) can tomatoes with green chiles
1 teaspoon chili powder
Tony Cachere's Creole Seasoning to taste
Salt and pepper to taste

Preheat oven to 275°. Brown ground beef with onion, celery, and garlic in skillet, stirring till ground beef is crumbly. Sauté sausage in skillet till brown and cooked through. Add sausage, cabbage, rice, tomatoes, chili powder, Creole seasoning, salt and pepper to ground beef mixture, and mix well. Spoon into a large Pam-sprayed baking dish. Bake 2 hours, stirring halfway through baking time. Serves 8.

Cooking in High Cotton

Zydeco

Zydeco is a musical genre that blends Cajun music, blues, and rhythm and blues. It evolved in southwest Louisiana by French Creoles. Usually having a fast tempo and dominated by the accordion and a washboard used for percussion, zydeco music was created and played at house dances, where families and friends gathered for socializing.

In 1946, Clifton Chenier, the "King of Zydeco," his brother Cleveland, and metal fabricator Willie Landry designed a wearable stainless steel washboard vest, known as a "frottoir," Cajun French meaning "vest to be rubbed." Made specifically for the genre solely as a percussion instrument, the frottoir is one of only a few musical instruments original to America, and is now in the permanent collection of the Smithsonian Institution.

PASTA, RICE, ETC.

Spinach & Lump Crabmeat Quiche

Quiche is one of those egg-based dishes that falls into the category of breakfast, lunch, or dinner. The variations to this dish are too numerous to count, but I'm sure the addition of crabmeat to the recipe is strictly Louisiana in origin. —Chef John Folse

¼ cup butter, melted
½ cup minced onion
¼ cup minced red bell pepper
¼ cup minced yellow bell pepper
1 tablespoon minced garlic
1 (10-ounce) package frozen spinach, thawed
1 cup grated Swiss cheese
1 cup grated Colby cheese
3 tablespoons all–purpose flour
6 eggs, beaten
1 cup half-and-half
Salt and pepper to taste
⅛ teaspoon nutmeg
½ pound jumbo lump crabmeat
2 (9-inch) unbaked pie shells

Preheat oven to 350°. In a heavy-bottomed sauté pan, heat butter over medium-high heat. Add onion, bell peppers, and garlic. Sauté 3–5 minutes, or till vegetables are wilted. Add spinach, and blend well into vegetable mixture, then cook 2 additional minutes. Remove pan from heat and add cheeses and flour. Mix well to incorporate, then set aside.

In a mixing bowl, combine eggs, half-and-half, salt, pepper, and nutmeg. Add spinach mixture to eggs, and mix well till all is incorporated. Distribute crabmeat evenly over bottom of the 2 pie shells, and top with spinach/egg mixture. Bake 45 minutes, or till quiche is set and lightly browned. Serves 8.

Hot Beignets & Warm Boudoirs

PASTA, RICE, ETC.

Muffuletta

The Muffuletta is an Italian sandwich created in the late 1800s. The sandwich originated when Italian merchants working in the market of New Orleans placed a mixture of broken green and black olives, found on the bottom of olive barrels, on loaves of round Italian bread known as "muffs." Over this mixture, they layered slices of ham, salami, and Provolone cheese. The most famous of all Muffuletta sandwiches are found at the historic Central Grocery on Decatur Street in New Orleans.

—Chef John Folse

OLIVE SALAD:
- ¼ cup black olives
- ¼ cup green olives
- ¼ cup pimentos
- ¼ cup capers
- ¼ cup cocktail onions
- 1 (6-ounce) jar artichoke hearts, undrained
- ¼ cup coarsely chopped celery
- 1 teaspoon celery seeds
- 1 teaspoon dried oregano
- 1 tablespoon chopped garlic
- ½ cup olive oil
- 2 tablespoons red wine vinegar

In a food processor, combine all ingredients and chop coarsely. Scrape into a bowl, and set aside.

SANDWICH:
- 1 loaf round Italian bread
- 2 tablespoons olive oil
- ¼ pound ham, thinly sliced
- ¼ pound Genoa salami, thinly sliced
- 3 slices mozzarella cheese
- ¼ pound Mortadella (Italian bologna), thinly sliced
- ¼ pound Provolone cheese, thinly sliced
- 1 cup prepared Olive Salad

Split bread lengthwise, and drizzle olive oil on each side. Layer bottom half of bread with meats and cheeses, then add Olive Salad. Cover with top of bread; cut and serve. Serves 4.

The Encyclopedia of Cajun & Creole Cuisine

Mardi Gras

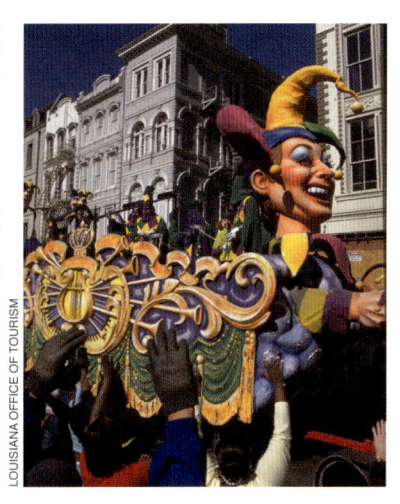

Mardi Gras means Fat Tuesday—a last fling followed by six weeks of Lenten fasting before Easter begins. It is a season of parades, balls, king cake parties, and "coming out" parties for young women. "Laissez Les Bons Temps Rouler!" . . . let the good times roll! And they have been rolling since March 3, 1699. Iberville, Bienville, and their men celebrated it as part of an observance of Catholic practice.

In 1856 six Creole businessmen gathered in New Orleans' French Quarter to organize a secret society to observe Mardi Gras with a formal parade, in which members are masked the whole time. They founded New Orleans' first and oldest krewe, the Mystick Krewe of Comus. Today, many krewes operate under a business structure whose membership is open to anyone who pays dues, and they are eligible to have a place on a parade float.

Parades moved out of the French Quarter in 1972 because of narrow streets and overhead obstructions. Major parades now follow a route along St. Charles Avenue and Canal Street.

In 1875 Louisiana declared Mardi Gras a legal state holiday. War, economic, political, and weather conditions sometimes led to cancellation of some or all major parades, but the city has always celebrated Carnival. The devastation caused by Hurricane Katrina in late 2005 did not stop the city's Mardi Gras celebrations, and though scaled back because so many had lost most or all of their possessions, the enthusiasm for Carnival was even more intense as an affirmation of life.

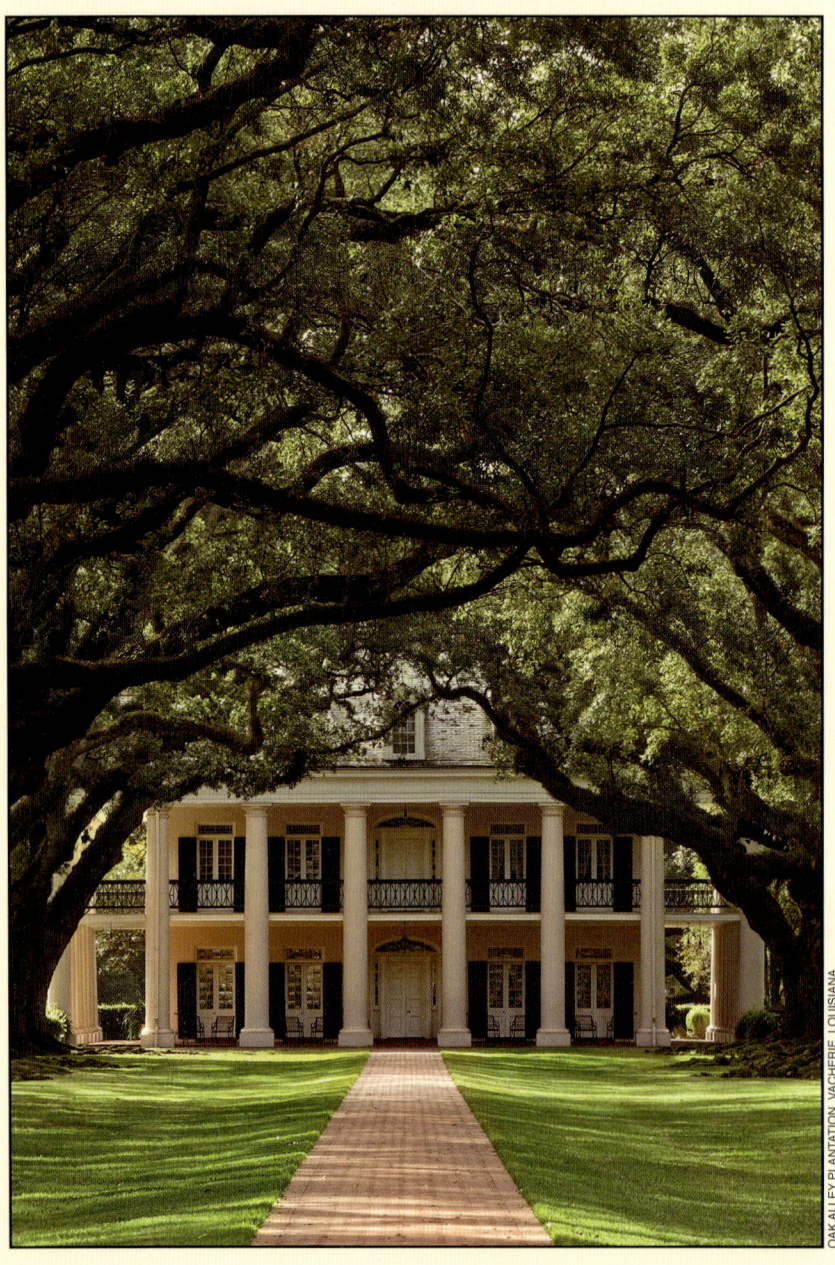

Oak Alley Plantation, Vacherie

Poultry

- Paulie's Poulet Dijonaise 126
- Chicken Fricassée 128
- Mitty Mitty's Chicken Breast 129
- Make-Ahead Chicken Casserole 129
- Bourbon Chicken 130
- Smothered Chicken 130
- Chicken Sauce Piquante 132
- Crawfish-Stuffed Chicken Breasts 133
- Chicken Cakes with Sherry Sauce 134
- Chicken and Waffle Sandwiches 135
- Creole Chicken & Biscuits 136
- Chicken and Black Bean Enchiladas 138
- Duck Breasts with Wine and Marmalade Sauce 139

Louisiana's fabled Great Mississippi River Road consists of a corridor approximately 70 miles between Baton Rouge and New Orleans. Along the road are the state's most famous and recognizable plantation houses, most built by wealthy sugar planters. A multicultural population developed along the river. The Creoles—a people descended from French and Spanish settlers and African Americans—had their own plantations. Unlike other parts of the South during that period, large populations of free people of color also existed in the area, and their influences in food, music, and culture helped shape the Louisiana of today.

Paulie's Poulet Dijonaise

4 skinless, boneless chicken breast halves
½ teaspoon ground black pepper
2 tablespoons tub margarine
⅓ cup Dijon mustard
1 tablespoon cornstarch
1 teaspoon mustard powder
1 (12-ounce) can evaporated skim milk
⅓ cup skim milk
¼ cup white wine
Fettuccine or linguine

Cut chicken into 1-inch strips and sprinkle with pepper. Sauté chicken in margarine in skillet over medium heat about 5 minutes, or till brown. Remove chicken; set aside.

Stir Dijon mustard into remaining margarine and juices in pan, scraping up bits. Blend cornstarch and mustard powder together. Slowly add 2–4 tablespoons of evaporated milk to the cornstarch, stirring till a smooth paste is formed. Continue to slowly blend in remaining milk. Then whisk milk mixture into margarine in pan. Stir wine into mixture, reduce heat, and cook sauce till it is reduced by one quarter. Stir or whisk frequently. It should be thick and velvety. Adjust seasonings and add chicken back to sauce. Serve over spinach fettuccine or linguine. Serves 4.

River Road Recipes III

River Road Recipes

The three "Rs" traditionally has meant "reading, 'riting, and 'rithmatic," but in Baton Rouge, it means *River Road Recipes*.

In 1959, the Baton Rouge Junior League published the original *River Road Recipes*. It has been reprinted 78 times. *River Road Recipes* has sold over 1.3 million copies, and has enabled the Junior League to contribute millions of dollars to projects that enrich the community. This phenomenally successful cookbook, considered "The Textbook of Louisiana Cuisine," along with their three subsequently published *River Road Recipes* cookbooks, is the All-Time Best-Selling Community Cookbook Series in the nation with over 1.9 million copies in print.

The amazing success of *River Road Recipes* brand is due to the dedicated commitment to excellence by the Junior League members who select, edit, test, and market these remarkable collections of recipes. The original Baton Rouge Junior League cookbook committee, led by Chairman Mrs. W. E. Robinson, Jr., spent two years (1957–59) gathering and perfecting the 600+ recipes that were chosen to be included in *River Road Recipes I*. These recipes feature classic Creole and Cajun dishes, with basic guidance like "how to make a roux."

River Road Recipes II: A Second Helping (1976) features more delicious recipes that utilize more up-to-date ingredients. In 1994, the Baton Rouge Junior League published *River Road Recipes III*, a collection of 341 recipes that bring Louisiana cooking into the health-conscious age. *River Road Recipes IV: Warm Welcomes* (2004) is full-color, hardcover, and features over 300 recipes and menus for every occasion.

River Road Recipes captures the full glory of Louisiana cooking. (See pages 256–257 for more information about these cookbooks.)

POULTRY

Chicken Fricassée

4 tablespoons cooking oil
1 large hen, cut up
4 tablespoons flour
2 onions, chopped
1 bunch green onions, chopped
3 cloves garlic, chopped
4 cups water
Salt, black pepper, red pepper to taste
4-5 sprigs parsley, chopped
3 cups hot cooked rice

Heat oil in iron pot, then add cut-up seasoned chicken and brown on all sides slowly. Remove chicken. On a low flame, gradually add flour to make a roux, stirring constantly with wooden spoon. When mixture turns a dark mahogany color (in about 35 minutes), add 4 cups water. Raise heat till mixture boils, and add onions, green onions, and garlic. Lower heat, cover, and cook 45 minutes.

Add chicken, and season to taste with salt, black pepper, and red pepper. Cook, covered, till chicken is done, approximately 1 hour. During the last 15 minutes, add a small amount of chopped parsley and green onions. Serve over cooked rice. Serves 8.

Tell Me More

Houmas House Plantation and Gardens, located in Burnside in Ascension Parish, was established as a sugar plantation in the late 1700s. It was named in honor of the Native American Houma people, who originally occupied this fertile land between the Mississippi River and Lake Maurepas to the north. In the late 1800s, "The Sugar Palace" was the largest sugar producer in the country, producing 20 million pounds per year. Houmas House Plantation and Gardens calls itself the Crown Jewel of Louisiana's River Road. There are 141 plantation homes in Louisiana that are on the National Register of Historic Places, or that have been designated as National Historic Landmarks. Like Houmas House, many of them offer tours.

Mitty Mitty's Chicken Breast

4 skinless, boneless chicken breasts
Salt and pepper to taste
2 packages dried onion soup mix

Cut heavy-duty foil into 4 (12-inch) squares. Preheat oven to 400°. Season chicken breasts with salt and pepper. Put 1 breast in center of each foil square. Sprinkle onion soup mix over chicken, coating well. Wrap chicken well, and seal. Bake 30–35 minutes. Open packages carefully, allowing steam to escape. Serve with wild rice and salad.

Skinny Cajun

Make-Ahead Chicken Casserole

1 (10-ounce) package frozen asparagus spears, thawed, drained
¼ cup corn oil
2 whole chicken breasts, skinned, boned, cut into 1- to 1½-inch squares
Salt and pepper to taste
1 (10¾-ounce) can cream of chicken soup
⅓ cup mayonnaise
½ teaspoon curry powder
1 teaspoon chopped pimento
1 teaspoon fresh lemon juice
¼ cup shredded Cheddar cheese

Place asparagus in single layer in a greased 2-quart shallow baking pan. Place oil in frying pan over medium heat. Add chicken; cook 5–7 minutes, or till browned. Sprinkle with salt and pepper to taste; drain. In medium bowl, mix soup, mayonnaise, curry powder, pimento, and lemon juice. Lay chicken over asparagus. Spoon soup mixture over chicken. Sprinkle on Cheddar cheese. Cover with foil. Casserole may be placed in refrigerator overnight, or baked immediately at 375° for 30 minutes till chicken is fork-tender, and sauce is bubbly. Serves 8.

Pots, Pans, and Pioneers V

POULTRY

Bourbon Chicken

6 skinless, boneless chicken breasts
½ teaspoon pepper
1 teaspoon garlic powder
¼ cup bourbon whiskey
¼ cup reduced-sodium soy sauce
1 (8-ounce) can crushed pineapple, in juice

Season chicken breasts to taste with pepper and garlic powder. Marinate for several hours in mixture of bourbon and soy sauce. Place chicken pieces and marinade in 9x13-inch glass baking dish. Top with crushed pineapple, including the juice. Bake in 325° oven about 25 minutes, or till chicken is well done. Baste several times during baking. Serves 6.

River Road Recipes III

Smothered Chicken

4 whole chicken breasts (or cut-up fryer)
Garlic salt to taste
1 stick butter
2 (10¾-ounce) cans cream of mushroom soup
1 (8-ounce) carton sour cream
1 (6-ounce) can French fried onions

Place chicken in greased baking dish, and add garlic salt to taste. Place small pats of butter on each chicken breast half. Spread thin layer of soup over chicken. Add dollops of sour cream on each piece. Sprinkle onions on top, cover with foil, and bake 2 hours at 350°. Serves 8.

Pots, Pans, and Pioneers IV

POULTRY

Bourbon Chicken

POULTRY

Chicken Sauce Piquante

1 hen, cut up and seasoned
2 pounds link sausage, sliced
½ cup oil
2 onions, chopped
3 cloves garlic, chopped
1 green bell pepper, chopped
1 (8-ounce) can tomato sauce
1 (10-ounce) can Ro-Tel tomatoes
½ cup roux
1 (10¾-ounce) can cream of mushroom soup
1 cup chopped green onions
Cooked rice

Put hen and sausage in a black cast-iron pot, and brown in oil. When brown, take out of pot; set aside. Sauté onions, garlic, bell pepper, tomato sauce, Ro-Tel tomatoes, roux, and mushroom soup. Cook till onions are clear in color. Add hen and sausage back in pot with ingredients, cover, and allow to cook at least 1 hour, or till hen is tender. Add water as needed. Serve over rice.

Amy's Cajun Recipes

Outside Duck Commander headquarters, West Monroe

POULTRY

Crawfish-Stuffed Chicken Breasts

8 boneless chicken breasts
Creole seasoning, salt, and pepper to taste
½ cup margarine
1 onion, chopped
1 bell pepper, chopped
½ cup chopped celery
1½ pounds crawfish tails
3 tablespoons Italian bread crumbs
5 tablespoons chopped parsley

Season chicken with Creole seasoning, salt, and pepper. Melt margarine in skillet. Add onion, bell pepper, and celery. Sauté 10 minutes or till onion is translucent. Add crawfish. Sauté 10 minutes over medium heat. Season with Creole seasoning, salt and pepper. Stir in enough bread crumbs to make of consistency of stuffing. Stir in parsley. Fill each chicken breast with stuffing and fold over, fastening edges with wooden picks or kitchen string to enclose the stuffing. Place in a single layer in a baking dish, and cover with foil.

Bake at 375° for 45 minutes. Remove foil. Bake 15 minutes longer, or till brown and cooked through. Remove all wooden picks and string before serving. Serves 8.

Roux To Do

Duck Dynasty is a popular American reality television series that portrays the lives of the Robertson family, who became wealthy from their family-operated business in West Monroe, which sells Duck Commander duck calls and other products for duck hunters. The show has broken several ratings records on both A&E and cable television as a whole, becoming the most-watched nonfiction cable series in history. Robertson brothers Phil and Si, and Phil's sons Jase, Willie, and Jep are known for their long beards as well as their outspoken Christian views. Miss Kay and the other Robertson women are known for their good cookin'—and trying to keep their men civilized.

POULTRY

Chicken Cakes with Sherry Sauce

CHICKEN CAKES:

2 tablespoons butter
1 small red bell pepper, seeded, chopped
8 green onion tops, sliced
3 garlic cloves, pressed
4 cups chopped cooked chicken (4 chicken breasts)
1 cup soft bread crumbs
2 tablespoons mayonnaise
2 tablespoons sherry
1 tablespoon Creole seasoning
2 eggs, lightly beaten
¼ cup vegetable oil, divided

Melt butter in a large nonstick skillet over medium heat. Add bell pepper, green onion tops, and garlic. Sauté till vegetables are tender. Process (pulse) cooked chicken in food processor till coarsely ground. Combine sautéed mixture, chicken, bread crumbs, mayonnaise, sherry, Creole seasoning, and eggs in a bowl, and mix well. Chill 10 minutes, so the ingredients will bind.

Shape chicken mixture into 8 (3½-inch) patties. Fry 4 patties in 2 tablespoons oil in a large skillet over medium heat for 3 minutes on each side or till golden brown. Drain on paper towels. Repeat with remaining oil and patties.

SHERRY SAUCE:

1 cup mayonnaise
1 garlic clove, pressed
2 tablespoons sherry
2 tablespoons ketchup
2 teaspoons Creole seasoning
5 green onion tops, sliced

Combine all ingredients in a bowl and mix well.

To serve, spoon Sherry Sauce over patties, and serve immediately. Serves 8.

Roux To Do

POULTRY

Chicken and Waffle Sandwiches

4 slices lower-sodium bacon, halved crosswise
3 tablespoons canola mayonnaise
1 tablespoon low-fat buttermilk
1 teaspoon cider vinegar
¼ teaspoon sugar
¼ teaspoon garlic powder
⅛ teaspoon freshly ground black pepper
8 frozen whole-grain waffles, toasted
6 ounces thinly sliced, lower-sodium deli chicken breast
8 (¼-inch thick) slices ripe tomato
4 Boston lettuce leaves

Cook bacon in a large nonstick skillet over medium heat till crisp. Drain on paper towels.

Combine mayonnaise, buttermilk, vinegar, sugar, garlic powder, and pepper. Spread mayonnaise mixture evenly over 4 waffles. Divide chicken, bacon, tomato, and lettuce evenly among servings. Top with remaining waffles. Serves 4.

Recipes from the Heart

Lee Circle

Lee Circle is a traffic circle located in New Orleans on St. Charles Avenue, where it intersects Howard Avenue. It was so named in the late 1870s, when a monument to Confederate General Robert E. Lee was erected in the center of the circle. Before then it was called Tivoli Circle or Tivoli Gardens, because of the Tivoli Carousel located there. From the beginning, it was an important point in the city, linking upriver and downriver, and a common meeting point and popular place to gather for Mardi Gras parades.

POULTRY

Creole Chicken & Biscuits

Although this recipe recommends biscuits as the perfect accompaniment to this Creole chicken, you may wish to serve it over rice or pasta. I often whip up a batch of my Cathead Biscuits to go along with this dish when company is coming. However, if I just have an urge for this wonderful regional dish, I sometimes use a can of "whack" biscuits.

—Chef John Folse

1 (3-pound) fryer, halved	2 tablespoons lemon juice
½ cup butter	1 tablespoon horseradish
½ cup diced onion	1 tablespoon chopped fresh thyme
¼ cup diced celery	
¼ cup diced green bell pepper	2 tablespoons chopped fresh basil
1 tablespoon diced garlic	
½ cup all-purpose flour	Salt and black pepper to taste
6 cups chicken stock	Creole seasoning to taste
2 (8-ounce) cans tomato purée	½ cup sliced green onions
1 (8-ounce) can tomato sauce	¼ cup chopped parsley

Prepare Captain John's Cathead Biscuits according to recipe (page 43), or use your favorite store-bought variety. Poach chicken by simmering in lightly seasoned water till tender, and meat has fallen from the bones. Remove chicken from liquid and reserve 6 cups of stock. Debone meat and set aside.

In a cast-iron Dutch oven, melt butter over medium-high heat. Add onion, celery, bell pepper, and garlic. Sauté 3–5 minutes, or till vegetables are wilted. Sprinkle in flour and, using a wire whisk, stir constantly till white roux is achieved. Add reserved 6 cups chicken stock, 1 cup at a time, till stew-like consistency is achieved. Add tomato purée, tomato sauce, lemon juice, and horseradish. Bring to a rolling boil; reduce to a simmer and cook 20 minutes, stirring occasionally. Add chicken, thyme, and basil, and season to taste with salt, pepper, and Creole seasoning. Cook an additional 10 minutes, then add green onions and parsley. If too acidic, add a tablespoon of sugar. Serve a generous portion of over open-faced biscuits. Serve 8–10.

Hot Beignets & Warm Boudoirs

POULTRY

Creole Chicken & Biscuits

POULTRY

Chicken and Black Bean Enchiladas

2 boneless, skinless chicken breasts
Salt and pepper to taste
3 tablespoons vegetable oil
12 corn or flour tortillas
1 (10-ounce) can tomatoes with chiles, drained
1 (15-ounce) can black beans, drained
1 cup salsa
1 tablespoon cumin
1 tablespoon chili powder
½ cup sour cream
1 cup shredded Cheddar cheese
1 cup shredded Monterey Jack cheese
1 handful cilantro, or to taste

Season chicken breasts with salt and pepper. Pan-fry in oil till done; set aside and let cool.

Shred cooled chicken with a fork. Place an equal portion of shredded chicken in each tortilla. Top each with tomatoes, black beans, and salsa. Mix cumin and chili powder with sour cream. Place an equal amount in each tortilla before rolling up. Arrange tortillas seam side down in a 9x13-inch baking dish. Sprinkle with both cheeses, and bake at 350° for 20–30 minutes, or till cheeses are melted. Garnish enchiladas with fresh cilantro.

Hint: Need a quick meal? Use a pre-cooked rotisserie chicken instead of cooking breasts.

Steel Magnolias in the Kitchen

POULTRY

Duck Breasts with Wine and Marmalade Sauce

Fileted breasts from 2 large ducks
Seasoning, such as Greek or Cajun
Flour
Salt and black pepper
12 ounces bacon
1 large onion, chopped
1 cup dry red wine
¾ cup orange marmalade

Sprinkle duck breasts generously with seasoning. Dredge in flour that has been seasoned with salt and pepper; shake off excess and allow to stand at room temperature.

Fry bacon till very crisp; remove to paper towels and drain. Sauté onion in hot bacon grease till limp; remove and set aside. Fry floured duck breasts in hot fat, turning once, till golden.

Mix wine and marmalade till thoroughly combined. Crumble bacon and add along with onion to the sauce. Stir well. Pour sauce over duck breasts; cover and reduce heat to medium. Allow to simmer 3–5 minutes. Do not overcook duck; the breasts should still be pink in center for best flavor. Serves 4.

Variations & Improvisations

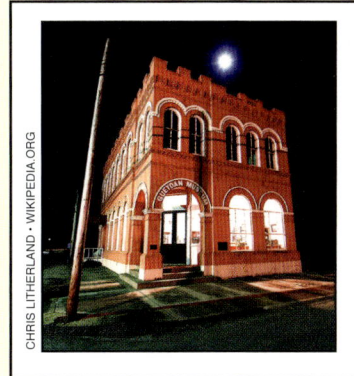

Gueydan is known as the "Duck Capital of America" in recognition of its abundance of waterfowl. The town is the site of the annual Duck Festival, which is held the weekend before Labor Day. The Louisiana state championships for duck and goose calling are held in conjunction with the festival. The Gueydan Museum (shown) offers attractions of local and historical interest.

CHRIS LITHERLAND · WIKIPEDIA.ORG

Louisiana's wild alligator is the king of the swamp.

Meats

Deluxe Weekend Dish 142
Mitty Mitty's Meatloaf.....143
Italian Meatloaf 143
Beef Bourguignon 144
Smothered Steak..............145
Slow Cooker Brisket 147
Easy Beef Brisket..............147
Grilled Beef Tenderloin
    with Mushroom
    Stuffing........................148
New Orleans Grillades 149
Cajun Pot Roast.................150
New Orleans Roast Beef..152

Deer Roast 152
Roast Beef Po-Boys 153
Leftover Roast Hash.........154
Meatball Fricassée............154
Pork Roast..........................155
Barbecued Spareribs 156
Alma's Pork Tenderloin
    in a Bed.......................157
Pork Medallions in Creole
    Mustard Sauce............158
Stuffed Pork Chops..........160
Breaded Pork Chops........161
Ted's Cochon de Lait 161

The American alligator is the largest reptile in North America. A typical male alligator reaches 13 to 14 feet in length, and can weigh over 600 pounds. Louisiana has the highest wild alligator population, estimated to be approaching two million. Alligator hunters currently harvest over 28,000 wild alligators per year. Louisiana's wild alligator season usually begins in late August/early September and continues for about one month. Alligators are native only to the United States and China.

MEATS

Deluxe Weekend Dish

This recipe is from an old Gourmet Galley column published in The Advocate *(Baton Rouge). This casserole freezes well. It can be frozen uncooked, or frozen cooked, or cut into squares for individual portions.*
—Corinne Cook

- 2 pounds ground beef round
- 2 tablespoons olive oil
- 1 (15-ounce) can tomato sauce
- 1 (12-ounce) can tomato paste
- 2 teaspoons dried basil
- 2 teaspoons dried oregano
- 1 (1-ounce) package dry onion soup mix
- 1 cup water
- 1–2 cloves garlic, minced
- 1 teaspoon salt, or to taste
- ½ teaspoon black pepper
- ¼ teaspoon red pepper or to taste
- ½ pound thin spaghetti, noodles or macaroni
- 1 pound mozzarella cheese, grated
- 1 (1-pound) carton small-curd cottage cheese
- 1 cup freshly grated Parmesan cheese

Brown meat in olive oil; drain. Stir in tomato sauce, tomato paste, basil, oregano, dry soup mix, water, garlic, salt, black pepper, and red pepper. Cover and simmer 20 minutes. Taste for seasoning.

Boil pasta in salted water till tender; drain. Layer in casserole sprayed with nonstick coating: pasta, mozzarella, meat, cottage cheese, and Parmesan cheese. Bake at 350° about 30 minutes, or till heated through. Serves 12.

Extra! Extra! Read More About It!

MEATS

Mitty Mitty's Meatloaf

2 pounds ground beef
Salt and pepper to taste
Louisiana red pepper sauce to taste
Cajun seasoning to taste
¾ cup finely chopped onion
¾ cup finely chopped green bell pepper
1 egg
⅓ cup Italian bread crumbs
1 (6-ounce) can tomato paste
1 (15-ounce) can tomato sauce

Season ground beef with salt, pepper, pepper sauce, and Cajun seasoning. Add onion, bell pepper, and egg; mix well. Add bread crumbs; mix well. Form mixture into a loaf shape in a 9x13-inch baking pan. Cover loaf completely with tomato paste, and pour tomato sauce over top. Cover with foil. Bake at 350° for 1 hour, basting about every 15 minutes with the tomato sauce in the pan. Serves 8–10.

Classic Cajun Deux

Italian Meatloaf

2 pounds lean ground beef
Salt, pepper, and oregano to taste
2 eggs, beaten
2 cups bread crumbs
1 (8-ounce) can tomato sauce, divided
1 package sliced pepperoni
8 ounces shredded mozzarella cheese

Combine and mix together beef, seasonings, eggs, bread crumbs, and ½ can tomato sauce. Pat meat mixture into lightly greased 10x16-inch rectangle on wax paper. Arrange pepperoni slices on meat rectangle. Sprinkle cheese over top. Roll up jellyroll-style; seal ends by pressing meat together. Place seam down in Pam-sprayed shallow pan. Bake at 350° for 1 hour. Top with remaining tomato sauce. Continue baking 10 minutes or till done. Serves 6.

Pots, Pans, and Pioneers II

MEATS

Beef Bourguignon

This recipe is typical of the country French techniques re-created in early New Orleans. In this dish, Burgundy wine is used for both flavoring and tenderizing the meat.

2½–3 pounds cubed beef chuck	1 cup sliced mushrooms
	3 cups Burgundy wine
Salt and black pepper to taste	4 cups beef broth
⅓ cup flour	1 tablespoon tomato paste
¼ cup vegetable oil	½ teaspoon dried thyme
4 slices bacon	1½ cups sliced green onions
2 cups diced onions	¼ cup chopped parsley
½ cup grated carrots	Hot cooked pasta
¼ cup minced garlic	

In a large mixing bowl, season meat with salt and pepper. Coat well with flour. In a cast-iron Dutch oven, heat oil over medium-high heat. Sauté bacon until golden brown. Drain on paper towels to cool; crush and keep warm. Add meat to Dutch oven in 3 separate batches. Brown meat on all sides, and allow it to caramelize in bottom of pot. Remove and keep warm.

Sauté onions, carrots, and garlic in meat drippings for 3–5 minutes, or until vegetables are wilted. Add mushrooms, wine, broth, and tomato paste. Scrape bottom of pot to release caramelized flavor. Return meat to Dutch oven. Add bacon and thyme. Cover, and simmer 1½ hours, or until meat is tender. Add green onions and parsley, then adjust seasonings, if necessary. Serve over hot pasta. Serves 6.

Note: The French title is Boeuf à la Bourguignonne, and some call it Beef Burgundy. It is delicious whatever you call it.

The Encyclopedia of Cajun & Creole Cuisine

MEATS

Smothered Steak

½ cup oil
Salt and pepper to taste
4 pounds chuck steak or
  round steak
1 pint water
½ cup flour (optional)*
1 large onion, thinly sliced

Line bottom of heavy Dutch oven or deep skillet with oil. Heat till hot; add seasoned meat. Brown on one side, then turn on other side and brown well. The meat may stick on the bottom of the pot, but that is okay, because it makes for a better gravy. Cook on medium-high heat, turning over occasionally, adding dabs of water as you turn. Just before meat is cooked, add sliced onions, and cook till they are done, approximately 20 minutes. The meat and onions will be done at the same time. Add a small amount of water to form gravy. Serve over rice. Serves 6.

*Editor's Extra: We like to combine salt and pepper with about ½ cup flour, and pat into steak before browning. Makes a nicer gravy.

Classic Cajun

Dixie

The word "Dixie" refers to privately issued currency originally from the Citizens State Bank (located in the French Quarter of New Orleans) and then other banks in Louisiana. These banks issued ten-dollar notes, labeled "Dix," French for "ten," on the reverse side. The notes were known as "Dixies" by English-speaking southerners, and the area around New Orleans and the French-speaking parts of Louisiana came to be known as "Dixieland." Eventually, usage of the term broadened to refer to the eleven southern states that seceded to form the Confederate States of America. They are, in order of secession: South Carolina, Mississippi, Florida, Alabama, Georgia, Louisiana, Texas, Virginia, Arkansas, North Carolina, and Tennessee.

Louisiana Timeline

1541–42: Hernando de Soto explored region; discovered Mississippi River

1682: Robert Cavalier and Sieur de La Salle claimed Mississippi watershed for France; named area for King Louis XIV

1714: Juchereau de St. Denis founded first permanent settlement in Louisiana (Natchitoches)

1718: Jean Baptiste le Moyne and Sieur de Bienville founded New Orleans

1723: New Orleans became capital of Louisiana

1762: King Louis XV gave Charles II of Spain all land west of Mississippi

1800: Spain ceded Louisiana back to France

1803: United States purchased Louisiana Territory

1812: Louisiana became 18th state

1815: British defeated by Andrew Jackson in Battle of New Orleans

1837: New Orleans held first Mardi Gras parade

1849: Baton Rouge became capital of Louisiana

1875: Louisiana declared Mardi Gras a legal holiday

1879: New state constitution adopted; mouth of Mississippi River deepened to allow large ocean vessels to reach New Orleans

1884: World's Fair held in New Orleans

1928: Huey P. Long elected governor

1932: Huey P. Long became U.S. senator; new capitol completed in Baton Rouge

1935: Huey Long assassinated on steps of state capitol

1956: Longest over-water bridge in world opened, Lake Pontchartrain Causeway

1966: National Football League awarded franchise to New Orleans Saints

1969: Hurricane Camille struck, killed 250 people

1975: Super Dome in New Orleans completed

1984: World's Fair held in New Orleans (for the second time)

1991: State legislature approved riverboat gambling

1992: Hurricane Andrew devastated south-central Louisiana

2005: Hurricane Katrina struck southeastern Louisiana, damaged levees, flooded New Orleans; Hurricane Rita caused major flooding in New Orleans

2010: New Orleans Saints won Super Bowl XLIV

Slow Cooker Brisket

1 (3- to 4-pound) beef brisket
1 teaspoon liquid smoke
1 (16-ounce) bottle barbecue sauce
2 tablespoons Worcestershire
Salt and pepper to taste
½ cup water

Place trimmed brisket on a piece of foil. Mix liquid smoke, barbeque sauce, Worcestershire, and salt and pepper. Pour mixture over brisket, and wrap foil securely around beef. Place water in bottom of slow cooker. Place foil-wrapped brisket in slow cooker, and cover. Cook on LOW 8–10 hours. Slice and serve. Serves 10 or more.

Come to the Table

Easy Beef Brisket

1 (5-pound) beef brisket
Celery salt
Garlic salt
Onion powder
1 (3-ounce) bottle liquid smoke
Salt and pepper to taste
Worcestershire

Sprinkle brisket generously with celery salt, garlic salt, and onion powder. Pour bottle of liquid smoke over brisket, cover with foil, and refrigerate overnight.

When ready to cook, preheat oven to 270°. Sprinkle brisket lightly with salt, pepper, and lots of Worcestershire. Cover and bake 6 hours. Serves 4–6.

The Landing Restaurant, Natchitoches
Louisiana's Best Restaurant Recipes

MEATS

Grilled Beef Tenderloin with Mushroom Stuffing

1 pound fresh mushrooms, sliced
1 cup chopped green onions
½ stick butter, melted
¼ cup chopped fresh parsley
1 (6- to 7-pound) beef tenderloin
½ teaspoon seasoned salt
¼ teaspoon lemon pepper
4 ounces blue cheese, crumbled
1 (8-ounce) bottle red wine vinaigrette
Crushed peppercorns

Sauté mushrooms and green onions in butter in a large skillet till tender; drain. Stir in parsley, and set aside. Trim any excess fat from beef. Cut lengthwise to within ¼ inch of the other edge, leaving one long side connected. Sprinkle with seasoned salt and lemon pepper. Spoon mushroom mixture into opening of beef, and sprinkle with cheese. Fold beef over to enclose filling, and secure with heavy kitchen string at 2-inch intervals. Place in a large shallow dish. Pour vinaigrette over beef. Marinate, covered, in refrigerator 8 hours, basting occasionally.

Preheat grill. Drain beef, discarding marinade. Press crushed peppercorns onto each side of beef, and place on grill rack. Grill over medium-hot coals 35 minutes or to 145° on meat thermometer for rare, or to 160° for medium. Place on platter, and slice to serve. Serves 12.

Cooking in High Cotton

MEATS

New Orleans Grillades

1½ pounds lean round steak, ½ inch thick
2–3 tablespoons beef or chicken broth or wine
1 tablespoon oil
2 tablespoons all-purpose flour
2 onions, chopped
3 cloves garlic, chopped
½ green bell pepper, chopped
1 stalk celery, chopped
1 (16-ounce) can chopped tomatoes, liquid reserved
Hot water plus reserved tomato liquid to equal 1½ cups
2 bay leaves, crumbled
¼ teaspoon thyme
2 tablespoons chopped parsley
¼ teaspoon salt
¼ teaspoon celery salt

Flatten steak with meat mallet to ¼-inch thickness; trim fat, and cut into 6 squares. Brown meat in a nonstick skillet. Add broth or wine, as needed, to prevent sticking. Remove meat; drain on paper towels. Add oil; blend in flour, and stir over medium heat till brown. Add onions, garlic, bell pepper, and celery, stirring frequently till vegetables soften. Add a little tomato liquid or water, if needed. Put vegetable mixture in crockpot, and add remaining ingredients. Mix well. Add browned steak, and slow cook 8 or more hours on LOW, or cook on stove till meat falls apart. Serve with Garlic Cheese Grits. Serves 6.

GARLIC CHEESE GRITS:

1 cup uncooked grits
½ teaspoon salt
3¾ cups water
⅓ cup skim milk
3 tablespoons margarine or butter
½ teaspoon garlic powder
4 ounces light Velveeta
1 cup grated reduced-fat sharp Cheddar cheese
1 tablespoon Worcestershire
Paprika to taste

Cook grits in salted water. Once cooked, stir in milk and cook a few more minutes. Add remaining ingredients. Stir until cheese has melted. Pour into casserole dish, and sprinkle with paprika. Bake in preheated 350° oven for 15–20 minutes.

River Road Recipes III

MEATS

Cajun Pot Roast

1 (3-pound) beef sirloin or chuck roast
2 large garlic cloves, cut into ¼- to ½-inch pieces
3 cayenne chiles or jalapeño peppers, cut into ¼- to ½-inch pieces
Salt and pepper to taste
1 large onion, chopped
1 green bell pepper, chopped
1 large garlic clove, minced
1 (4-ounce) can whole or sliced mushrooms, drained
1 tablespoon Worcestershire
Creole seasoning to taste

Cut ½- to ¾-inch slits into beef. Stuff one piece of garlic and one piece of jalapeño into each slit. Season roast with salt and pepper. Heat a large heavy nonstick saucepan over medium heat. Add beef, and brown well on all sides. Add onion, bell pepper, and minced garlic, and sauté till tender. Add water to saucepan to cover beef. Stir in mushrooms and Worcestershire, and season with Creole seasoning. Simmer, covered, 3–4 hours or till tender, adding additional water if needed to keep the liquid level halfway up the beef.

You may stir 1 tablespoon all-purpose flour mixed with 1 cup cold water into liquid near end of cooking for a thicker gravy. Serves 6.

Marshes to Mansions

Louisiana is Happy!

There's a lot to be happy about. In 2014, researchers at Harvard University and the University of British Columbia did nationwide research, and voted Lafayette the happiest city in America, followed by Houma, third Shreveport-Bossier City, fourth Baton Rouge, fifth Alexandria, eighth Lake Charles, and Monroe made the top twenty! We're happy all over the place! Good food, good music, and good times make for happy folks.

MEATS

Cajun Pot Roast

MEATS

New Orleans Roast Beef

1 (3½-pound) beef eye of
   round roast
1 tablespoon plus 2 teaspoons
   cooking oil, divided
10 whole garlic cloves, peeled
½ teaspoon onion powder
2 tablespoons Worcestershire
¾ teaspoon salt
½ teaspoon black pepper
4–5 dashes pepper sauce

Make a horizontal slit through the roast. In a small saucepan, heat 2 teaspoons oil on medium-high heat. Sauté garlic cloves 4 minutes, stirring often. Allow garlic cloves to cool. In a small bowl, combine remaining ingredients; mix well; set aside. When garlic is room temperature, push cloves into slit in roast till they fill the slit. Rub oil mixture over entire roast. Place roast in baking dish. Roast at 350° for 1 hour 15 minutes or till desired doneness. Serve immediately. Serves 6.

Skinny Cajun

Deer Roast

1 deer roast
¼ cup Smart Balance
   margarine
3 medium onions, chopped
1 medium green bell pepper,
   chopped
3 ribs celery, chopped
1 (12-ounce) can regular beer

Brown roast in a heavy Dutch oven with margarine on medium heat. Remove from pot. Add onions, bell pepper, and celery; sauté. Deglaze bottom of pot by adding beer. Put roast back into pot, and cover. Put Dutch oven in 350° oven and bake 1 hour 30 minutes. Turn roast over and bake at 400° uncovered 30 minutes. Remove roast from heat.

Note: To make a great thick brown gravy, add 1 tablespoon cornstarch and ½–⅔ cup beef broth. Bring to a boil, stirring constantly. Season gravy to your taste with salt and pepper.

Skinny Cajun

MEATS

Roast Beef Po-Boys

Your guests will need at least 3 napkins, because it is very messy, but very good!

1 (13- to 14-pound) boneless sirloin tip roast	2 or 3 (10¾-ounce) cans golden mushroom soup
3 envelopes onion soup mix	Roast drippings
6 cups water	Brown gravy mix
4 large onions, chopped	French bread

Trim excess fat from roast. (Roast may be cut into quarters for faster cooking.) Place roast in large roaster; sprinkle with soup mix, and add water. Cover and bake at 350° for 4–4½ hours. Remove roast from pan. Let meat and drippings cool thoroughly; refrigerate. When meat is cold, remove and slice, saving meat drippings for gravy.

Sauté onions over low heat till transparent; do not brown. Add 2 or 3 cans soup, depending upon how much gravy you want. Cook about 15 minutes, stirring often. Add meat drippings, and bring to a boil. To thicken gravy, add gravy mix. Layer sliced beef and gravy in a roasting pan. Heat at 350° for about 30 minutes, or till hot. Serve on French bread with lettuce, tomatoes, and onions. Serves 20–30.

Down the Bayou

A key ingredient that differentiates **po-boys** from submarine sandwiches is the bread. Typically, the French bread comes in 10-ounce, 32-inch long "sticks." Standard sandwich sizes might be a "Shorty," measuring 5 to 7.5 inches; a quarter po-boy, 8 inches; half po-boy, about 16 inches, and a full po-boy, at about 32 inches long. A "dressed" po-boy has lettuce, tomato, and mayonnaise; pickles and onions are optional. The Oak Street Po-Boy Festival is an annual one-day festival dedicated to the po-boy; it features live music, arts, and food vendors with multiple types of po-boys. It is held in mid-November along a commercial strip of Oak Street in New Orleans.

Leftover Roast Hash

1 large onion, chopped
2 potatoes, cubed
2 tablespoons bacon drippings
2 tablespoons flour
1 cup roast broth or beef bouillon
1 clove garlic, chopped
3 cups chopped cooked roast
½ tablespoon chili powder
1 teaspoon seasoned salt
Pepper to taste

Brown or sauté onion and potatoes in bacon drippings. Add flour and brown; add broth. Add remaining ingredients; simmer till tender. Serves 4–6.

Pots, Pans, and Pioneers III

Meatball Fricassée

2 pounds ground meat (pork or beef)
1 onion, chopped
1 (5-ounce) can evaporated milk
¾ cup bread crumbs
1 egg
Salt and pepper to taste
Flour for coating
⅓ cup oil
1 pint roux (or more if desired thicker)
4 cups water
3 potatoes, peeled, diced
2 carrots, diced
Cooked white rice

In a bowl, mix together ground meat, onion, evaporated milk, bread crumbs, egg, and salt and pepper to taste. Shape into meatballs. Roll meatballs in plain flour for frying.

In a pot, put oil, and heat on medium. When oil is hot, add a few meatballs. Fry till all meatballs are brown. Take meatballs out of pot; set aside. In the pot, add roux and water, and boil till roux is dissolved. Add meatballs, potatoes, and carrots to roux mixture, and season. Allow to boil till carrots and potatoes are tender, and gravy is thick. Serve over white rice. Serves 6–8.

Amy's Cajun Recipes

MEATS

Pork Roast

¼ cup finely chopped onion
4 cloves garlic, finely chopped
1 teaspoon salt
½ teaspoon pepper
1 (4-pound) pork roast
Additional salt and pepper to taste
¼ cup oil
2 cups water

Combine chopped onion and garlic in a small dish. Season with salt and pepper. Cut slit in the middle of roast, and stuff all the onion mixture inside. Season outside of roast with salt and pepper. Heat oil in heavy roasting pot. Place roast in pot; brown all sides, adding small amounts of water occasionally. After roast is browned on all sides, add the rest of the water; cover. Cook on low heat about 3 hours. This also makes a wonderful gravy. Serve over rice. Serves 6–8.

Note: May cook beef roast in the same manner.

Classic Cajun

The Wildest Show in the South

Begun in 1965, the Angola Prison Rodeo, staged at the Louisiana State Penitentiary, is the longest running prison rodeo in the United States. It is held on one weekend in April and on every Sunday in October. Various prisoner organizations sell food at concession stands. As part of the prison rodeo, there is a biannual Arts and Crafts Festival, where prisoners make handmade work to sell. The rodeo raises funds for religious educational programs for prisoners. There is always a sell-out crowd; the 2013 spring rodeo raised $450,000. The rodeo's slogan is "The wildest show in the South."

MEATS

Barbecued Spareribs

1 cup vinegar
2 tablespoons Worcestershire
1 teaspoon salt
1 teaspoon paprika
1 clove garlic, minced

2 tablespoons sugar
½ cup ketchup
1 teaspoon dry mustard
⅛ teaspoon pepper
2–3 pounds spareribs

Combine all ingredients except ribs in saucepan. Cover and simmer 15 minutes. Place ribs on rack in baking pan. Bake in very hot (500°) oven for 10–15 minutes. Reduce heat to 325°, and bake 1–1½ hours or till ribs are tender, brushing frequently on both sides with barbecue sauce. Serves 4.

Pots, Pans, and Pioneers I

Gardens of the American Rose Center

The Gardens of the American Rose Center in Shreveport is comprised of 118 acres of botanical gardens dedicated to rose varieties. The headquarters of the American Rose Society since 1974, these gardens include some 20,000 rose varieties, arranged in 65 individual gardens, such as the newest rose hybrids, All-America Rose Selections, miniature roses, single-petaled roses, etc. Taken together, the gardens are described as the largest park in the United States dedicated to roses. The gardens are open daily March 30th through October 31st.

IMAGES: AMERICAN ROSE SOCIETY

156

MEATS

Alma's Pork Tenderloin in a Bed

2 (1-pound) pork tenderloins
Salt and pepper to taste
4 potatoes or red potatoes
2 loaves French bread
4 sprigs rosemary
4 garlic cloves, divided
⅓–½ pound bacon slices
Olive oil

Preheat oven to 375°. Rinse tenderloins and pat dry. Season with salt and pepper. Peel potatoes and cut into chunks. Cut bread loaves to the length of each tenderloin. Remove soft interior of bread, leaving a shell. Place each tenderloin inside of a hollowed loaf. Place a sprig of rosemary under and on top of each tenderloin. Place a garlic clove on top of each tenderloin. Wrap loaves with bacon slices, and tie with clean kitchen string.

Arrange loaves in a roasting pan. Arrange potatoes and remaining 2 garlic cloves around them. Sprinkle with salt, and drizzle with olive oil. Reduce heat to 350°, and bake tenderloin loaves 45 minutes to 1 hour, or till cooked through. Cut each loaf into slices to serve. Serve with potatoes. Makes 4 servings.

Da Cajn Critter

MEATS

Pork Medallions in Creole Mustard Sauce

1 (2-pound) pork tenderloin
1 teaspoon salt
1 teaspoon pepper
½ cup flour
1 stick butter, divided
1 tablespoon minced garlic
2 tablespoons vermouth
1–2 tablespoons Creole mustard
1 cup half-and-half
4–5 slices Swiss cheese
16 ounces fettuccini or vermicelli

Cut tenderloin into ¼-inch-thick slices. Sprinkle with salt and pepper. Dredge in flour.

Heat ½ stick butter in a heavy skillet till melted. Add pork. Cook till lightly browned on both sides. Remove from skillet and keep warm. Add remaining ½ stick butter to skillet and heat till melted. Add garlic and sauté. Stir in vermouth and mustard. Reduce heat to low. Stir in half-and-half. Add cheese and cook till cheese melts. Return pork to skillet. Bring to a simmer. Simmer for 10–15 minutes.

Cook fettuccini using package directions; drain. Place fettuccini on a serving platter. Arrange pork and sauce over the top. Serves 6–8.

Secret Ingredients

MEATS

Pork Medallions in Creole Mustard Sauce

MEATS

Stuffed Pork Chops

6 (1½-inch-thick) pork chops
Salt and pepper to taste
Louisiana hot sauce to taste
4 tablespoons butter
1 small onion, finely chopped
¼ cup finely chopped green onions with tops
1 small green bell pepper, finely chopped
3 cloves garlic, finely chopped
4 slices bread
¼ cup milk

Cut slits horizontally in chops to make pockets. Season with salt, pepper, and pepper sauce; set aside. Melt butter in saucepan. Add onions, bell pepper, and garlic; sauté till softened. Season to taste. Soak bread in milk, and squeeze out. Add bread to sautéed vegetables; mix well. Stuff mixture into pockets of chops. Lay chops side-by-side in a pan sprayed with nonstick cooking spray; cover. Bake at 350° for 1½ hours, turning chops once halfway through. Uncover, and bake 30 minutes longer. Serves 6.

Classic Cajun Deux

BILLY HATHORN • WIKIPEDIA.ORG

Winnsboro, the "Stars and Stripes Capital of Louisiana," is one of the most patriotic cities in America. On Memorial Day, July 4th, Veteran's Day, Labor Day, and other special occasions, approximately 350 American flags fly proudly along Highway 15.

Breaded Pork Chops

4 center-cut pork chops
Salt, pepper, garlic powder, and pepper sauce to taste
2 cups bread crumbs
Egg substitute equaling 2 eggs, beaten
3 tablespoons cooking oil

Season pork chops with seasonings. Coat well with bread crumbs on both sides. Dip in egg substitute, and place back into bread crumbs, coating well on both sides again. Heat oil in frying pan, and cook pork chops over medium heat till brown on the outside and cooked internally. Serves 4.

Skinny Cajun

Ted's Cochon de Lait

1 (70-pound) hog, cleaned
2 large bottles Italian salad dressing
Tony's Chachere's Creole Seasoning
2 liters 7-Up

The night before, marinate the hog in a large ice chest with Italian salad dressing and Tony's. Baste it repeatedly. Put pig on the spit. Let it roast all day, or till done. While pig is turning on the hot spit, and while the fire is hot (just before it is done), spray with 2 liters of 7-UP to "crack the cracklin's." Cool down. Pull cracklin's. Pull pork. Figuring one pound per person, this hog should feed 70 people. Enjoy!

deBellevue Williams Cochon de Lait

Locals hold traditional crawfish boils, where folks gather to feast on well-seasoned crawfish boiled with small potatoes, broken ears of corn, and sausage pieces . . . all thrown in for tasty good eatin'!

Seafood

Crabmeat Cheesecake 164
Louisiana Crab Cakes with Sauce Ravigotte 166
Crabmeat au Gratin 168
Shrimp Luncheon Dish ... 168
Perfect Boiled Shrimp 169
Barbecue Shrimp 170
Ron's Bar-B-Que Shrimp . 171
Shrimp Rémoulade 171
Shrimp and Grits with Artichokes 172
Dot's New Year's Eve Shrimp 173
Mama's Shrimp Creole ... 174
Grilled Garlic Shrimp Fajitas 175
Sautéed Shrimp and Peppers over Cheese Grits 176

Stella and Stanley's Crawfish Etouffée 178
Easy Crawfish Casserole . 178
Oliver's Crawfish Boulettes 179
Southern-Fried Catfish and Hushpuppies 180
Baked Catfish à la Melissa 181
Catfish Courtbouillon 182
Trout Meunière 183
Trout Pecan 183
Andouille-Crusted Fish with Cayenne Butter Sauce 184
Barbecued Redfish 185
Oyster Po-Boys 186
Oysters Larose 187
Passion Cocktail Sauce 188

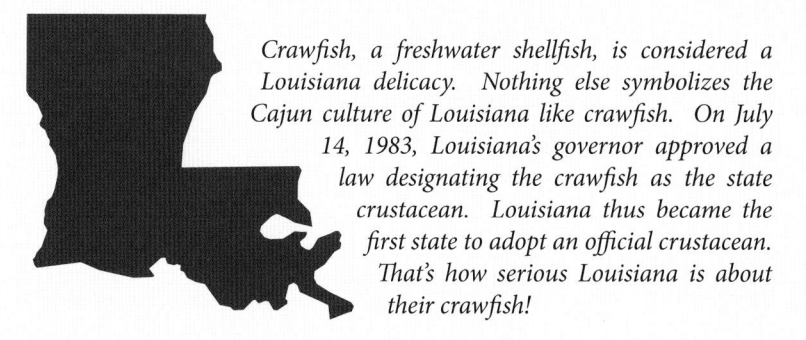

Crawfish, a freshwater shellfish, is considered a Louisiana delicacy. Nothing else symbolizes the Cajun culture of Louisiana like crawfish. On July 14, 1983, Louisiana's governor approved a law designating the crawfish as the state crustacean. Louisiana thus became the first state to adopt an official crustacean. That's how serious Louisiana is about their crawfish!

SEAFOOD

Crabmeat Cheesecake

PECAN CRUST:

¾ cup pecans
1 cup all-purpose flour
¼ teaspoon salt

5 tablespoons butter, cold
3 tablespoons ice water

Preheat oven to 350°. Finely grind pecans in a food processor. Transfer to a large mixing bowl. Add flour and salt; mix well. Cut in butter, working butter into flour with two knives until dough is in crumbs the size of small peas. Add ice water and evenly incorporate into mixture, which should remain fairly crumbly. Roll out dough to a ⅛-inch thickness on a lightly floured surface. Press dough into sides and bottom of a greased 9-inch tart pan. Bake crust for 20 minutes, or until golden.

FILLING:

½ cup small diced onion
1 tablespoon butter
4 ounces crabmeat
8 ounces cream cheese, room temperature
⅓ cup Creole cream cheese or sour cream

2 eggs
1 tablespoon hot pepper sauce (we use Crystal brand hot sauce in this recipe)
Kosher salt and white pepper to taste

Sauté onion in butter until translucent. Add crabmeat and cook just until heated through, then remove from heat. Blend cream cheese until smooth in a mixer fitted with a paddle, or by hand using a wooden spoon. Add Creole cream cheese and mix well. Mix in eggs one at a time. Gently fold in crabmeat mixture. Stir in hot sauce and season to taste with salt and white pepper. Spoon filling into prepared crust. Bake at 300° for 30–40 minutes, or until firm to the touch.

(continued)

(Crabmeat Cheesecake, continued)

MEUNIÈRE SAUCE:

1 lemon, peeled and quartered	Kosher salt and white pepper to taste
½ cup Worcestershire	
½ cup hot pepper sauce	2 cups sliced mixed wild mushrooms
¼ cup heavy whipping cream	
1 pound butter, cold, cut into small cubes	2 tablespoons butter, softened
	24 crab claw fingers

Combine lemon, Worcestershire, and hot pepper sauce in a heavy saucepot. Reduce over medium heat, stirring constantly with a wire whisk until mixture becomes thick and syrupy. Whisk in heavy whipping cream. Reduce heat to low and slowly blend in 1 pound butter, one cube at a time, adding additional butter only after previously added butter has completely incorporated into the sauce. Remove from heat and continue to stir. Season with salt and pepper to taste. Strain through a fine strainer, and keep warm. Sauté mushrooms in 2 tablespoons butter until tender and all moisture has cooked off. (Excess water from mushrooms may break your sauce if it isn't cooked off.) Stir mushrooms into Meunière Sauce. Continue to keep warm.

GARNISH:

1 tablespoon butter   24 crab claw fingers

Melt butter in a sauté pan and warm crab claws over low heat.

TO SERVE:

Slice cheesecake and top each piece with warm Meunière Sauce and three crab claws. Serves 8.

Palace Café: The Flavor of New Orleans

SEAFOOD

Louisiana Crab Cakes with Sauce Ravigotte

This recipe comes from Fertitta's Bistro 6301, a family-owned restaurant that has enjoyed local success in the Arkansas, Louisiana, and Texas area for more than thirty years.

SAUCE RAVIGOTTE:

1½ cups mayonnaise
Worcestershire to taste
Tabasco to taste
⅛ teaspoon white pepper
½ cup chopped drained capers
½ cup chopped drained dill pickles
¼ cup chopped fresh parsley

Combine first 4 ingredients in a bowl; mix well. Stir in capers, dill pickles, and parsley. Chill, covered, in refrigerator.

CRAB CAKES:

5 eggs, divided use
¼ cup Creole mustard
¼ cup mayonnaise
Cayenne pepper to taste
1 pound Louisiana lump crabmeat, drained, shells and cartilage removed
¼ finely chopped green onions
¼ cup bread crumbs or cracker crumbs
1 cup milk
1½ cups all-purpose flour
Tony Chachere's Creole Seasoning to taste
Olive oil

Lightly beat 3 eggs in a bowl. Add mustard and mayonnaise; season with cayenne. Fold in crabmeat; do not break up lumps. Gently stir in green onions and bread crumbs; the mixture should be moist. Shape mixture into patties, 3 inches by ¾ inch thick. Arrange on a baking sheet lined with wax paper; chill till firm.

Whisk milk and remaining 2 eggs in a bowl till blended. Mix flour and Tony's Creole Seasoning in a separate bowl. Dip each crab cake in egg mixture, and coat lightly with flour mixture. Heat enough olive oil in skillet to measure ¼ inch, and fry crab cakes till golden brown; drain. Serve with Sauce Ravigotte. Makes 6–8 crab cakes.

Mardi Gras to Mistletoe

SEAFOOD

Louisiana Crab Cakes with Sauce Ravigotte

SEAFOOD

Crabmeat au Gratin

⅔ cup chopped onion
¼ cup chopped green bell pepper
½ cup butter
3 tablespoons flour
1 (5-ounce) can evaporated milk
Salt and pepper to taste
3 cups lump crabmeat
¼ cup chopped or minced parsley
½ cup grated cheese
2 tablespoons paprika

Sauté onion and bell pepper in butter. Slowly stir in flour, stirring constantly. Slowly stir in evaporated milk, stirring constantly. Add salt and pepper to taste, crabmeat, and parsley. Pour into individual foil crab shells, or a casserole dish that has been sprayed with nonstick spray. Sprinkle cheese and paprika over top of casserole. Bake at 350° till hot and bubbly, about 20 minutes. Serves 6.

Classic Cajun

Shrimp Luncheon Dish

½ stick margarine
1 medium green bell pepper, chopped
1 medium onion, chopped
½ cup chopped celery
1 (14-ounce) can Italian stewed tomatoes
1 cup uncooked rice
1 cup water
2 (7-ounce) cans cooked shrimp, drained
1 (4-ounce) can mushrooms (optional)
1 teaspoon salt
1 teaspoon pepper
1 tablespoon Worcestershire

Sauté first 4 ingredients. Add remaining ingredients. Cook, covered, very slowly for 30 minutes (electric skillet is good for this). If using Minute Rice, cook only 2 or 3 minutes and let stand 10 minutes or more. Serves 4–6.

Pots, Pans, and Pioneers IV

SEAFOOD

Perfect Boiled Shrimp

No guesswork—perfect every time.

Water
1 onion, peeled, quartered
2 cloves garlic
2 tablespoons vegetable oil
½ lemon, sliced
1 tablespoon vinegar
½ teaspoon Tabasco
½ teaspoon black pepper
2 pounds unpeeled headless shrimp
2 teaspoons liquid crab boil (or 1 seasoning bag)
3 tablespoons salt

Fill 5-quart pot half full of water; bring to a boil. Add all ingredients, except shrimp, crab boil, and salt; return to a boil, and add shrimp and crab boil. Boil 5 minutes, then stir in salt to dissolve. Cover, remove from heat, and let set 30 minutes. Remove drained shrimp to a large bowl and cover with ice. Serve right away or chilled. Serves 4–6.

Note: If you can't get crab boil, do without. Spread out newspaper and bring on the sauce! I promise when you serve these boiled shrimp, you will surely "pass a good time." —*Gwen McKee*

The Little New Orleans Cookbook

Shrimp boats are a-comin'...

SEAFOOD

Barbecue Shrimp

This book wouldn't be complete without a barbecue shrimp recipe. I played around in the kitchen to ensure the recipe included tons of sauce to dip the French bread, as that is the best part. Serve with French bread and angel hair pasta. —Holly Clegg

¼ cup olive oil
¼ cup fat-free Italian or creamy onion dressing
1 tablespoon minced garlic
1 teaspoon onion powder
¼ teaspoon cayenne
¼ cup Worcestershire
2 teaspoons dried thyme leaves
2 teaspoons dried oregano leaves
1 tablespoon paprika
Salt and pepper to taste
2 pounds large shrimp, not peeled
⅓ cup light beer
½ cup clam juice or fat-free chicken broth

In large nonstick skillet, combine oil, Italian dressing, garlic, onion powder, cayenne, Worcestershire, thyme, oregano, paprika, and salt and pepper over medium heat till sauce begins to boil. Add shrimp; cook 5 minutes. Add beer and broth; cook another 5–7 minutes, or till shrimp are done. Serves 4–6.

Note: Peeled shrimp may be used, if desired, but peeling the shrimp is tons of fun—just have plenty of paper towels.

Gulf Coast Favorites

Big fun fishin' on the bayou

SEAFOOD

Ron's Bar-B-Que Shrimp

If you don't "sop" your bread in the sauce, it's your mistake!

2 dozen jumbo shrimp in shells
½ stick butter
Cajun injector Creole Garlic Marinade
Black pepper
½ fresh lemon

Wash shrimp thoroughly. Pinch off portion of head from eyes forward. Melt butter in a large skillet. Place shrimp in a single layer in the butter. Shake marinade well and pour over shrimp till almost covered. Cover top with black pepper. Cook 5 minutes, occasionally shaking skillet in a back-and-forth motion; do not stir. Just before removing shrimp from heat, squeeze fresh lemon on top of shrimp and sauce. Remove from heat; serve immediately in bowls with hot French bread on the side. Serves 2.

Chef Reese Williams, Cajun Injector, Inc.
Louisiana's Best Restaurant Recipes

Shrimp Rémoulade

6 tablespoons olive oil
1 tablespoon paprika
4 green onions, chopped
4 tablespoons Creole style mustard
½ teaspoon white pepper
½ teaspoon salt
2 ribs celery, chopped fine
Chopped parsley to taste
¼ head lettuce, shredded
2 pounds cleaned, cold, boiled shrimp
2 hard-boiled eggs, separated, chopped

Combine all ingredients, except lettuce, shrimp, and eggs. Place shrimp on plate of shredded lettuce. Pour rémoulade over shrimp and garnish with chopped eggs. Serves 4–6.

Pots, Pans, and Pioneers II

SEAFOOD

Shrimp and Grits with Artichokes

CHEESE GRITS:

½ cup grits
1 cup shredded Pepper Jack cheese
½ cup Cheez Whiz
2 tablespoons butter, softened
¼ teaspoon Worcestershire
¼ teaspoon white pepper

Cook grits according to package instructions. Combine with remaining ingredients in a large bowl, and mix well; set aside.

SHRIMP:

3 tablespoons butter
1¼ cups sliced fresh mushrooms
1 small onion, chopped
1 (14-ounce) can artichoke hearts, drained, quartered
2 tablespoons white wine
2 pounds fresh shrimp, cooked, peeled, deveined

Melt butter in skillet, and add mushrooms and onion. Sauté till tender, then stir in artichokes. Cook till heated through, then stir in wine. Cook till wine evaporates, stirring occasionally.

Add artichoke mixture and shrimp to Cheese Grits, and mix well. Spread shrimp mixture in buttered 9x13-inch baking dish.

WHITE SAUCE:

3 tablespoons butter
3 tablespoons all-purpose flour
2 cups milk
1 teaspoon hot sauce
½ teaspoon salt

Melt 3 tablespoons butter in saucepan, and add flour. Cook till bubbly, stirring constantly. Stir in milk and bring to a boil. Cook till thickened, stirring constantly. Blend in hot sauce and salt. Spread White Sauce over shrimp mixture.

(continued)

SEAFOOD

(Shrimp and Grits with Artichokes, continued)

TOPPING:

½ cup fine bread crumbs
¼ cup grated Parmesan cheese
1 stick butter, melted

Toss bread crumbs and cheese in bowl, and sprinkle over top. Drizzle with melted butter.

Bake at 350° for 20 minutes, or till brown and bubbly. Serves 8–10.

Note: You may prepare up to 1 day in advance, and store, covered, in refrigerator. Let stand at room temperature for 1 hour before baking.

Mardi Gras to Mistletoe

Dot's New Year's Eve Shrimp

4 cloves garlic, finely minced
1 bunch green onions, washed, chopped
½ cup salted butter
2 pounds fresh large shrimp, peeled, deveined
2 or more tablespoons dry white wine
1 teaspoon dill weed
Juice of 1 lemon
½ teaspoon white pepper
Salt to taste
Cooked angel hair pasta (for 4)

In large skillet, sauté garlic and green onions in butter till slightly tender. Keep the heat on low; add shrimp and remaining ingredients, except pasta, and stir gently. Cook only till shrimp are pink and tender. Serve over pasta. Serves 4.

Who Dat Cookin'

SEAFOOD

Mama's Shrimp Creole

This is another family recipe. It is the Shrimp Creole that my mother taught me to make when I was a teenager. The golden roux and seasonings make a delicious gravy to serve over hot rice.—Corinne Cook

⅓ cup vegetable oil
¼ cup all-purpose flour
1 cup chopped onion
½ cup chopped green bell
  pepper
¼ cup chopped celery
1 (8-ounce) can tomato sauce
2 pounds fresh shrimp,
  peeled, deveined

¼ cup water or wine (red or
  white)
Salt, black pepper, and
  cayenne pepper to taste
½ cup chopped green onions
  (tops only)
½ cup chopped fresh parsley

In a large heavy skillet make a golden brown roux with flour and oil. Add onion, bell pepper, celery, and tomato sauce. Cook covered 20 minutes. Add raw shrimp and water or wine. Cover and cook over low heat 10–15 minutes. Add seasonings to taste. Add green onions and parsley. Stir and serve over hot cooked rice. Serves 6–8.

Extra! Extra! Read More About It

What is Creole?

Like the Creole people, Creole food is a blend of the various cultures of New Orleans, including Italian, Spanish, African, German, Caribbean, Native American, and Portuguese. It is thought of as somewhat aristocratic, with classical European styles adapted to local foods. Traditionally, slaves in the kitchens of well-to-do members of society prepared the food. They had an abundance of time and resources, including access to an array of spices to make their soups and sauces creamy and exotic and delicious. A rémoulade sauce, for example, might consist of a dozen ingredients. Creole cuisine has become famous the world over.

SEAFOOD

Grilled Garlic Shrimp Fajitas

Fajitas are simple to prepare and quite tasty as a lunch or dinner item. The good news is that with so many ready-to-use products on supermarket shelves, including prepared guacamole and tortilla shells, there is no reason for you not to have fajitas often. —Chef John Folse

6 flour tortillas
½ cup butter
6 cloves garlic, minced
1½ pounds (21- to 25-count) shrimp, peeled, deveined
1 tablespoon cumin
¼ cup chopped cilantro
¼ teaspoon chili powder
Salt and black pepper to taste
Granulated garlic to taste
¾ cup sour cream
¾ cup prepared guacamole
¾ cup diced tomatoes
3 cups shredded lettuce

Dampen a large kitchen towel with cold water and ring dry. Place flour tortillas onto towel and fold over to cover completely. Place on a 10-inch plate, and set aside.

In a medium saucepan, melt butter over medium heat. Add minced garlic, and sauté 1–2 minutes. Add shrimp, cumin, cilantro, and chili powder. Season to taste using salt, pepper, and granulated garlic. Stir-fry till shrimp are pink and curled. Set aside and keep warm.

Place towel-wrapped tortillas into microwave and heat 30 seconds, checking temperature. The dampened towel softens the tortillas and warms them nicely. When ready to serve, place a tortilla on each plate, top with shrimp, sour cream, guacamole, tomatoes, and lettuce, and drizzle with spoon of pan drippings. Serve warm. Serves 6.

Hooks, Lies & Alibis

SEAFOOD

Sautéed Shrimp and Peppers over Cheese Grits

The red and green peppers and Canadian bacon make this casserole pretty and satisfying.

½ cup chopped Canadian bacon
1 cup red bell pepper strips
1 cup green bell pepper strips
1 (10-ounce) can diced tomatoes with green chiles, drained
1½ pounds shrimp, peeled, deveined
½ cup chopped green onions

Brown bacon in skillet. Stir in bell peppers, and cook 10 minutes, stirring frequently. Add tomatoes; mix well. Cook 5 minutes, stirring occasionally. Stir in shrimp and cook 3 minutes longer, or till shrimp turn pink, stirring occasionally. Mix in green onions. Remove from heat, and cover to keep warm. Spoon shrimp mixture over grits on a serving platter. Serves 6–8.

CHEESE GRITS:
1⅔ cups milk
1 (16-ounce) can chicken broth
1 cup instant grits (yellow or polenta preferred)
1 cup (4 ounces) shredded sharp Cheddar cheese

Bring milk and broth to a boil in saucepan, and stir in grits. Return grits mixture to a boil; reduce heat. Cook 5 minutes, stirring occasionally. Add cheese to grits and stir till melted.

Warm Welcome (River Road Recipes IV)

SEAFOOD

Sautéed Shrimp and Peppers over Cheese Grits

SEAFOOD

Stella and Stanley's Crawfish Etouffée

1 medium onion, chopped
2 cloves garlic, finely chopped
2 stalks celery, chopped
1 small green bell pepper, chopped
⅓ cup vegetable oil
2 medium tomatoes, peeled, chopped
1 cup fish stock
½ teaspoon basil
¼ teaspoon thyme
1 bay leaf
Freshly ground black pepper
1 teaspoon Tabasco
1 pound crawfish, peeled
½ cup chopped green onions

Sauté onion, garlic, celery, and bell pepper in oil about 5 minutes, or till clear. Add tomatoes, stock, basil, thyme, bay leaf, and pepper to taste. Bring to a boil, stirring constantly. Reduce heat and simmer 15 minutes, or till it thickens to a sauce. Add Tabasco, crawfish, and green onions, and simmer for an additional 5 minutes, or till the crawfish are cooked. Remove bay leaf and serve. Serves 4.

A Streetcar Named Delicious

Easy Crawfish Casserole

This dish takes 1ˢᵗ prize in two categories; easy and delicious!

1 pound crawfish tails (rinse and drain, if frozen)
1 (10¾-ounce) can cream of onion soup
1 (10¾-ounce) can cream of mushroom soup
⅔ cup uncooked long-grain rice
¼ teaspoon red pepper
¼ cup water

Mix all ingredients well. Bake, covered, in a buttered 2-quart casserole in a 350° oven for 1 hour and 10 minutes. Serves 4.

So Good . . . Make You Slap Your Mama! II

SEAFOOD

Oliver's Crawfish Boulettes

½ cup minced onion
½ cup minced celery
¼ cup minced green bell pepper
1 tablespoon sunflower oil
1 pound minced crawfish tails
2 tablespoons minced parsley
¼ cup minced green onions
¼ cup egg substitute
1 cup Italian bread crumbs
½ teaspoon salt
¼ teaspoon cayenne pepper
Vegetable oil spray

Sauté onion, celery, and green pepper in sunflower oil till light brown and limp. Place in large bowl. Add crawfish, parsley, green onions, egg substitute, bread crumbs, and seasonings. Mix thoroughly till it resembles meatball consistency. Roll by tablespoon-size portions into balls; place on baking sheet previously sprayed with vegetable coating. Bake at 350° for 20–25 minutes. Makes 6 servings.

Who Dat Cookin'

Jazz Fest

The New Orleans Jazz Festival celebrates the music and culture of New Orleans and Louisiana, including blues, R&B, gospel music, Cajun music, zydeco, Afro-Caribbean, folk music, Latin, rock, rap music, country music, bluegrass . . . and all that jazz. Food booths have typical Louisiana items made locally—no carnival food here. Craft booths, in the atmosphere of a true marketplace, display a variety of wares from the city, the country, and the world. Held on the last weekend of April and the first weekend of May, the festival is a major tourism destination, rivaled only by Mardi Gras.

SEAFOOD

Southern-Fried Catfish and Hushpuppies

The Cajuns of Bayou County were a very resourceful people, often using the scraps and leftovers from one meal to create a side dish or make a new meal for the next day. This unique recipe is no exception; the leftover batter used to fry the catfish is transformed into hushpuppies to serve alongside the entrée. —Chef John Folse

Peanut oil for deep-frying
2 cups stone-ground corn flour
Salt and black pepper to taste
Cayenne pepper to taste
Granulated garlic to taste
1 large egg
2 cups buttermilk
3 pounds catfish fillets

Preheat oven to 200°. In a Dutch oven or home-style electric deep-fryer (such as a FryDaddy), heat oil to 375° according to manufacturer's instructions. Place 2 wire racks on 2 baking sheets, and set aside. In a shallow bowl, add corn flour, season to taste using salt, peppers, and granulated garlic, then set aside.

In a medium bowl, whisk together egg and buttermilk. Add fish fillets, and turn to coat well. Working in batches, remove fillets from buttermilk mixture, allowing excess batter to drip back into bowl. Dredge in seasoned corn flour, shaking off excess. Carefully slip each fillet into hot oil. Do not overcrowd pot. Fry 3–5 minutes, or till golden brown on both sides, turning once. Using a slotted spoon or tongs, remove fillets from oil, and place on wire racks to dry. Place fish in 200° oven, and keep warm till all fish are fried. Allow oil temperature to return to 375° between batches.

HUSHPUPPIES:
1¾ cups stone-ground yellow cornmeal
1 teaspoon baking powder
1 teaspoon baking soda
½ cup thinly sliced green onions

(continued)

(Southern-Fried Catfish and Hushpuppies, continued)

Into the leftover buttermilk mixture, add cornmeal, baking powder, and baking soda; mix well to combine. Add leftover seasoned corn flour (¼–½ cup) to batter, a little at a time, just till batter is thick enough to be spooned. Fold in green onions, and set aside.

Return oil to 375°. Using 2 teaspoons, carefully drop batter by spoonfuls into oil. Fry approximately 3 minutes, or till golden brown and floating. Using a slotted spoon or tongs, remove hushpuppies from oil, and place on wire rack to drain. Repeat till all batter is fried. Serve immediately alongside fried catfish with Louisiana Tartar Sauce for dipping. Serves 8.

Hooks, Lies & Alibis

Baked Catfish à la Melissa

4 medium-sized catfish fillets (can use whole fish)
Salt, pepper, garlic salt, Cajun seasoning, and Louisiana Hot Sauce to taste
1 large onion, cut into wedges
½ medium green bell pepper, cut into strips
2 large garlic cloves, chopped
2 lemons, sliced
2 large tomatoes, diced
2 ribs celery, sliced lengthwise
3 green onions, tops only, chopped
½ cup water

Wash fish; season according to your taste, rubbing seasoning mixture into fish. Preheat oven to 350°. Spray casserole dish with nonstick cooking spray. Place fish in bottom of dish and layer remaining ingredients, except water, over fish. Pour water over all, and cover tightly with foil. Bake 45 minutes, or till fish flakes easily with a fork. Serves 4.

Skinny Cajun

SEAFOOD

Catfish Courtbouillon

1 cup chopped onion
⅔ cup chopped green onion tops
¾ cup chopped green bell pepper
¼ cup chopped celery
4–6 pounds catfish steaks
Salt and pepper to taste
½ cup oil
1 (10¾-ounce) can tomato soup
Cooked rice

Mix together chopped onion, onion tops, bell pepper, and celery. Season catfish with salt and pepper. Line bottom of heavy pot with oil. Layer catfish steaks and chopped vegetable mixture till all is used. (Put catfish layer first, then cover with mixed vegetables.) Cover and bring to a slow boil on medium-high heat. Uncover and pour tomato soup on top of last layer. Lower to medium heat. Do not boil fast, because the fish will break up. Allow to cook 1 hour, partially covered. If gravy is too thin, thicken by mixing ¼ cup water with 1 tablespoon cornstarch, adding hot gravy to cornstarch mixture till well blended, then add to gravy in pot. Serve over rice. Serves 4–6.

Classic Cajun

Louisiana contains some 6,084 square miles of water surface, and 41 percent of the coastal marshlands in the United States. Speckled trout (shown here), redfish, and flounder are caught in coastal lakes, bays, and marshes. Saltwater species include mackerel, grouper, snapper, and tuna. Principal freshwater sport fish of Louisiana are largemouth bass, spotted bass, crappie, bream, white bass, catfish, and striped bass. Louisiana's mild climate allows freshwater fishing year-round. Louisiana is home to the oldest fishing tournament in the nation, the Grand Isle Tarpon Rodeo, established in 1928.

SEAFOOD

Trout Meunière

4 fillets tenderloin trout
¼ cup butter
1 tablespoon Worcestershire
¼ cup chopped green onions
2 teaspoons lemon juice
½ teaspoon garlic powder
½ teaspoon salt
¼ teaspoon cayenne pepper
Parsley and lemon slices for garnish

Place clean, dry fish in a glass baking dish. Combine remaining ingredients except garnish; microwave on HIGH 1 minute. Pour over fillets, and cover with wax paper. Microwave on HIGH 6 minutes, or till fish flakes easily with fork. Garnish with parsley and lemon slices. Serves 4.

Pots, Pans, and Pioneers III

Trout Pecan

1 tablespoon fresh lemon juice
4 large trout fillets
Salt and pepper to taste
8 tablespoons bread crumbs, divided
1 cup toasted pecans
2 teaspoons dried rosemary
1 egg
2 teaspoons water
⅓ cup all-purpose flour
2 tablespoons vegetable oil
2 tablespoons butter

Sprinkle lemon juice over fillets. Season with salt and pepper; let stand at room temperature 10 minutes. Finely grind 2 tablespoons bread crumbs and pecans in a food processor. Mix with remaining 6 tablespoons bread crumbs and rosemary. Remove mixture to a plate. Beat egg and water in a shallow dish. Dredge fillets in flour, then dip in egg mixture. Press fillets skin side up into crumb mixture to coat. Heat half the oil and half the butter in a large skillet over medium-high heat. Fry 2 fillets skin side up for 3 minutes or till golden brown. Flip carefully and fry 3 minutes, or till no longer transparent. Remove to a plate; keep warm. Repeat with remaining oil, butter, and fillets. Serves 4.

Crescent City Collection

SEAFOOD

Andouille-Crusted Fish with Cayenne Butter Sauce

CHIVE AÏOLI:

¼ cup chopped garlic
⅔ cup blend of 80% vegetable oil and 20% olive oil
1 bunch chives, divided
2 tablespoons chopped parsley

2 egg yolks
1 teaspoon Dijon mustard
Juice of 1 lemon
Salt to taste

Cook garlic in oil blend in a saucepan over medium heat for 20 minutes, stirring frequently; do not brown. Strain oil into a bowl and cool; discard garlic. Reserve 8 chive pieces for garnish. Purée remaining chives and parsley in a food processor. Add egg yolks, and pulse to mix well. Add cooled garlic oil gradually, processing constantly. Add Dijon mustard, lemon juice, and salt; mix, adding a small amount of water, if necessary, for a thin mayonnaise-like consistency. Spoon into a pastry tube or plastic squeeze bottle, and chill for up to several days.

CAYENNE BUTTER SAUCE:

¾ cup Crystal Hot Sauce

2 sticks chilled butter, chopped

Cook hot sauce in a small saucepan over medium heat until reduced by a third. Reduce heat to low, and whisk in butter a few pieces at a time, mixing well after each addition. Keep warm.

ANDOUILLE-CRUSTED FISH:

6 ounces andouille sausage or smoked pork sausage, coarsely chopped
1 onion, coarsely chopped
5 tablespoons blend of 80% vegetable oil and 20% olive oil, divided

1 cup bread crumbs
4 (8-ounce) skinless, boneless fish fillets
Kosher salt and white pepper to taste

(continued)

SEAFOOD

(Andouille-Crusted Fish with Cayenne Butter Sauce, continued)

Grind andouille in a food processor. Sauté ground andouille with onion in 2 tablespoons oil blend in a skillet over medium heat until sausage is brown and onion is transparent. Purée mixture in food processor. Add bread crumbs, and pulse until mixed.

Preheat oven to 350°. Season fish on both sides with kosher salt and white pepper. Heat remaining 3 tablespoons oil blend in an ovenproof skillet over high heat. Add fish fillets and sear for 2 minutes. Turn fillets over and drain skillet. Press andouille mixture onto fish to form a crust. Bake 5 to 10 minutes or until fish flakes easily and crust is golden brown.

To serve, ladle Cayenne Butter Sauce onto each serving plate. Place 1 fish fillet on each plate, and drizzle Chive Aïoli across fish in a zigzag pattern. Top with reserved chives. Serves 4.

Palace Café: The Flavor of New Orleans

Barbecued Redfish

1 stick butter
5 ounces Worcestershire
2 ounces Pickapeppa sauce
3 tablespoons Tabasco
Lime juice to taste
Ketchup to thicken
1 large redfish fillet with skin

Combine first 6 ingredients in a 1-quart saucepan. Bring to simmer and cook 10–15 minutes. Brush on both the skin and meat side of the fish. Grill fish over hot coals approximately 10–15 minutes, beginning with meat-side down. After turning the skin side down, baste with additional sauce. Serves 2–4.

Tell Me More

SEAFOOD

Oyster Po-Boys

"A recipe for po-boys? You're kidding! Everybody knows how to make po-boys." Well, just in case....

Oysters (about 1 per inch of bread), drained
Corn flour seasoned with salt and pepper or Cajun seasoning
Po-boy bread or French mini-loaves
Mayonnaise, salad dressing, or tartar sauce
Tomato slices
Shredded lettuce
Dill pickle slices (optional)
Salt and pepper to taste

Dip drained oysters in seasoned corn flour and fry quickly in very hot oil; drain on paper towels. Heat bread in oven just long enough to get hot—do not toast. Split bread, and spread generously with mayonnaise. Cover with hot oysters, tomato slices, lettuce, and a few pickles, if desired. Season with salt and pepper to taste. Put the top half on and give it one good mash with the palm of your hand, then chomp in! Have ketchup handy . . . and Tabasco.

Note: Fried shrimp, roast beef and gravy, ham and cheese, soft-shell crab, and crawfish are other popular choices. Be sure to order your po-boy "dressed" if you want to get lettuce and tomatoes. And if you want to make these with any other kind of bread, go ahead, but you'll have to call it something else. It just ain't a real po-boy if you don't have that light-on-the inside, crusty-on-the-outside New Orleans French bread! —*Gwen McKee*

The Little New Orleans Cookbook

SEAFOOD

Oysters Larose

4 dozen oyster shells
1 gallon oysters
4 large onions, finely chopped
1–2 cups butter, divided
8 cloves garlic, minced
2 (8-ounce) cans mushrooms, finely chopped
½ cup chopped fresh parsley, or ¼ cup parsley flakes
1 cup chopped shallots
1 (8-ounce) can seasoned bread crumbs
Salt, pepper, and Tabasco to taste
Garlic powder (optional)
1 cup Sauterne
2 cups fine cracker meal
1 box rock salt

Wash and scrub oyster shell halves with soap and water; rinse well and let dry. Simmer oysters in own liquid till edges curl. Remove from liquid (reserving liquid), and chop fine. Sauté onions in half of butter till wilted. Add garlic and mushrooms; stir well, and add chopped oysters. If mixture sticks, add more butter. Add oyster liquid gradually, stirring constantly. Add parsley and shallots; sauté for 1 minute. Add bread crumbs till liquid is absorbed, and mixture is thick and pasty. Add salt, pepper, and Tabasco to taste. Adjust seasoning, adding garlic powder, if necessary, to have a definite garlic flavor. Stir in Sauterne. Spray inside of shells with vegetable oil, and add enough oyster mixture to cover bottom of shell ½ inch thick. Dust each with cracker meal, and top with ¼ teaspoon melted butter.

Preheat oven to 450°. Sprinkle rock salt in large baking tray(s), place shells on tray(s), and heat 10–12 minutes. Makes 4 dozen.

Down the Bayou

SEAFOOD

Passion Cocktail Sauce

Not to be confused with ho-hum sauce, this one will make your nose tingle!

1 cup ketchup	½ teaspoon Tabasco
1 tablespoon lemon juice	1 teaspoon Worcestershire
4 tablespoons horseradish	¼ teaspoon onion powder

Mix and store in a jar in the refrigerator.

Note: Superb with boiled shrimp and crawfish, and perfect for raw oysters.

I was just a little girl when my daddy brought home a sack of oysters. He opened one and I thought the shell was very pretty. The oyster, however, didn't look like something I'd want to eat! I watched my daddy slide it off the shell into his mouth, and his facial expression said that it was some kind of good! He opened one and offered it to me. I trusted my daddy explicitly, so I cautiously accepted it. Didn't go down very gracefully, as I recall, but it pleased my daddy so much that I took another. And another. We made up this sauce, and before long I was anxiously waiting for him to pry those shells open! That was a very special night—I became a full-fledged raw oyster lover, and my daddy and I developed a very special bond. (My mother checked on me all night to be sure I was still breathing.) —Gwen McKee

The Little New Orleans Cookbook

Avery Island

Avery Island is better known as the birthplace of Tabasco Sauce. The island was named after the Avery family, who settled there in the 1830s. Before the Civil War, Edmund McIlhenny joined the Avery family by marrying Mary Eliza Avery. In 1868, McIlhenny began manufacturing Tabasco brand pepper sauce.

The island occupies roughly 2,200 acres and sits atop a deposit of solid rock salt thought to be deeper than Mount Everest is high. Geologists believe this deposit is the remnant of a buried ancient seabed, pushed to the surface by the sheer weight of surrounding alluvial sediments.

Avery Island is surrounded on all sides by bayous, salt marsh, and swampland; it sits about 140 miles west of New Orleans. The island was a sugar plantation formerly known as Petite Anse Island. (Petite Anse means "Little Cove" in Cajun French.) Access to the island is via toll bridge, which charges only inbound traffic.

Today, Avery Island remains the home of the TABASCO® brand pepper sauce factory, as well as Jungle Gardens and its Bird City wildfowl refuge. The Tabasco factory and the gardens are open to the public. For tourism information, visit www.TABASCO.com.

Wooden bonfire structures

Cakes

King Cake with Cream Cinnamon Filling 192
King Cake 193
Praline Cake 194
Tortuga Rum Cake 195
Joie de Vivre Heavenly Hash Cake 196
Gahto ah la Booyee 198
Sour Cream Somersault Cake 199
Pumpkin Upside-Down Cake 200
Pineapple-Coconut Cake 201
Regal Almond Cake 202
Grandmother Garrison's 14-Carat Cake 204
Millionaire Cake 205
Moist and Yummy Yam Cake 206
Cheesecake 208
Turtle Cheesecake Des Amis 209

Every Christmas Eve, over one hundred 30-foot-tall-bonfire structures built of wood, firecrackers, and occasionally bamboo are lit along the Mississippi River levee near the town of Lutcher. The American flags are removed, the structures are laced with kerosene, then all are ignited simultaneously at 7 p.m. to light the way for Papa Noel. Long before the levees were built, bonfires were used to help friends of the family find the inlets coming off the river to the homes of those they wanted to visit on Christmas Eve. Posters display a pirogue with Papa Noel being pulled by his special alligators, led by Alphonse.

The lighting of the bonfires is enjoyed with a pot of gumbo, fireworks, and a lawn-chair. There are even special riverboats that offer bonfire cruises down the Mississippi River.

CAKES

King Cake with Cream Cinnamon Filling

Now, you can make a quick King Cake recipe in your own home any time, without worrying about a complicated yeast dough. Kids love helping with this cake year round—try red and pink colors for Valentine's Day, pastels for Easter, and red and green for Christmas! —Holly Clegg

- 2 (8-ounce) cans reduced-fat crescent rolls
- 4 ounces reduced-fat cream cheese, softened
- 2 tablespoons confectioners' sugar
- 1 teaspoon vanilla
- 2 tablespoons butter
- ⅓ cup light brown sugar
- 1 tablespoon ground cinnamon

Preheat oven to 350°. Coat a 10-inch round pizza pan with nonstick cooking spray. Separate crescent rolls at perforations, into 16 slices. Place slices around prepared pan with points in the center. Press seams together from center out about halfway.

In mixing bowl, beat cream cheese, confectioners' sugar, and vanilla till creamy. Spread on dough in center where seams have been pressed together.

In another small bowl, combine butter, brown sugar, and cinnamon with a fork till crumbly. Sprinkle over cream cheese. Fold dough points over filling, then fold bottom of triangle over points forming circular roll like King Cake. Bake 20–25 minutes or till golden brown. Cool slightly and drizzle with colored Mardi Gras Icing.

MARDI GRAS ICING:
The Mardi Gras colors represent power (yellow), faith (green), and justice (purple).

- 1 cup confectioners' sugar
- 1–2 tablespoons skim milk
- ½ teaspoon vanilla extract
- Yellow, green, red, and blue food coloring

(continued)

CAKES

(King Cake with Cream Cinnamon Filling, continued)

In a small bowl, combine all ingredients, except food coloring. Divide mixture into 3 bowls. In first bowl, add a few drops of yellow food coloring. In second bowl, add a few drops of green food coloring. In third bowl, add equal amounts of drops of red and blue food coloring to create purple. Drizzle separately over cooled cake. Serves 16.

Gulf Coast Favorites

King Cake

2 (8-ounce) cans crescent rolls
2–3 Granny Smith apples, chopped
1 (8-ounce) package cream cheese, softened
1 egg, separated (save white)
1 teaspoon vanilla
1½ cups powdered sugar
Cinnamon

Lay crescent rolls in star shape on baking stone or pizza pan. Cream remaining ingredients, except egg white. Place mixture in middle of rolls. Fold edges over and tuck points under. Bake in 400° oven 25–30 minutes. Brush top with egg white before baking, if desired. Add baby to cake after baking, if desired. Glaze.

GLAZE:
2 ounces cream cheese
Powdered sugar
Milk
Food coloring in Mardi Gras colors (green, yellow, purple)

Mix and drizzle over cake.

Mane Ingredients III

CAKES

Praline Cake

1½ cups cake flour, sifted
1½ teaspoons baking powder
¼ teaspoon salt
¼ cup shortening

¾ cup sugar
1 teaspoon vanilla
1 egg
⅔ cup milk

Sift together flour, baking powder, and salt. Cream shortening, sugar, and vanilla. Beat in egg thoroughly. Add flour mixture alternately with milk, beating just till smooth after each addition. Pour into well-greased, heat-resistant glass, round cake dish. Bake in 325° oven about 40 minutes. Cool slightly in dish.

ICING:

½ cup brown sugar
4 teaspoons flour
2 tablespoons water

4 tablespoons butter, softened
¾ cup chopped pecans

Mix together all ingredients. Carefully spread on top of slightly cooled cake. Return to oven and bake 10 minutes.

River Road Recipes I

Steen's

Steen's cane syrup is a traditional American sweetener made by the simple concentration of cane juice through long cooking in open kettles. It is sweeter than molasses, because no refined sugar is removed from the product. Produced in Abbeville by Steen's Syrup Mill since 1910, it is the world's largest syrup plant. Four generations of the Steen family have produced this syrup, which is still sold in an old-fashioned, bright yellow can. "Great when poured over hot biscuits!"

CAKES

Tortuga Rum Cake

1 (18¼-ounce) box yellow cake mix
1 (3-ounce) package vanilla instant pudding
4 eggs
½ cup vegetable oil
½ cup water
½ cup Tortuga Rum (or any premium rum)
½ cup chopped pecans

Heat oven to 350°. Mix cake mix, pudding, eggs, oil, water, and rum. Beat 2 minutes. Spray Bundt pan with nonstick cooking spray. Sprinkle pecans on bottom of pan. Pour batter into pan and bake 1 hour. Cool. Invert on cake plate. Prick holes in cake with toothpick.

GLAZE:
1 stick butter
1 cup sugar
¾ cup rum

Melt butter in saucepan. Mix in sugar and rum. Heat till sugar is melted. Slowly pour Glaze over cake, letting liquid absorb into cake.

Vedros Family Recipes

CAKES

Joie de Vivre
Heavenly Hash Cake

This one was recommended by a close friend from Uptown. She got it from her mother, who got it from hers, who got it from . . . well, you get the picture. Joie de vivre means the joy of life, and after you take a bite of this cake, you'll understand our joy. —Todd-Michael St. Pierre

- 4 eggs, beaten lightly
- 2 cups sugar
- 3 sticks butter, divided (2 softened)
- 1½ cups self-rising flour
- 2 cups chopped Louisiana pecans
- 1 teaspoon vanilla
- 2 tablespoons plus 4 teaspoons cocoa, divided
- 1 pound powdered sugar
- 8 teaspoons evaporated milk
- 1 bag miniature marshmallows

Combine eggs, sugar, 2 sticks softened butter, flour, pecans, vanilla, and 2 tablespoons cocoa in large mixing bowl. Mix well. Pour into a greased 9x13-inch baking pan, and bake at 350° for 40 minutes.

Prepare glaze by mixing remaining 4 teaspoons cocoa, 1 stick butter, powdered sugar, and milk in saucepan, and heat till spreading consistency. Place marshmallows on top of baked cake. Heat in oven till marshmallows are melted. Spread glaze (or drizzle heavily) over marshmallows. Cut into squares to serve.

Taste of Tremé

Heavenly Hash Eggs are a product of the **Elmer Chocolate Company**, which was founded in 1855 in New Orleans, and now relocated in Ponchatoula. They are famous primarily for their seasonal chocolate boxes (Christmas, Valentines, Easter), but they still produce the individually wrapped candies—Gold Brick, Heavenly Hash, and Pecan Egg—during Easter. Heavenly Hash is the oldest of the three, first produced in 1923. These candies are sold throughout the Gulf Coast states.

CAKES

Joie de Vivre Heavenly Hash Cake

CAKES

Gahto ah la Booyee
(Pudding Cake)

Pronounced "Got-toe ah la Boo yee."

1 (18¼-ounce) box Duncan Hines cake mix (white or yellow)

Mix cake according to package directions. Pour into greased and floured 9x13-inch baking pan. Set aside. (Do not bake yet!)

BOOYEE (PUDDING):

2 (12-ounce) cans evaporated milk	8 tablespoons cornstarch
2 cans water	2 eggs
1 cup sugar	2 teaspoons vanilla
	1 cup butter

Bring milk and water to a boil in saucepan. In a small bowl, mix sugar and cornstarch. Add eggs and mix well. As soon as milk boils, put several large spoons of hot milk into egg/sugar mixture. Stir and add sugar/egg mixture to saucepan of hot milk. Stir and add vanilla and butter to pudding. Cook over low heat till thick. Immediately pour pudding into center of unbaked cake and spoon into corners of pan. Bake in preheated 350° oven for 45 minutes or till done. Serves 8–10.

Note: This pudding cake may be served hot, warm, or cold. It is easier to spoon into serving plates than to cut into squares.

Pots, Pans, and Pioneers V

CAKES

Sour Cream Somersault Cake

Margarine
½ cup sugar
2 tablespoons cinnamon
1 cup finely chopped pecans
1 (18¼-ounce) box yellow cake mix
4 eggs
1 (3.5-ounce) package instant vanilla pudding mix
¾ cup water
1 cup sour cream
1 teaspoon vanilla extract
¼ cup cooking oil

Grease a Bundt cake pan heavily with margarine. Mix sugar, cinnamon, and pecans. Use part of this mixture to coat all sides of pan well. Save the rest to use between layers.

Blend remaining ingredients with electric mixer in large mixing bowl for time indicated on cake mix box. In prepared Bundt pan, alternate layers of batter with cinnamon mixture. Bake at 350° for 1 hour. Cool completely before removing from pan. If desired, you can wrap it in foil, and let stand 2 or 3 days. Stays fresh for 2 weeks. Freezes very well.

River Road Recipes II

Some sayings you might hear in Louisiana:

- **Lagniappe:** French for a little extra or a bonus. Pronounced lan-yap.
- **Laissez les bon temps roulez:** French for "let the good times roll." Never taken lightly in New Orleans.
- **Making groceries:** Shopping for food.
- **Voodoo:** New Orleans has its own brand of voodoo—it is a fusion of the voudon religion of Senegambian slaves and the Catholicism of the European colonists. Marie Laveau was the city's most famous practitioner. From the 1830s to the 1870s, she attended mass at the St. Louis Cathedral every day. There continues to be a few authentic sources for voodoo in the city.
- **Who Dat:** The chant of "Who dat? Who dat say dey gonna beat dem Saints?" originated in minstrel shows of the late 1800s and was then taken up by jazz and big band performers in the 1920s and 30s. It has become the theme for the New Orleans Saints.

CAKES

Pumpkin Upside-Down Cake

1 (16-ounce) can pumpkin
1 (12-ounce) can evaporated milk
2 cups sugar, divided
3 eggs
2 teaspoons cinnamon
1 (18¼-ounce) package yellow cake mix
1 cup chopped pecans
2 sticks butter, melted
1 (8-ounce) package cream cheese, softened
12 ounces nondairy whipped topping

Line a 9x13-inch baking pan with wax paper. Combine pumpkin, evaporated milk, 1 cup sugar, eggs, and cinnamon in bowl; mix well. Pour into prepared pan. Sprinkle dry cake mix over pumpkin mixture. Sprinkle pecans over cake mix. Drizzle butter over layers. Bake at 350° for 1 hour. Cool in pan. Invert onto flat plate.

Combine cream cheese, remaining 1 cup sugar, and whipped topping in bowl; mix well. Spread over top of cake. Chill 1–2 hours, or longer. Cut into 1-inch squares. Serves 24.

Secret Ingredients

John James Audubon Bridge

The beautiful John James Audubon Bridge (shown on opposite page) opened in 2011. At 3,186 feet, it is considered to be the longest cable-stayed span in North America. The $409 million bridge crosses the Mississippi River between Pointe Coupee and West Feliciana parishes in south central Louisiana, and serves as the only bridge structure on the Mississippi River between Natchez, Mississippi, and Baton Rouge (approximately 90 river miles). The bridge replaced the ferry between the communities of New Roads and St. Francisville.

Pineapple-Coconut Cake

1 (18¼-ounce) package Duncan Hines pineapple cake mix
½ cup sugar
½ cup cooking oil
1 cup buttermilk, with 1 teaspoon baking soda added
4 eggs, beaten
1 teaspoon vanilla

Mix all ingredients together; bake in 3 greased round baking pans at 350° till done (25–30 minutes).

PINEAPPLE-COCONUT ICING:

1 (8-ounce) can crushed pineapple
¼ cup water, mixed with 2 tablespoons cornstarch
1½ cups sugar
1 stick margarine
1 teaspoon vanilla
1 (7-ounce) can coconut, divided (reserve half to sprinkle on top of cake)

Combine all Icing ingredients and cook, stirring till thick. Cool. Spread between layers and on sides and top. Sprinkle reserved coconut over all.

Mane Ingredients III

The John James Audubon Bridge

CAKES

Regal Almond Cake

1 cup plus 2 tablespoons butter, softened, divided
1 cup sliced almonds
2 cups plus 2 tablespoons sugar, divided
3¼ cups sifted cake flour
4 teaspoons baking powder
1½ teaspoons salt
1½ cups milk
4 eggs, separated
2 teaspoons vanilla
1½ teaspoons grated lemon peel
½ teaspoon almond extract

Butter bottom, sides, and tube of 10-inch tube pan with 2 tablespoons butter; sprinkle with sliced almonds, rotating pan till sides and bottom are evenly coated. Sprinkle 2 tablespoons sugar over almond-coated sides and bottom. Cream together 1 cup butter and 2 cups sugar till light and fluffy.

Sift together flour, baking powder, and salt; add to creamed mixture alternately with milk. Add egg yolks, beating thoroughly. Add vanilla, lemon peel, and almond extract.

Beat egg whites till stiff, and gently fold into batter. Turn into tube pan. Bake at 325° about 1 hour and 20 minutes, or till cake tests done. Let cool in pan about 10 minutes, then invert onto wire rack to finish cooling. No frosting is needed, as the almonds are the crowning touch.

Pots, Pans, and Pioneers III

Nottoway Plantation and Resort

Nottoway Plantation is the South's largest remaining antebellum mansion. Located in its namesake's town of White Castle, this stunning historic plantation is on the River Road between Baton Rouge and New Orleans. It was completed in 1859 for the John Hampden Randolph family at a cost of about $80,000. Mr. Randolph had the ballroom painted white to show off the natural beauty of all the women. A dramatic, multimillion-dollar renovation has restored this historic plantation to her days of glory as well as adding luxury resort amenities and corporate and social event venues. Nottoway was listed on the National Register of Historic Places in 1980. Plantation tours are given every day of the week.

CAKES

Grandmother Garrison's 14-Carat Cake

2 cups cake flour
2 teaspoons baking powder
1½ teaspoons baking soda
1½ teaspoons salt
2 teaspoons cinnamon
4 eggs
2 cups sugar

1½ cups vegetable oil
2 cups shredded carrots
1 (8-ounce) can crushed pineapple, drained
1 (3½-ounce) can coconut
1 cup chopped nuts

Stir together first 5 ingredients. Beat eggs, sugar, and oil together. Add dry ingredients and beat at low speed till blended. Fold in carrots, pineapple, coconut, and nuts. Pour into 3 greased and floured 9-inch pans. Bake at 325° for 40 minutes, or till cake tests done.

BUTTERMILK GLAZE:

1 cup sugar
1½ teaspoons baking soda
½ cup buttermilk

½ cup butter
1 tablespoon molasses
1 teaspoon vanilla

Bring all ingredients, except vanilla to a boil. Boil 5 minutes; stir often. Remove from heat, and add vanilla. Pour over hot cake layers in pans. Let stand 15 minutes. Remove and cool layers.

CREAM CHEESE FROSTING:

¾ cup butter, softened
11 ounces cream cheese, softened

3 cups sifted powdered sugar
1½ teaspoons vanilla

Beat butter and cream cheese together till smooth. Add powdered sugar and vanilla. Beat till smooth. Frost and stack cooled layers.

Note: May line pans with wax paper then grease and flour; it makes it easy to remove.

Come to the Table

CAKES

Millionaire Cake

1 (18¼-ounce) package chocolate cake mix
1 (14-ounce) package caramels, unwrapped
1 stick butter
1 (14-ounce) can sweetened condensed milk
2 cups chopped pecans
2 cups semisweet chocolate chips

Preheat oven to 350°. Prepare cake mix using package directions. Pour ½ of batter into a greased 9x13-inch cake pan. Bake 15 minutes. Melt caramels with butter and condensed milk in saucepan over low heat, stirring constantly. Pour over cake layer. Sprinkle pecans over caramel mixture. Pour remaining cake batter over pecans. Top with chocolate chips. Bake 20 minutes longer. Cool in pan before serving. Serves 4–6.

Something to Talk About

A Palace of Dreams

The Strand Theatre in Shreveport was built in 1925 at a cost of $750,000. The 2,400-seat theatre had a huge pipe organ, crystal chandeliers, and gilt mirrors. The "Million Dollar Theatre" was air conditioned, and in the early days had its own full-time orchestra on staff. By the mid 70s, The Strand, sadly in decline, closed. In 1976 the newly formed Strand Theatre of Shreveport Corporation got the community involved in its restoration. The lost chandeliers were copied from photos, the opera boxes were replaced, the original marquee was replicated, and the exterior was sandblasted to the original facade. In December of 1984, the Strand reopened to a standing-room-only crowd. Since then the six murals of the "Muses of the Strand" have been re-created, and today it is recognized as one of the top five glitziest theatres for live performance anywhere in the country.

CAKES

Moist and Yummy Yam Cake

This versatile batter is perfect for muffins or bread. —Chef John Folse

1½ cups vegetable oil
2 cups sugar
4 eggs
2 cups all-purpose flour
3 teaspoons baking powder
3 teaspoons baking soda
1 teaspoon salt
2 teaspoons cinnamon
1½ cups Bruce's mashed yams
1 cup chopped pecans
1 tablespoon pure vanilla
Raisins to taste, optional

Preheat oven to 350°. In a large mixing bowl, cream oil and sugar until well blended. Add eggs, 1 at a time, whisking after each addition. In a separate bowl, combine flour, baking powder, baking soda, salt, and cinnamon. Slowly add dry mixture to egg mixture, blending well. Fold in yams, pecans, vanilla, and raisins, if desired. Pour batter evenly into 3 greased and floured 9-inch cake pans. Bake 40 minutes or until toothpick inserted in center comes out clean. Cool, then remove from pans.

PINEAPPLE FILLING:

1 (20-ounce) can crushed pineapple
1½ tablespoons cornstarch
1 cup sugar

While cake is baking, make filling by combining pineapple, cornstarch, and 1 cup sugar. Bring to a low boil over medium-high heat, stirring constantly for 5 minutes. Once mixture thickens, remove from heat and let cool.

CREAM CHEESE ICING:

8 ounces cream cheese, softened
½ stick butter, softened
1 pound powdered sugar
1 tablespoon pure vanilla

Combine cream cheese, butter, powdered sugar, and vanilla. Beat on low speed until fluffy and smooth; set aside.

When cakes cool, spread Pineapple Filling between layers. Coat with Cream Cheese Icing and serve.

The Encyclopedia of Cajun & Creole Cuisine

CAKES

Moist and Yummy Yam Cake

CAKES

Cheesecake

CRUST:

15 sugar cookies   6 tablespoons butter, melted

Grind cookies in food processor till fine; mix with melted butter. Press mixture in bottom and side of 8½-inch springform pan that has been coated with nonstick cooking spray.

FILLING:

3 pounds cream cheese, softened
2 cups sugar
6 eggs, beaten

1 cup sour cream
2 tablespoons pure vanilla extract

Preheat oven to 350°. In a bowl, beat cream cheese, sugar, eggs, sour cream, and vanilla with electric mixer till creamy. Pour over Crust. Wrap bottom of pan with aluminum foil, enough to cover sides, so that water from water bath does not get into pan. Bake in water bath for 45 minutes to 1 hour, till firm. Refrigerate, preferably overnight, before serving. Makes 12 slices.

The Grapevine Café and Gallery, Donaldsonville
Louisiana's Best Restaurant Recipes

Oakley Plantation

St. Francisville is a popular tourism destination with a number of restored historic plantations open daily for tours, including Rosedown Plantation, Butler Greenwood Plantation, The Myrtles, The Cottage Plantation, and Greenwood Plantation, as well as several antebellum gardens. The Audubon State Historic Site near St. Francisville is the anchor of a lush 100-acre park graced by Oakley House, built in 1806. The famed nature painter, John James Audubon lived here in 1821 and created some 32 paintings.

CAKES

Turtle Cheesecake Des Amis

In this cheesecake, the "turtle" mixture of pecan and caramel is not only used as a topping for the cake, but also is baked between the crust and filling. Almonds or walnuts can be substituted, but Louisianians prefer pecans. —Chef John Folse

- 15 Oreo cookies
- 6 tablespoons butter, melted
- 1 (14-ounce) bag caramel candy, unwrapped
- 1 (5-ounce) can evaporated milk
- 2 cups chopped pecans, divided
- ½ cup sour cream
- 1½ pounds cream cheese, softened
- 4 large eggs
- ½ cup sugar
- 2 tablespoons pure vanilla extract
- ½ cup semisweet chocolate chips

Preheat oven to 350°. Spray a 9-inch springform pan with cooking spray, and set aside. In a food processor, chop cookies to fine crumbs, then toss with melted butter. Press evenly into pan to form a crust, then set aside.

In a microwave-safe bowl, combine caramel and evaporated milk. Microwave on HIGH at 2-minute intervals, stirring until smooth and creamy. Allow caramel topping to cool 10 minutes, or until slightly thickened. Pour half of caramel topping over cookie crust, and top with 1 cup chopped pecans.

In a large mixing bowl, blend sour cream and cream cheese with an electric mixer. Add eggs and sugar, continuing to blend until smooth. Stir in vanilla, then pour batter into pan. Bake 45–60 minutes, or until toothpick inserted into center comes out clean. Remove from oven, and allow cake to cool 30 minutes. Top cake with chocolate chips, remaining caramel topping, and remaining 1 cup pecans. Refrigerate overnight. Serves 6–8.

The Encyclopedia of Cajun & Creole Cuisine

Louisiana's state bird, the brown pelican, is one of the best known and most prominent birds found in coastal areas.

Cookies & Candies

- Coconut Macaroons 212
- Toffee Crunch Cookies 212
- Gamoo's Almond Iced Tea Cakes 213
- McKenzie's Turtle Cookies 214
- Shortbread Cookies 216
- Robert's Sand Tarts 216
- Chocolate Graham Cracker Bars 217
- Pecan Pie Surprise Bars .. 217
- Pumpkin Bars 218
- Seven Layer Cookies 219
- Lisa's Peanut Butter Squares 219
- Bodacious Brownies 220
- "Everything But the Kitchen Sink" Bar Cookies 220
- Strawberry Fudge Balls .. 222
- Almond Bark Candy 222
- Pat's Pralines 223
- Creole Pralines 223
- Mom's Peanut Butter Fudge 224
- Toasted Pecan Clusters 224

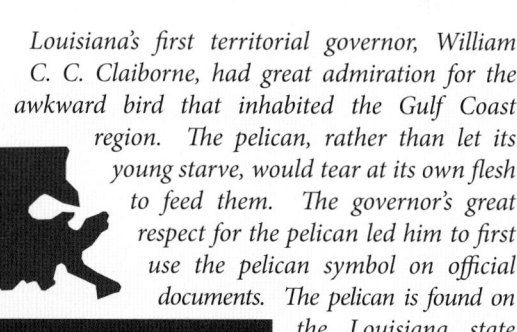

Louisiana's first territorial governor, William C. C. Claiborne, had great admiration for the awkward bird that inhabited the Gulf Coast region. The pelican, rather than let its young starve, would tear at its own flesh to feed them. The governor's great respect for the pelican led him to first use the pelican symbol on official documents. The pelican is found on the Louisiana state seal and the state flag. The official nickname of Louisiana is the "Pelican State."

COOKIES & CANDIES

Coconut Macaroons

4 cups shredded coconut
½ cup all-purpose flour
2 teaspoons vanilla

1⅓ cups sweetened condensed milk

Mix coconut and flour in a bowl. Mix vanilla with condensed milk. Add to coconut mixture, and stir with a wooden spoon till combined. Drop by teaspoonfuls 2 inches apart onto a greased cookie sheet. Bake in preheated 325° oven for 15 minutes or till golden brown. Remove to a wire rack to cool. Store in airtight container. Makes about 40 macaroons.

Crescent City Moons / Dishes and Spoons

Toffee Crunch Cookies

1 stick butter, softened
1 (18¼-ounce) package yellow butter cake mix with pudding

2 eggs, lightly beaten
1½ cups almond butter chips or Heath candy pieces
½ cup chopped pecans

Combine butter, cake mix, and eggs in bowl; mix well. Stir in butter chips and pecans. Drop by rounded teaspoonfuls on a greased cookie sheet. Bake at 350° for 8–10 minutes. Remove to wire rack to cool. Makes 5 dozen.

Secret Ingredients

COOKIES & CANDIES

Gamoo's Almond Iced Tea Cakes

2 sticks butter, softened
2 cups sugar
4 eggs
6 cups all-purpose flour
2 teaspoons baking powder
Pinch of baking soda
Pinch of salt
1 tablespoon almond extract
¼ cup milk

Cream butter and sugar well. Add eggs and mix well. Mix dry ingredients in a separate bowl, then add slowly to egg mixture. Add almond extract, then mix in milk carefully. Make into a big ball and chill several hours. Roll on floured wax paper. Use seasonal cookie cutters to make various shapes. Place on foil-lined baking sheets. Bake at 350° for only 3–5 minutes (for chewy cakes). Be careful not to overcook!

ALMOND ICING:

1 stick butter
1 (1-pound) box confectioners' sugar
2 tablespoons almond extract
2 tablespoons (or more) milk

Melt butter; slowly mix in confectioners' sugar, almond extract, and milk. The Icing should be thin enough to firm when brushed (with a pastry brush) on the back of a cooled tea cake. Makes 4 dozen or so.

deBellevue Williams Cochon de Lait

The **Port of South Louisiana** is the largest tonnage port district in the Western Hemisphere. Over 4,000 oceangoing vessels and 55,000 barges call at the port each year, making it the top ranked in the country for export tonnage and total tonnage. Located between New Orleans and Baton Rouge, it stretches 54 miles along the Mississippi River within St. Charles, St. John the Baptist, and St. James parishes, with headquarters in LaPlace.

McKenzie's Turtle Cookies

A New Orleans tradition for over 70 years, McKenzie's Bakery closed in 2001. These are the best cookies on earth, y'all.
—Todd-Michael St. Pierre

COOKIE:
- 1 stick butter, softened
- ½ cup light brown sugar, packed
- 1 whole egg
- 1 egg, separated
- ¼ teaspoon vanilla
- 1 teaspoon maple flavoring
- 1½ cups all-purpose flour
- ¼ teaspoon salt
- ¼ teaspoon baking soda
- Pecan halves (about 120)

Preheat oven to 350°. Cream butter with sugar till light and fluffy. Beat in egg, egg yolk, vanilla, and maple flavoring; set aside. Sift together flour, salt, and baking soda. Add dry ingredients gradually to the creamed mixture till you have a smooth dough; then chill 2 hours.

Shape teaspoons of dough into oval-shaped balls (like a turtle body). Dip bottoms into egg white. Press slightly onto greased cookie sheet on which a group of 5 pecan halves have already been placed to form head and 4 feet of turtles. Bake 10–12 minutes, or till set, and when cool, frost.

CHOCOLATE FROSTING:
- 2 ounces solid baking chocolate
- ¼ cup milk
- 1 tablespoon butter
- 1 pound powdered sugar

Melt chocolate with milk and butter. Beat in powdered sugar till smooth. Frost cookies. Makes about 2 dozen cookies.

Taste of Tremé

COOKIES & CANDIES

McKenzie's Turtle Cookies

215

COOKIES & CANDIES

Shortbread Cookies

4 cups all-purpose flour
2 cups butter, softened
1 cup sugar

Combine all ingredients and knead by hand. Roll into logs; refrigerate till firm. Remove from fridge; slice and bake on ungreased cookie sheets at 350° for 10 minutes. Makes about 3 dozen.

Pots, Pans, and Pioneers III

Robert's Sand Tarts

2 stick margarine, softened
2 teaspoons vanilla
2½ cups chopped pecans
5 tablespoons powdered sugar
2 cups all-purpose flour
Additional powdered sugar

Combine first 5 ingredients; mix well. Drop by teaspoonfuls onto greased cookie sheet. Bake at 350° for 30 minutes, or till light brown. Immediately after taking out of oven, roll in additional powdered sugar, twice.

Pots, Pans, and Pioneers III

Satchmo

Louis Armstrong (August 4, 1901–July 6, 1971) nicknamed Satchmo, was a jazz trumpeter and singer from New Orleans. Coming to prominence in the 1920s as an "inventive" trumpet and cornet player, Armstrong was a foundational influence in jazz, shifting the focus of the music from collective improvisation to solo performance. Renowned for his charismatic stage presence and voice almost as much as for his trumpet-playing, Armstrong's influence extends well beyond jazz music. In 2001, the airport was renamed Louis Armstrong New Orleans International Airport in his honor.

COOKIES & CANDIES

Chocolate Graham Cracker Bars

12 double graham crackers
1 cup butter
1 cup light brown sugar
1 (12-ounce) package milk chocolate chips
1 cup chopped pecans

Line a jellyroll or metal pan with foil. Place graham crackers on foil as close together as possible. Melt butter and light brown sugar. Boil 3 minutes (be sure to boil, not cook), stirring constantly. Should be thick. Pour over graham crackers and spread evenly. Bake at 400° for 5 minutes. Watch closely so it does not burn. Sprinkle milk chocolate chips (must be milk chocolate) over sugar-butter mixture, and spread till even. Sprinkle pecans over melted chocolate. Cut into squares.

Tell Me More

Pecan Pie Surprise Bars

1 (18¼-ounce) package yellow cake mix
⅓ cup butter, melted
4 eggs, divided
1½ cups dark corn syrup
½ cup firmly packed brown sugar
1 teaspoon vanilla
1 cup chopped pecans

Reserve ⅔ cup dry cake mix; combine remaining cake mix, butter, and 1 egg. Press into greased bottom and sides of a 9x13-inch baking pan. Bake at 350° for 15–20 minutes until light golden brown. Combine corn syrup, brown sugar, vanilla, reserved dry cake mix, and remaining 3 eggs. Beat at medium speed 1–2 minutes. Pour over partially baked crust, then sprinkle with pecans. Return to oven and bake 30–35 minutes till filling is set.

Pots, Pans, and Pioneers II

COOKIES & CANDIES

Pumpkin Bars

1 (16-ounce) can pumpkin
1 (14-ounce) can sweetened condensed milk
½ cup sugar
3 eggs
1 teaspoon cinnamon
1 (18¼-ounce) package white cake mix
1 cup chopped pecans
½ cup butter, melted

Line a 9x13-inch baking pan with wax paper. Mix pumpkin, condensed milk, sugar, eggs, and cinnamon in a bowl till smooth. Pour into prepared pan. Sprinkle with dry cake mix and pecans, and pat into pumpkin mixture. Pour butter over top. Bake at 350° for 50–60 minutes. Cool in pan 5–10 minutes. Invert onto a tray and remove wax paper.

CREAM CHEESE FROSTING:
1 (8-ounce) package cream cheese, softened
1 cup confectioners' sugar
1 (8-ounce) carton whipped topping

Combine cream cheese and confectioners' sugar, and beat till smooth; mix in whipped topping. Spread Frosting over cooled pumpkin bars. Cut into bars to serve. Serves 15.

Roux To Do

The oil and gas industry, as well as its subsidiary industries such as transport and refining, have dominated Louisiana's economy since the 1940s. In 2014, the oil and gas industry in Louisiana employed 300,000 people, ranked fourth in petroleum production, and was the second largest gas-producing state.

ExxonMobil's refinery in Baton Rouge as seen from the state capitol tower

COOKIES & CANDIES

Seven Layer Cookies

1 stick butter
1 cup graham cracker crumbs
½ (12-ounce) package chocolate chips
½ (12-ounce) package butterscotch chips
1 (14-ounce) can sweetened condensed milk
1 (3-ounce) can shredded coconut
½ cup chopped pecans or walnuts

Melt butter in a 9x13-inch baking pan. Pat in crumbs. Pour chocolate chips on top, then butterscotch chips on top of chocolate chips. Pour condensed milk evenly over top. Sprinkle coconut, then nuts on top. Bake at 350° for 30 minutes. Cool, then cut into 2-inch squares.

Pots, Pans, and Pioneers III

Lisa's Peanut Butter Squares

3 sticks butter, melted
8 ounces graham cracker crumbs
4 cups confectioners' sugar
2 cups peanut butter
1 (12-ounce) package milk chocolate chips

Combine butter, graham cracker crumbs, confectioners' sugar, and peanut butter in a bowl; mix well. Pat over the bottom of a buttered 9x13-inch baking pan. Place chocolate chips in a microwave-safe bowl, and microwave till melted (about 2 minutes). Spread over prepared layer.

Chill, covered, till set. Cut into squares. Serve at room temperature, or slightly chilled. Store in an airtight container. Makes 3–4 dozen squares.

Crescent City Moons, Dishes and Spoons

COOKIES & CANDIES

Bodacious Brownies
A.K.A. "Big Booty Brownies"

Easy and SO Good!

1 (18¼-ounce) package chocolate cake mix
2 cups chopped walnuts
4 eggs, divided use
½ cup butter, melted
1 (8-ounce) package cream cheese, softened
1 (1-pound) package confectioners' sugar

Mix cake mix, walnuts, 1 egg, and butter in a bowl. (The batter will be stiff.) Press into a buttered 9x13-inch baking pan. Beat cream cheese, remaining 3 eggs, and confectioners' sugar in mixing bowl till smooth. Spread over top of batter. Bake at 350° for 45 minutes. Cool in pan before cutting. (Pipe with chocolate frosting, if desired.) Makes 1 dozen.

Roux To Do

"Everything But the Kitchen Sink" Bar Cookies

1 (18-ounce) roll refrigerator chocolate chip cookie dough
1 (7-ounce) jar marshmallow crème
½ cup creamy peanut butter
1½ cups corn Chex cereal
½ cup M&M Chocolate Candies

Pat cookie dough over bottom of greased 9x13-inch baking pan. Bake at 350° for 13 minutes. Drop teaspoonfuls of marshmallow crème and peanut butter over the top. Sprinkle with cereal and chocolate candies, and bake 7 minutes longer. Cool in pan on wire rack, and cut into 2-inch bars. Makes 3 dozen bars.

Mardi Gras to Mistletoe

COOKIES & CANDIES

Bodacious Brownies

COOKIES & CANDIES

Strawberry Fudge Balls

Made like bourbon balls, with crushed vanilla wafers, melted chocolate, and strawberry preserves, along with cream cheese and pecans.

- 1 (8-ounce) package cream cheese, softened
- 1 cup semisweet chocolate morsels, melted
- ¾ cup vanilla wafer crumbs
- ¼ cup strawberry preserves
- ½ cup toasted, finely chopped pecans

Beat cream cheese at medium speed with a hand-held electric mixer till creamy. Beat in melted chocolate till smooth. Stir in vanilla wafer crumbs and strawberry preserves; cover and chill 1 hour. Shape into 1-inch balls; roll in toasted chopped pecans; chill.

Note: To toast nuts, spread out in a single layer on a baking sheet. Toast in 350° oven, stirring occasionally, 10–15 minutes. Or, toast in an ungreased skillet over medium heat, stirring, till golden brown and aromatic.

A Confederacy of Scrumptious

Almond Bark Candy

- 3 cups chopped pecans or sliced almonds
- 3 tablespoons butter, melted
- 6 squares almond bark (vanilla, chocolate, or butterscotch)

Heat oven to 300°. Toast nuts with butter on baking pan in oven for 25 minutes; don't let burn! In a saucepan, heat almond bark till melted. (You can also melt almond bark in microwave for 2 minutes on HIGH). Stir till smooth. Remove from heat. Add toasted pecans or almonds to melted bark; stir well. Drop by teaspoonfuls onto wax paper, and let harden.

Vedros Family Recipes

COOKIES & CANDIES

Pat's Pralines

1 stick butter
1½ cups white sugar
¾ cup brown sugar
1¼ cups milk
1 tablespoon vanilla
2 cups chopped or halved pecans

Cook all ingredients in a large saucepan till temperature reaches 238° (or a drop hardens in cool water). Let cool till thickened. Drop by tablespoons onto wax paper. Let cool completely.

Hey, Good Lookin', What's Cooking?

Creole Pralines

3 cups unrefined sugar
1 stick butter
1 cup milk
2 tablespoons corn syrup
2 cups chopped pecans
1 teaspoon vanilla

Place all ingredients except pecans and vanilla in a 3-quart (or larger) saucepan. Bring to a boil, then cook about 20 minutes longer, stirring occasionally. Add pecans, and cook mixture till a small amount of mixture dropped into cold water forms a soft ball. Add vanilla, stirring well. Drop by tablespoonfuls onto wax paper with several sheets of newspaper beneath wax paper.

Down the Bayou ... and Back Again

French settlers brought the praline recipe to Louisiana. French pralines are a combination of almonds and caramelized sugar. Since both sugar cane and pecan trees were plentiful in Louisiana during the 19th century, New Orleans chefs substituted pecans for almonds, added cream to thicken the confection, and thus created what became known throughout the American South as the praline. Pralines have a creamy consistency, similar to fudge. (Pronounced *peh-cahn praw-leens*.)

COOKIES & CANDIES

Mom's Peanut Butter Fudge

¾ cup butter or margarine
3 cups sugar
1 (5-ounce) can evaporated milk
½ cup creamy peanut butter
1 (7-ounce) jar marshmallow crème
1 (10-ounce) bag peanut butter chips
1 teaspoon vanilla

In a 2-quart saucepan, melt butter over medium-low heat. Add sugar and evaporated milk. Increase heat to medium and bring mixture to a boil, stirring constantly. Boil 5 minutes, stirring constantly. Remove from heat, and add peanut butter, marshmallow crème, peanut butter chips, and vanilla. Stir till smooth and fully mixed. Pour into a buttered 9x13-inch pan; cool. When set, cut into squares.

Steel Magnolias in the Kitchen

Toasted Pecan Clusters

6 tablespoons butter
6 cups pecans pieces
1 (24-ounce) package chocolate candy coating*

Preheat oven to 300°. Melt butter in a 10x15-inch baking pan in oven. Add pecans, and stir to coat. Spread pecans over baking pan. Bake in preheated oven for 30 minutes, stirring every 10 minutes.

Melt candy coating in heavy saucepan over low heat. Remove from heat, and let cool 2 minutes. Stir in pecans. Drop by rounded teaspoonfuls onto wax paper, and let cool completely. Store in airtight container in refrigerator. Serves 40.

*May substitute chocolate bark or white chocolate almond bark for chocolate candy coating.

Marshes to Mansions

Some Notables Born in Louisiana

CULINARY

John Besh
Tony Chachere
Leah Chase
John Folse

Paul Prudhomme
Susan Spicer
Justin Wilson

POLITICAL / LITERARY

James Carville politician
Truman Capote author
Ernest Gaines author
Lillian Hellman playwright

John Kennedy Toole author
Huey Long politician
Anne Rice author

ENTERTAINMENT

Trace Adkins singer, songwriter
Louis Armstrong musician, singer
Clifton Chenier zydeco musician
Van Cliburn concert pianist
Harry Connick, Jr. musician, actor
Ellen DeGeneres comedian
Fats Domino musician, songwriter
Donna Douglas actress
Dr. John musician
Pete Fountain musician
Mickey Gilley musician, actor
Bryant Gumbel television newscaster
Buddy Guy singer, musician
Al Hirt musician
Earl Holliman actor
Mahalia Jackson singer
Randy Jackson musician, former
   American Idol judge
Dorothy Lamour actress
John Larroquette actor

Jerry Lee Lewis singer, musician
Lil Wayne rapper
Ellis, Ellis, Jr., Branford, and Wynton
   Marsalis musicians
Tim McGraw singer
Garrett Morris actor
Jelly Roll Morton musician
Aaron Neville singer
Tyler Perry actor, director
Professor Longhair musician
Louis Prima musician
Willie Robertson family reality stars
Britney Spears singer
Irma Thomas singer, "Soul Queen of
   New Orleans"
Allen Toussaint musician, songwriter
Hank Williams, Jr. singer
Lucinda Williams singer, songwriter
Reese Witherspoon actress

SPORTS

Terry Bradshaw football
Bill Russell basketball
Eli Manning football
Peyton Manning football

Richard Simmons fitness
Freddie Spencer motorcycle racer
Carl Weathers actor, football player

French Quarter, New Orleans

Pies & Other Desserts

- Sweet Potato Pie 228
- Yam Pecan Pie in Gingersnap Crust 229
- Southern Pecan Pie..........230
- Mystery Pecan Pie............230
- Magnolia (Buttermilk) Pie..................................232
- Fluffy Peanut Butter Pie..................................232
- Grand Finale Pie 233
- Blackberry Cobbler..........234
- Strawberry Pie..................234
- Champion Cobbler at Ruston Peach Festival..........................235
- Kind Stranger's Bread Pudding with Whiskey Sauce............................237
- Pineapple Bread Pudding........................238
- Diet Bread Pudding 239
- White Chocolate Blueberry Bread Pudding 240
- White Chocolate/ Macadamia Crème Brûlée 241
- Strawberry 'n Cream Shortcakes...................242
- Raspberry-Peach Trifle....244
- Bouillie 245
- Cajun Amaretto Freeze ...245
- Louisiana Strawberry Sherbet 246
- Lemon Sherbet.................246
- Bananas Foster Soufflé with Vanilla Ice Cream.......247

The French Quarter, also known as "The Quarter," is the oldest neighborhood in the city of New Orleans. The district as a whole has been designated as a National Historic Landmark, with numerous buildings that are separately deemed significant. Most of the French Quarter's architecture was built during the late 18th century and the period of Spanish rule over the city, which is reflected in the architecture of the neighborhood. Bourbon Street is the most well known of the French Quarter streets.

PIES & OTHER DESSERTS

Sweet Potato Pie

2 tablespoons butter, softened
¾ cup light brown sugar
3 large eggs
½ teaspoon salt
½ teaspoon nutmeg
¼ teaspoon ground cloves
¼ teaspoon cinnamon
1 cup evaporated milk
1½ cups cooked mashed sweet potatoes
1 (9-inch) pie shell, unbaked
Toasted, chopped pecans, or whipped cream for topping (optional)

Preheat oven to 425°. Cream butter and sugar together. Add eggs, salt, and spices. Add evaporated milk and mashed sweet potatoes. Bake in pie shell 30–35 minutes, or till firm. This pie is good when topped with toasted, chopped pecans, or with whipped cream.

Lea's Lunch Room, Lecompte
Louisiana's Best Restaurant Recipes

Lea's Lunchroom

Lea's Lunchroom in Lecompte has been the place to stop since 1928 for signature ham sandwiches, plate lunch specials, strong Louisiana coffee, and homemade pies. Geographically located exactly between New Orleans and Shreveport on Highway 71, it was the perfect lunch break... and still is. Lea's has been expanded four times, and welcomes visitors from all over the world. The restaurant's fame got Lea Johnson on the *Johnny Carson Show*, where he was so entertaining, he was asked to stay longer. In March 2001, the Louisiana Legislature proclaimed Lecompte the Pie Capital of Louisiana. Lea's went from making two pies a week in 1928 to almost 65,000 pies a year, many of which are sold online (leaslunchroom.com).

Yam Pecan Pie in Gingersnap Crust

When you can't decide between pecan or sweet potato pie, have them both! The gingersnap crust sets the stage for the perfect blend of pecan filling and sweet potato mixture that captures the best of what Louisiana has to offer. —Holly Clegg

1¼ cups gingersnap cookie crumbs
2 tablespoons butter, melted
1½ teaspoons vanilla
1 (15-ounce) can sweet potatoes (yams), drained, mashed, or 1 cup fresh, cooked mashed yams
2 eggs, divided
¼ cup light brown sugar
½ teaspoon ground cinnamon
¼ teaspoon ground nutmeg
3 eggs whites
⅔ cup dark corn syrup
½ cup sugar
2 teaspoons vanilla
⅔ cup chopped pecans

Preheat oven to 350°. Combine gingersnap crumbs, butter, and vanilla in pie plate; press up sides. Bake 10 minutes, remove from oven.

In mixing bowl, blend together yams, 1 egg, brown sugar, cinnamon, and nutmeg. Spread evenly on bottom of pie crumb crust.

In another mixing bowl, beat together remaining egg, egg whites, corn syrup, sugar, and vanilla, till mixture is creamy. Stir in pecans. Carefully spoon over yam layer. Bake 50–60 minutes, or till filling is set around edges, or till knife inserted halfway between center and edge comes out clean. Cool, then serve. Serves 8–10.

Gulf Coast Favorites

PIES & OTHER DESSERTS

Southern Pecan Pie

Prepare your favorite pie shell.

PECAN PIE MIXTURE:

1 cup granulated sugar
1 cup white Karo syrup
2 tablespoons butter, melted
¼ teaspoon salt
3 eggs, beaten
1½ cup pecan halves

Mix all ingredients; pour into unbaked pie shell. Bake at 400° for 15 minutes. Reduce heat to 350°, and bake another 30 minutes. Remove from oven, and let cool on cake rack.

Tell Me More

Mystery Pecan Pie

1 (8-ounce) package cream cheese, softened
¼ teaspoon salt
1 egg
⅓ cup sugar
1 teaspoon vanilla
1¼ cups chopped pecans
1 unbaked pie shell

Combine all ingredients except pecans, and spread in bottom of unbaked pie shell. Sprinkle with pecans.

TOPPING:

3 eggs
1 cup light or dark corn syrup
¼ cup sugar
1 teaspoon vanilla

Mix all Topping ingredients together. Gently pour Topping over pecans. Bake at 375° for 35–45 minutes.

Recipes from the Heart

PIES & OTHER DESSERTS

Southern Pecan Pie

PIES & OTHER DESSERTS

Magnolia (Buttermilk) Pie

2 cups sugar
1 stick butter, softened
4 tablespoons flour
3 eggs, slightly beaten
1 cup buttermilk
1½ teaspoons vanilla
1 (9-inch) unbaked pie shell

In a large bowl, cream together sugar, butter, and flour. Add eggs, buttermilk, and vanilla. Pour into unbaked pie shell, and bake 1 hour at 325°.

Steel Magnolias in the Kitchen

Fluffy Peanut Butter Pie

1 (8-ounce) package cream cheese, softened
½ cup peanut butter, creamy or crunchy
1 cup powdered sugar
½ cup milk
1 (8-ounce) carton Cool Whip, thawed
1 (9-inch) graham cracker crumb crust
1 cup finely chopped peanuts

Whip cream cheese till soft and fluffy. Beat in peanut butter and sugar. Slowly add milk, blending thoroughly into mixture. Fold in Cool Whip. Pour into prepared crust. Sprinkle with chopped peanuts. Freeze till firm.

Pots, Pans, and Pioneers II

Anne Rice is an American author of Gothic fiction and Christian literature. She is perhaps best known for her popular and influential series of novels, *The Vampire Chronicles*, books which were the subject of two film adaptations, *Interview with the Vampire: The Vampire Chronicles* in 1994, and *Queen of the Damned* in 2002. Born in New Orleans, Rice moved to Texas, then to San Francisco, then back to New Orleans where she remains a vocal advocate for the city and related relief projects.

WWW.ANNERICE.COM

PIES & OTHER DESSERTS

Grand Finale Pie

BUTTERY CARAMEL SAUCE:

1¼ cups sugar
⅓ cup bourbon
¾ cup whipping cream
3 tablespoons unsalted butter, cut in pieces

Stir sugar and bourbon in heavy saucepan over low heat till sugar dissolves. Increase heat to medium-high; boil without stirring till mixture turns deep amber, brushing sides occasionally with a wet pastry brush. Remove from heat. Add cream to saucepan; sugar mixture will boil up rapidly. Whisk till the caramel is smooth. Return to a boil, whisking constantly. Remove from heat, add butter, and stir till smooth. Set aside. Makes 1½ cups.

PIE:

¼ cup butter
1 cup chopped pecans
6 ounces flaked coconut
1 (8-ounce) package cream cheese, softened
1 (14-ounce) can sweetened condensed milk
1 (8-ounce) container whipping cream
2 (8-inch) pie shells, baked

In heavy iron skillet, melt butter, and add pecans and coconut. Cook on low, stirring often, till brown. Set aside.

Mix cream cheese and condensed milk in a large bowl. Use electric mixer to whip whipping cream to soft peaks. Beat into cream cheese mixture. Pour cream mixture into baked pie crusts, dividing evenly. Sprinkle coconut mixture over top, and drizzle with Buttery Caramel Sauce. Freeze pies for at least 4 hours. Remove from freezer, cut each pie into 6–8 wedges, and serve immediately. Makes 2 pies.

Note: Store any unused Butter Caramel Sauce in the refrigerator. It will keep for 1 week.

Variations & Improvisations

PIES & OTHER DESSERTS

Blackberry Cobbler

2½ cups blackberries, mixed
   with ⅓ cup sugar
1 cup all-purpose flour
1 cup sugar
¼ teaspoon salt
2 teaspoons baking powder
¾ cup milk
1 stick margarine, melted

Mix all dry ingredients in bowl. Add milk, and stir well. Pour into greased baking dish; pour melted butter over dough. Place blackberries on top, and bake at 350° till dough rises to top and is golden brown (45 minutes to 1 hour). Serves 6–8.

Hey, Good Lookin', What's Cooking?

Strawberry Pie

3 pints Louisiana strawberries
2 graham cracker pie crusts
2½ cups sugar
3 heaping tablespoons
   cornstarch
2½ cups water
1 (6-ounce) box strawberry
   gelatin
1 (12-ounce) container Cool
   Whip

Wash, stem, and drain strawberries. Slice and place in pie crusts (the crusts should be full). In a 2-quart saucepan, mix sugar, cornstarch, and water. Boil till thick. Stir in gelatin. Pour over strawberries in crust. Cool till set, and cover. Top with Cool Whip before serving. Makes 2 pies.

Main Street Restaurant, Franklinton
Louisiana's Best Restaurant Recipes

USS Kidd Veterans Memorial Museum

PIES & OTHER DESSERTS

Champion Cobbler at Ruston Peach Festival

FILLING:

8 or 9 peaches, peeled, sliced
½ cup water
2 tablespoons all-purpose flour
Pinch of salt
1½ cups sugar
½ cup margarine or butter, melted

Cook peaches in water till tender. Combine flour, salt, and sugar; add to peaches, and mix. Add melted margarine or butter. Pour half the peaches into a 9x13-inch baking dish.

PASTRY FOR COBBLER:

1 cup all-purpose flour
½ teaspoon salt
⅓ cup shortening
4 tablespoons sweet milk, or enough for stiff dough

Blend flour, salt, and shortening to a coarse meal texture. Add milk. Chill. Roll out on floured board. Cut enough pastry dumplings (save some for lattice strips) to cover first layer of peaches, and place on top of peaches in baking dish. Pour remaining peaches over dumplings. Cover with lattice strip pastry top. Bake at 350° for 40–50 minutes, or till top is brown.

River Road Recipes II

USS Kidd Veterans Memorial Museum

The *USS Kidd* was selected to serve as a memorial for Louisiana World War II veterans. *Kidd* was towed from Philadelphia to Baton Rouge, arriving May 23, 1982. The *USS Kidd* was never modernized and is the only destroyer to retain its World War II appearance. The *Kidd*'s special mooring in the Mississippi River is designed to cope with the annual change in river depth, which can be up to forty feet; for half the year she floats in the river, the other half of the year she is dry-docked out of the water. She is now on public view as a museum vessel, and provides youth group overnight encampments.

Louisiana's Rich Cultural History

The **Acadian Cultural Center** in Lafayette tells stories of the origins, migration, settlement, and contemporary culture of the Acadians (Cajuns). Ranger programs, films, exhibits, and events share a variety of local traditions, including music, story-telling, dance, and food. Visitors can also explore the mysteries of the Atchafalaya Basin, Louisiana's wildest place, by boat. The center bookstore sells music, books, and crafts.

Opened in 1990, **Vermilionville** is a living history museum and folklife park that preserves and represents the cultural resources of the Acadian, Native American, and Creole cultures—from the time period 1765 to 1890. The park is on a 23-acre site on the banks of Bayou Vermilion with 19 attractions, including seven restored original homes with local artisans who provide demonstrations on a variety of essential crafts performed by the early settlers.

Acadian Village in Lafayette offers an authentic vision of Acadian society in south Louisiana during the 19th century. The village showcases authentic homes with wooden pegs, mud walls, hand-hewn cypress timbers, and high-peaked roofs. All buildings are furnished with native Louisiana antiques. A replica of a general store and Acadian chapel enhance the atmosphere of a quaint village that is surrounded by ten acres of gardens and woodlands.

PIES & OTHER DESSERTS

Kind Stranger's Bread Pudding with Whiskey Sauce

Yes, Blanche, the kindness of strangers can be so very . . . uh . . . kind!

4 cups broken bread (best with stale bread)
3 cups milk
¼ cup butter, melted
½ cup sugar
2 eggs, slightly beaten
¼ teaspoon salt
½ cup raisins
1 teaspoon cinnamon

In a large bowl, tear bread into small chunks. In a saucepan, scald milk, and pour over bread; cool, and add remaining ingredients, mixing well. Pour into a 1½-quart casserole dish coated with cooking spray. Place dish in a pan of hot water (1 inch deep) and bake at 350° for 1 hour, or till a table knife inserted into pudding comes out clean.

WHISKEY SAUCE:

8 tablespoons butter
1 cup sugar
1 egg
¼ cup whiskey

Cook butter and sugar together in double boiler till mixture is hot and thick, and sugar is dissolved. Remove from heat. Add egg and beat. Cool slightly; add whiskey. Serve over pudding.

A Streetcar Named Delicious

PIES & OTHER DESSERTS

Pineapple Bread Pudding

4 eggs
2 cups sugar
1 teaspoon cinnamon
1 teaspoon nutmeg
1 teaspoon vanilla
2 cups milk
1 (20-ounce) can crushed pineapple, undrained
1 medium-size loaf French bread, broken up
1 stick butter

Mix eggs, sugar, cinnamon, nutmeg, and vanilla. Add milk and pineapple. Mix thoroughly. Place broken-up bread in a 9x13-inch baking dish; pour mixture over bread, and let soak 30 minutes. Mash mixture with end of spatula. Cut butter into pats and place evenly over mixture. Bake in 350° oven 60–80 minutes. Take out when peaks turn brown. Serves 8–10.

Come to the Table

Preservation Hall

No food or drinks . . . a worn wooden floor . . . only a few wooden benches for seating . . . and yet this happening place is always stompin'. In 1961, Preservation Hall was established to preserve, perpetuate, and protect one of America's truest art forms—traditional New Orleans jazz. Operating as a music venue, a record label, a nonprofit organization, and a touring band that has included performances at Carnegie Hall, the Kennedy Center, the Hollywood Bowl, the United Nations, and Austin City Limits, Preservation Hall continues their mission today as a cornerstone of New Orleans music and culture. It presents intimate, acoustic New Orleans jazz concerts seven nights a week on St. Peter Street in the heart of the French Quarter.

"Preservation Hall. Now that's where you'll find all of the greats."
— Louis Armstrong

PIES & OTHER DESSERTS

Diet Bread Pudding
(Diabetic)

4 cups day-old French bread, torn into bits and pieces
1 cup water
1 (12-ounce) can skim evaporated milk
1½ teaspoons vanilla
¾ cup raisins
12 packets artificial sweetener
3 tablespoons Smart Balance margarine, melted
3 egg yolks
1 (8-ounce) can unsweetened pineapple chunks, drained

Place bread and water in a greased 7x12x2-inch baking dish. Let soak about 1 hour. Beat milk, vanilla, raisins, sweetener, margarine, and egg yolks. Pour over soaked bread. Mix all ingredients thoroughly. Place in 400° oven, and bake 15 minutes. While this is baking, prepare Meringue.

MERINGUE:
3 egg whites
⅛ teaspoon salt
¼ teaspoon cream of tartar
6 packets sweetener

Beat egg whites, salt, and cream of tartar till frothy. Add sweetener, 1 packet at a time, beating after each till soft peaks form when beaters are lifted. Remove pudding from oven. Reduce heat to 350°. Pour Meringue over pudding, being careful NOT to seal sides of dish. This causes large bubbles, which tend to fall flat as pudding cools. Bake till light brown; about 10 minutes. Serves 6.

Skinny Cajun

PIES & OTHER DESSERTS

White Chocolate Blueberry Bread Pudding

12–18 miniature croissants
12 eggs
2 cups sugar
1 cup sweetened condensed milk
¼ cup vanilla extract
4 cups fresh blueberries
½ cup chopped pecans
1 cup butter
5⅓ cups white chocolate chips
6 tablespoons whiskey

Tear croissants into pieces and spread over bottom of a greased 9x13-inch baking dish. Combine eggs, sugar, sweetened condensed milk, and vanilla in a bowl; mix well. Pour evenly over croissants. Sprinkle blueberries and pecans over top. Bake in preheated 350° oven for 50 minutes. Remove to wire rack.

Combine butter and white chocolate chips in top of a double boiler over simmering water. Cook till mixture is melted and smooth, whisking constantly. Stir in whiskey just before serving. Serve bread pudding with sauce over top or on the side. Serves 24.

Marshes to Mansions

The Louisiana Purchase

In 1803, the United States paid France $15 million for the Louisiana Territory, 828,000 square miles of land west of the Mississippi River. The lands acquired stretched from the Mississippi River to the Rocky Mountains, and from the Gulf of Mexico to the Canadian border, thereby doubling the size of the United States. All or part of thirteen states were created from the land gained from the Louisiana Purchase.

PIES & OTHER DESSERTS

White Chocolate/Macadamia Crème Brûlée

8 ounces white chocolate
1 quart heavy cream
8 egg yolks, beaten
4 ounces chopped macadamia nuts, divided

8 tablespoons unrefined sugar, or sugar in the raw, divided

Preheat oven to 325°. Place white chocolate into a stainless steel bowl. Place cream into a pot, and bring to a simmer. Pour cream over white chocolate and stir till mixture is smooth. Temper in egg yolks. Divide mixture into 8 (6-ounce) soufflé cups. Place 1 tablespoon macadamia nuts into each cup. Bake in a pan with a water bath for 40 minutes or till custard looks firm. Take out of oven and let custard cool 15 minutes. Sprinkle 1 tablespoon sugar on top of each custard. Caramelize sugar using a culinary blowtorch or salamander, and serve. Serves 8.

Bella Fresca Restaurant, Shreveport
Louisiana's Best Restaurant Recipes

The Louisiana Purchase (shown in white) was one of several territorial additions to the United States.

PIES & OTHER DESSERTS

Strawberry 'n Cream Shortcakes

STRAWBERRIES:

2 pints whole strawberries, hulled, rinsed, divided
½ cup sugar
1 tablespoon fresh lemon juice

In large bowl, combine 1 pint strawberries and sugar. Crush berries. Slice remaining pint of strawberries, reserving 4–6 whole berries for garnish. Stir sliced berries into crushed berry mixture. Mix in lemon juice. Refrigerate 1 hour.

CREAM SHORTCAKES:

1 cup all-purpose flour
1 cup cake flour
3 tablespoons sugar
1 tablespoon baking powder
¼ teaspoon salt
1 stick butter, cut into pieces
1 cup plus 1 tablespoon heavy whipping cream, divided

Combine flours, sugar, baking powder, and salt. Cut in butter with pastry blender or 2 table knives till mixture resembles coarse crumbs. Gradually add 1 cup cream, tossing with a fork till dough is evenly moistened. Transfer dough to a work area and knead gently till dough just holds together. Roll or pat dough to ½-inch thickness. Cut into circles using a 3-inch cutter. Place on a well-greased or foil-lined baking sheet. Brush tops with remaining 1 tablespoon cream. Bake at 400° for 18–20 minutes, or till tops are golden brown. Cool.

CREAM MIXTURE:

1 cup heavy whipping cream
2 tablespoons powdered sugar
3 tablespoons sour cream
1 teaspoon vanilla

In a large bowl, beat cream and powdered sugar till soft peaks form. Add sour cream and vanilla; beat till stiff.

To serve, split Cream Shortcakes in half horizontally. Spoon Strawberries and 1½ cups Cream Mixture evenly among bottom halves. Replace cake tops, and dollop remaining Cream Mixture on top of each. Garnish with reserved strawberries.

Classic Cajun Deux

PIES & OTHER DESSERTS

Strawberry 'n Cream Shortcakes

PIES & OTHER DESSERTS

Raspberry-Peach Trifle

I have been serving this captivating fruit trifle for thirty years. I serve it for dinner parties, feature it in cooking classes, and have demonstrated it on television cooking segments. It matters not where I introduce it—it draws rave reviews. —Marlyn Monette

- 1 (11-ounce) frozen Sara Lee pound cake, thawed
- ⅓ cup amaretto liqueur
- ⅔ cup raspberry preserves
- 1 (3½-ounce) package vanilla instant pudding
- 1 (12-ounce) carton Cool Whip, thawed, divided
- ⅔ cup chopped almonds, toasted
- 1 (16-ounce) package frozen peach slices, thawed, drained well

Slice cake in half lengthwise. Reserving 1 tablespoon liqueur, sprinkle remaining liqueur over cake. Spread with preserves. Cut each half into eighths; set aside.

Prepare pudding mix as directed on package, except use only 1½ cups milk. Fold in 2 cups Cool Whip and the almonds. In a 2-quart glass bowl, layer a third of the cake slices, a third of the pudding mixture, and a third of the peaches. Repeat layers, ending with cake. Add reserved liqueur to remaining Cool Whip, and spread over last cake layer. Top with additional almonds, if desired. Chill overnight, or several hours. Serves 10–12.

So Good . . . Make You Slap Your Mama! II

Named a UNESCO World Heritage Site in 2014, Poverty Point is the largest and most complex Late Archaic (540 BC–480 BC) earthwork occupation and ceremonial site yet found in North America. This 3400-year-old earthen construction was developed by Native American hunter-gatherers between 1650 and 700 BCE. The site is located in Epps, near Monroe.

PIES & OTHER DESSERTS

Bouillie
(Old-Fashioned Custard)

1 (5-ounce) can evaporated milk
1 (14-ounce) can sweetened condensed milk
1 quart whole milk
8 eggs, separated
½ cup sugar, divided
3 tablespoons cornstarch
¼ cup butter
1 cup crushed pineapple, drained (optional)
¼ teaspoon cream of tartar

Combine milks in 5-quart saucepan; bring to a boil. Beat egg yolks; add ¼ cup sugar and cornstarch. Add yolk mixture to boiling milk. Beat with electric mixer over medium heat till creamy and thick. Remove from heat; add butter. Add pineapple, if desired.

In large bowl, beat egg whites till frothy; add remaining ¼ cup sugar and cream of tartar; beat till semi-stiff. Fold into cooked milk custard. Serve hot or cold. Serves 8–10.

Down the Bayou

Cajun Amaretto Freeze

2–3 jiggers amaretto
4–6 scoops vanilla ice cream
Nutmeg to taste
1 maraschino cherry

Combine amaretto and ice cream in blender. Process till smooth, but not watery. Spoon into brandy snifter. Sprinkle with nutmeg. Top with cherry. Serve with biscotti. Serves 1.

Da Cajn Critter

PIES & OTHER DESSERTS

Louisiana Strawberry Sherbet

This is a favorite dessert of mine; so few ingredients and so much taste describe these simple scrumptious treats. Serve them in pretty stemmed glasses, and wait for the compliments. Don't worry about not liking the buttermilk; I don't either, but you cannot taste the buttermilk in it. —Corinne Cook

4 cups fresh strawberries, rinsed, hulled, patted dry
2 cups sugar
2 cups buttermilk

Place strawberries and sugar in food processor. Pulse until berries are coarsely chopped. Add buttermilk and blend well. Pour mixture into a 9x13-inch baking dish and freeze 1 hour (center will still be mushy). Transfer mixture to food processor and whip again. Return to freezer for at least 4 more hours. Serve in pretty stemmed glasses or small bowls. Serves 6.

Extra! Extra! Read More About It!

Lemon Sherbet

Luray Eshelman sent me this recipe on a sticky note attached to her Christmas card, saying, "It was the best, easiest and fastest dessert ever." With that description and only four ingredients, I made it, and agreed with her. It can easily be doubled or tripled. My daughter Julie loves serving this dessert. —Corinne Cook

1 cup whipping cream (not whipped)
1 cup milk
1 cup sugar
Juice and finely grated zest of 1 lemon

In plastic bowl or freezer container, add all ingredients. Stir till well mixed and sugar is dissolved; cover and freeze. Serve in a footed glass or dessert dish. It can be served alone or with fruit on top. Serves 4–6.

Extra! Extra! Read More About It!

PIES & OTHER DESSERTS

Bananas Foster Soufflé with Vanilla Ice Cream

2 tablespoons butter, divided
2–3 teaspoons granulated sugar
6½ ounces bananas (4 ounces peeled)
1 tablespoon plus 2 teaspoons brown sugar, divided
¼ teaspoon cinnamon
2 tablespoons dark rum
2 egg whites
Pinch of kosher salt
Pinch of cream of tartar
4 ounces vanilla ice cream

Arrange oven rack in middle position, and then preheat oven to 400°. Coat inside of 4 (6-ounce) ramekins with 1 tablespoon butter, and sprinkle with granulated sugar; tap ramekins to remove any excess sugar. Cut bananas into ¼-inch slices.

Melt remaining 1 tablespoon butter with 1 tablespoon brown sugar in a 10-inch sauté pan over medium heat, stirring occasionally till sugar dissolves. Add bananas and cook 2 minutes, stirring constantly. Stir in cinnamon, and increase heat to high. Add rum, and carefully tilt side of pan to flame in order to ignite the rum. Allow flames to subside, and cook 1 minute longer. Remove banana mixture to a bowl to cool.

Combine egg whites and salt in mixing bowl, and beat with mixer fitted with a whisk attachment till foamy. Add cream of tartar, followed by remaining 2 teaspoons brown sugar, beating constantly at medium-high speed till stiff peaks form. Spoon egg whites into a medium bowl. Spoon cooled banana mixture into same mixing bowl that held the egg whites; do not clean bowl before adding banana mixture. Beat at high speed 2 minutes. Using a rubber spatula, fold into egg whites till completely incorporated. Divide banana mixture evenly among the 4 prepared ramekins, and smooth the tops. Bake 11 minutes, or till soufflés rise and are brown. Top each serving with equal scoops of vanilla ice cream, and serve immediately. Makes 4 soufflés.

Cooking with a Private Chef

Contributing Cookbooks

All recipes in this book have been selected from the cookbooks shown on the following pages. Individuals who wish to obtain a copy of any particular book may do so by sending a check or money order to the address listed by each cookbook. Please note the postage and handling charges that may be required. State residents add tax only when requested. Prices and addresses are subject to change, and the books may sell out and become unavailable. Retailers are invited to call or write to same address for discount information.

Amy's Cajun Recipes
by Amy Cormier and the Cormier Family
950 W. Laurel Avenue • Eunice, LA 70535
337-457-1484 • kolinthia@sunsports1988

Amy's Cajun Recipes is a cookbook filled with 245 of the best of Cajun recipes. From her kitchen to yours, you will get a taste of what Cajun cooking and traditions are all about.

   $12.00   Retail price
     $1.08   Tax for LA residents
     $5.00   Postage and handling
Make check payable to Kolinthia Labbe

Classic Cajun
by Lucy Henry Zaunbrecher
17362 Zaunbrecher Road • Jones, LA 71250
800-257-5829 • www.lpb.org/programs/lucy

Classic Cajun is a must for those interested in the culture and cuisine of south Louisiana. Besides good recipes, Lucy has also included much of the history of her own family and of the Cajun people as a whole. 206 pages, hardcover, spiral-bound.

   $16.95   Retail price
     $1.19   Tax LA residents
     $3.50   Postage and handling
Make check payable to Classic Cajun
ISBN 978-0-9640748-0-4

Classic Cajun Deux
by Lucy Henry Zaunbrecher
17362 Zaunbrecher Road • Jones, LA 71250
800-257-5829 • www.mslucy.com

More culture and cooking Cajun style is Lucy Zaunbrecker's gift to you. Enjoy reading more interesting facts about South Louisiana and relish the delicious recipes within, some from Lucy's mother's old recipe file box. 206 pages, hardcover, spiral-bound.

   $16.95   Retail price
     $1.19   Tax LA residents
     $3.50   Postage and handling
Make check payable to Classic Cajun
ISBN 978-0-9640748-1-1

CONTRIBUTING COOKBOOKS

Come to the Table
St. Edmond Knights of Columbus Ladies Auxiliary
106 Pilgrimage Drive • Lafayette, LA 70506
337-984-7975 • mdup22@yahoolcom

Come to the Table is a collection of recipes by the Knights of Columbus Ladies Auxiliary and members of St. Edmond Catholic Church in Lafayette, Louisiana. The cookbook includes 325 recipes and is 174 pages. Proceeds go to the church.

   $12.00   Retail price
     $5.00   Postage and handling

Make check payable to Knights of Columbus Ladies Auxiliary

A Confederacy of Scrumptious
by Todd-Michael St. Pierre
www.LouisianaBoy.com

Good gracious, Ignatius! Don't suffer the trauma of another downward cycle! Open up that pyloric valve with some flawless French Quarter flavor and spice! Delectable! Distinctive! And oh so very Divine! Because man cannot live on Lucky Dogs alone! Join the Confederacy, grab a Dr. Nut, and enjoy!

www.amazon.com/1456593269
   $11.95

Cooking in High Cotton
Junior League of Monroe, Inc.
2811 Cameron St. • Monroe, LA 71201
318-322-3236 • www.jlmonroe.org
Jrleague@centurytel.net

A collection of classic southern dishes and unique creations from some of our area's finest kitchens. This beautiful hardbound cookbook contains 192 pages with 222 delicious recipes

   $24.95   Retail price   VISA, MC, Discover
     $9.95   Tax LA residents
                Postage and handling varies for location

Make check payable to Junior League of Monroe
ISBN 978-0-9602364-2-8

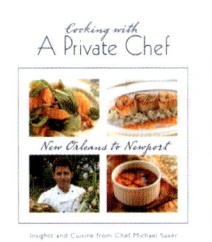

Cooking with a Private Chef:
New Orleans to Newport
by Michael Saxer

1033 Josephine St. Apt A • New Orleans, LA 70130
504-460-7171 • www.michaelsaxer.net
msaxer22@gmail.com

Contemporary regional cuisine—classic dishes made light and modern. A national award winner with a story spanning twelve years for a single employer internationally. Over 100 recipes; 143 pages. Guests range from British royalty to Mardi Gras royalty.

   $29.95   Retail price

Make check payable to Saxtastic, LLC or Michael Saxer
ISBN 978-0-9798935-0-6

CONTRIBUTING COOKBOOKS

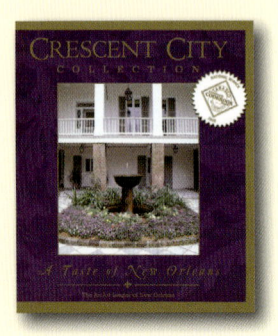

Crescent City Collection:
A Taste of New Orleans
Junior League of New Orleans
4319 Carondelet Street • New Orleans, LA 70115
504-891-5845 • Fax: 897-9496 • info@jlno.org • www.jlno.org

Combines New Orleans' love of good food with its rich architecture—recipes for sumptuous dishes are interspersed with fabulous photographs of some of New Orleans' grandest residences. Winner of the Tabasco Community Cookbook Award in 2000.

$26.95 Retail price   Visa/MC
$2.43   Tax LA residents
$8.00   Postage and handling

Make check payable to Junior League of New Orleans
ISBN 0-9604774-0-3

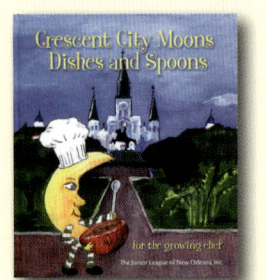

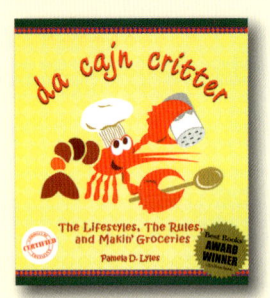

Crescent City Moons, Dishes and Spoons for the growing chef
Junior League of New Orleans
4319 Carondelet Street • New Orleans, LA 70115
504-891-5845 • Fax: 897-9496 • info@jlno.org • www.jlno.org

The collection includes dishes for all age groups, as well as international recipes, recipes addressing specific dietary needs, and dishes from popular New Orleans chefs. Best yet, all of the included dishes were tested and approved by children!

$15.00 Retail price   Visa/MC
$1.35   Tax LA residents
$8.00   Postage and handling

Make check payable to Junior League of New Orleans
ISBN 0-9604774-0-3

Da Cajn Critter
The Lifestyles, The Rules, and Makin' Groceries
P. O. Box 57082 • New Orleans, LA 70157
504-522-9905
info@dacajncritter.com • www.dacajncritter.com

Da Cajn Critter is a gumbo of 185 old family, friends, and personal recipes from Louisiana and the world. These are easy, simple recipes that use everyday ingredients. It's about breaking the rules and making cooking fun. Be the first "critter" on your block!

$14.95 Retail price   Visa/MC
$1.35   Tax LA residents
$6.00   Postage and handling

Make check payable to Lyles Ventures LLC
ISBN# 978-0-9800236-0-2

deBellevue Williams Cochon de Lait
Edited by Patricia Ellyn Powell
2126-A Jackson. St. • Alexandria, LA 71301
318-609-4013 • www.mycirco.com • Profpatti@aol.com

C'est bon! Nearly 200 pages contain over 400 Deep South, French influenced recipes! The cochon de lait, or suckling pig, is celebrated in all her glory, and accompanied by all that spreads a good table while you pass a good time.

$16.95 Retail price   Check or money orders only
$5.00   Postage and handling

Make check payable to Patricia Powell

CONTRIBUTING COOKBOOKS

Down the Bayou
Bayou Civic Club Inc.

Larose Regional Park & Civic Center
P. O. Box 1105 • Larose, LA 70373 • 985-693-7355
www.bayoucivicclub.org • jasmineayo@bayoucivicclub.org

There's no place on earth quite like "down the bayou." This collection of favorite Cajun recipes is dedicated to our community people—their uniqueness, culture, and love of life. Hardcover, spiral-bound, 254 pages, the book is in its sixth printing.

    $18.95   Retail price   Visa, MC, AMEX, Discover
      $1.84   Tax LA residents
      $3.50   Postage and handling

Make check payable to Larose Civic Center
ISBN 0-9613375-0-8

Down the Bayou…and Back Again
Bayou Civic Club Inc.

Larose Regional Park & Civic Center
P. O. Box 1105 • Larose, LA 70373 • 985-693-7355
www.bayoucivicclub.org • jasmineayo@bayoucivicclub.org

Second in the *Down the Bayou* collection, this book invites you to join in the good Cajun life, "down the bayou"—through original artwork and fascinating narrative, along with old and new favorite family recipes. Hardcover, spiral-bound, 254 pages.

    $21.95   Retail price   Visa, MC, AMEX, Discover
      $1.91   Tax LA residents
      $3.50   Postage and handling

Make check payable to Larose Civic Center
ISBN 978-0-9779068-0-2

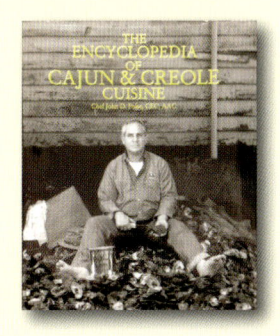

The Encyclopedia of Cajun & Creole Cuisine
by Chef John Folse

Chef John Folse & Company
2517 South Philippe Avenue • Gonzales, LA 70737
225-644-6000 • www.jfolse.com

Chef Folse has hand-picked 700 of his very best recipes from roux to cochon de lait to give you this authoritative collection of Louisiana's culture and cuisine. In 850-full color pages, you will learn hows, whats, whys, and history, helping you to develop a new understanding and love of Cajun and Creole cuisine.

    $55.95   Retail price   Hardcover
   Plus shipping and handling

Make check payable to Chef John Folse & Company

Extra! Extra! Read MORE About It!
by Corinne Cook

P. O. Box 82477 • Baton Rouge, LA 70884
225-293-9470 • corinnecook@cox.net

Corinne Cook, FOOD columnist, has been featuring recipes in *The Advocate* newspaper for over 37 years. You can become an accomplished cook by following these simple-to-follow, step-by-step instructions for truly delicious recipes.

    $19.95   Retail price
      $1.80   Tax LA residents
    $21.75   includes postage

Make check payable to Corinne Cook
ISBN# 978-0-615-55932-2

CONTRIBUTING COOKBOOKS

Good Gumbo Weather
by Todd-Michael St. Pierre
www.LouisianaBoy.com
This new collection of Cajun favorites will guide you through all things Gumbo and beyond! First cool snap? Warm January? Chilly April? Raining cats and dogs? Rare sneauxfall? Hurricane blowing? Here in the Bayou State, no matter the forecast, it's always . . . *Good Gumbo Weather*!
Send orders to amazon.com/144213996X
$12.95

Hey, Good Lookin', What's Cooking?
Curves of Destrehan
42496 Meadow Wood Dr. • Ponchatoula, LA 70454
sgrayson1961@att.net
A group of women enjoying exercise and fun at a Curves location compiled these recipes to enjoy. 86 pages, spiral-bound 207 recipes.

    $10.00   Retail price
      $3.00   Postage and handling
Make check payable to Suzanne L. Grayson

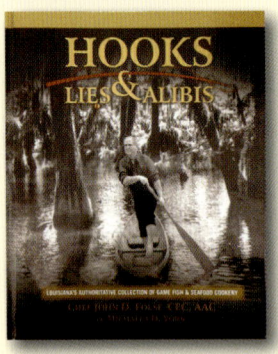

Hooks, Lies and Alibies
by Chef John Folse with co-author Michaela D. York
Chef John Folse & Company
2517 South Philippe Avenue • Gonzales, LA 70737
225-644-6000 • www.jfolse.com
A tribute to Louisiana's time-honored fish and seafood tradition and cuisine, "This cookbook offers folks new ways of preparing the fish and shellfish we all love to eat." Folse took special care to include in this 920-page volume a variety of cooking methods to showcase Louisiana's brimming waters.

    $59.95   Retail price   Hardcover
    Plus shipping and handling
Make check payable to Chef John Folse & Company

Holly Clegg's Trim & Terrific Gulf Coast Favorites
by Holly Clegg
1-800-88HOLLY • Fax 225-752-4689
Finally, Louisiana and southern food can be good for you! This practical cookbook, with over 200 recipes and full-color photographs, provides southern cuisine lovers with all of their regional and southern favorites, using recipes that are effortless, pantry-friendly, and nutritious.

    $24.95   Retail price
      $2.25   Tax LA residents
      $4.00   Postage and handling
Make check payable to Holly B. Clegg, Inc.
ISBN: 978-0-9815640-0-5 / 0-9815640-0-3

CONTRIBUTING COOKBOOKS

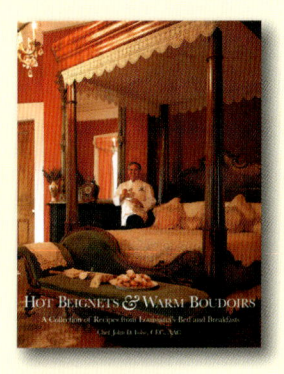

Hot Beignets & Warm Boudoirs
by Chef John Folse

Chef John Folse & Company
2517 South Philippe Avenue • Gonzales, LA 70737
225-644-6000 • www.jfolse.com

As much a romance novel as it is a cookbook, John Folse takes you on a tasty rendezvous through 26 of Louisiana's premier bed and breakfasts. With beautiful color photographs and 200 fantastic recipes, this is an anthology on the origin of breakfast as an event in New Orleans.

    $24.95   Retail price   Hardcover
    Plus shipping and handling

Make check payable to Chef John Folse & Company

The Little Gumbo Book
by Gwen McKee

Quail Ridge Press • P. O. Box 123 • Brandon, MS 39043
1-800-343-1583 • info@quailridge.com

Carefully created recipes include explanations, definitions, and step-by-step directions that will enable everyone to enjoy the special experience of gumbo. Recipes, Roux, Rice, Stock, Seasoning—it's all in this charming little book. Hardbound, illustrated.

    $9.95   Retail price
      $.70   Tax MS residents
    $3.00   Postage and handling

Make check payable to Quail Ridge Press
ISBN 978-0-937552-17-9

The Little New Orleans Cookbook
by Gwen McKee

Quail Ridge Press • P. O. Box 123 • Brandon, MS 39043
1-800-343-1583 • info@quailridge.com

Capture the cuisine of New Orleans with this nifty little hardcover cookbook that recreates 57 classic Creole recipes that made New Orleans famous. Fascinating secrets, hints, history, origins of recipes, and tales of the Crescent City. Illustrated, photographs.

    $9.95   Retail price
      $.70   Tax MS residents
    $3.00   Postage and handling

Make check payable to Quail Ridge Press
ISBN 978-0-937552-42-1

Louisiana's Best Restaurant Recipes
Compiled by John M. Bailey

Quail Ridge Press • P. O. Box 123 • Brandon, MS 39043
1-800-343-1583 • info@quailridge.com

Imagine preparing signature dishes from one hundred of Louisiana's most popular restaurants right in your own kitchen! These 262 recipes enable you to do just that! This cookbook also serves as a statewide guide to Louisiana's finest dining-out experiences.

    $19.95   Retail Price
      $1.40   Tax MS residents
      $5.00   Postage and handling

Make check payable to Quail Ridge Press
ISBN 978-1-893062-96-2

CONTRIBUTING COOKBOOKS

Mane Ingredients III
Bossier Central Lions Club
P.O. Box 5295
Bossier City, LA 71171

The members of the Bossier City Lions Club thank all their friends, family members and co-workers for submitting their cherished family keepsake recipes. Proceeds from *Mane Ingredients III* help us support our major projects: The Louisiana Lions Children's Camp in Leesville, and the Louisiana Lions Eye Foundation in New Orleans. Currently out of print.

Mardi Gras to Mistletoe
Junior League of Shreveport-Bossier
2601 Line Avenue, Suite B • Shreveport, LA 71104
318-221-6144 • Fax 318-221-4601
jrleaguesb@bellsouth.net • www.jlsb.org

More than 200 recipes for entertaining, with a photographic tour of the area through its special celebrations. Each chapter portrays a month of the year, focusing on unique heritage and festivals, delightful seasonal recipes, cooking tips, and culinary trivia.

   $26.95   Retail price
    $6.00   Postage and handling

Make check payable to Junior League of Shreveport-Bossier
ISBN 0-9602246-0-2 / 978-0-9602246-0-9

Marshes to Mansions
Junior League of Lake Charles, Inc.
1019 Lakeshore Drive • Lake Charles, LA 70601
337-436-4025 • 337-436-4013 Fax
jllc1019@bellsouth.net • www.jllc.net

A unique culinary adventure across South Louisiana. In addition to delicious recipes, the book boasts beautiful pictures that capture the culture of people living in southwest Louisiana.

   $28.95   Retail price   VISA, MC, Amex, Discover
    $1.16   Tax for LA residents
    $5.14   Postage and Handling

Make check payable to Junior League of Lake Charles, Inc.
ISBN 978-0-9607524-4-7

Palace Café: The Flavor of New Orleans
by Dickie Brennan, Gus Martin, Leslie Brennan
Palace Café
605 Canal Street • New Orleans, LA 70130
504-523-1661 • info@palacecafe.com

This lovely cookbook tells the story of a restaurant, a city, and the Brennan family. It features home-cook-friendly recipes, sample menus, and serving tips. The color food photography and stylish black-and-white photos of the nationally acclaimed French Quarter restaurant make this book a delight to the eye and the palate. Currently out of print.

CONTRIBUTING COOKBOOKS

Pots, Pans, and Pioneers
Telephone Pioneers in Louisiana • Attn: Keint Jeffrey
3115 Dee St., Room 300 • Shreveport, LA 71105
318-670-1165
www.attpioneersvolunteers.org/Louisiana24/cookbooksLA24.ittmc
These recipes have been collected from employees and families of the telephone industry, and come to life as the handiwork of many. This huge volume, published in 1976, has some 2,000 recipes, and has been reprinted many times.
  $12.00   Retail price
  $4.00   Postage and handling
Make check payable to ATT Pioneers
ISBN 0-934474-22-2

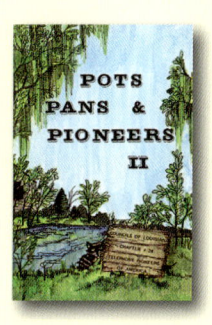

Pots, Pans, and Pioneers II
Telephone Pioneers in Louisiana • Attn: Keint Jeffrey
3115 Dee St., Room 300 • Shreveport, LA 71105
318-670-1165
www.attpioneersvolunteers.org/Louisiana24/cookbooksLA24.ittmc
This second huge volume of recipes was published in 1979. Like its predecessor, it has been reprinted over and over, having also sold hundreds of thousands of copies. Simply good Louisiana cooking from the Pioneers.
  $12.00   Retail price
  $4.00   Postage and handling
Make check payable to ATT Pioneers
ISBN 0-934474-15-X

Pots, Pans, and Pioneers III
Telephone Pioneers in Louisiana • Attn: Keint Jeffrey
3115 Dee St., Room 300 • Shreveport, LA 71105
318-670-1165
www.attpioneersvolunteers.org/Louisiana24/cookbooksLA24.ittmc
Published in 1983, this third volume is evidence that the Telephone Pioneers of Louisiana Chapter 24 really know how to cook! Another Louisiana Pioneer cookbook laden with delicious recipes.
  $12.00   Retail price
  $4.00   Postage and handling
Make check payable to ATT Pioneers
ISBN 0-934474-25-7

Pots, Pans, and Pioneers IV
Telephone Pioneers in Louisiana • Attn: Keint Jeffrey
3115 Dee St., Room 300 • Shreveport, LA 71105
318-670-1165
www.attpioneersvolunteers.org/Louisiana24/cookbooksLA24.ittmc
This volume is wire-o-bound and contains lots of helpful hints besides more great recipes from Louisiana Pioneers. Published in 1993, the cooking just keeps getting better.
  $12.00   Retail price
  $4.00   Postage and handling
Make check payable to ATT Pioneers

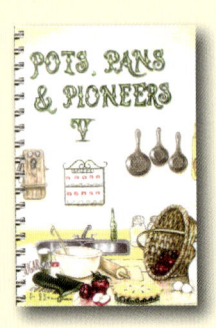

CONTRIBUTING COOKBOOKS

Pots, Pans, and Pioneers V
Telephone Pioneers in Louisiana • Attn: Keint Jeffrey
3115 Dee St., Room 300 • Shreveport, LA 71105
318-670-1165
www.attpioneersvolunteers.org/Louisiana24/cookbooksLA24.ittmc

Pots, Pans, and Pioneers introduces us to yet another of its popular cookbooks to add to their popular series. All from employees, spouses, and friends of AT&T Pioneers, the Louisiana flavor is outstanding.

   $12.00   Retail price
     $4.00   Postage and handling
Make check payable to ATT Pioneers

Recipes from the Heart
Lifeshare Blood Centers
8910 Linwood Avenue • Shreveport, LA 71106
318-222-770 • Ffax 318-673-1448
www.lifeshare.org • donna.bascle@lifeshare.org

A collection of 492 recipes contributed by Lifeshare Blood Centers employees, donors, and friends, bringing a little of the generosity, love and compassion from our community into your home.

   $12.00   Retail price
     $1.03   Tax LA residents
     $6.00   Postage hand handling
Make check payable to Lifeshare Blood Centers
ISBN 240656-12

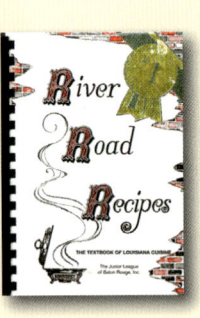

River Road Recipes
Junior League of Baton Rouge, Inc.
9523 Fenway Avenue • Baton Rouge, LA 70809
225-924-0298

River Road Recipes is the nation's #1 best-selling community cookbook series. A must for collectors, this original cookbook features 650 classic Creole and Cajun recipes, and sets the standard for capturing Louisiana's unique flavors, richly preserved in authentic gumbos, jambalayas, pralines, and more. Truly, this is the textbook on Louisiana cooking.

   $19.95   Retail Price
     $1.80   Tax LA residents
     $3.25   Shipping and handling
Make check payable to Junior League of Baton Rouge

River Road Recipes II: A Second Helping
Junior League of Baton Rouge, Inc.
9523 Fenway Avenue • Baton Rouge, LA 70809
225-924-0298

Welcome to a Second Helping of dishes that are full of flavor from the Cajun-Creole region. This is a collection of the finest dishes from individual homemakers who pride themselves on the perfection of their Louisiana cooking. It is now available in a new hardback concealed wire-o binding.

   $19.95   Retail Price
     $1.80   Tax LA residents
     $3.25   Shipping and handling
Make check payable to Junior League of Baton Rouge

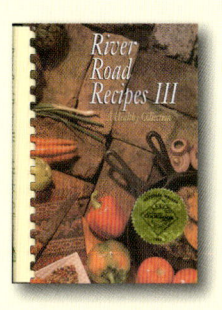

CONTRIBUTING COOKBOOKS

River Road Recipes III: Healthy Collection
Junior League of Baton Rouge, Inc.
9523 Fenway Avenue • Baton Rouge, LA 70809
225-924-0298

These recipes take the bounty of Louisiana cuisine, old favorites and new dishes, and modify them to fit today's healthier lifestyle. Creole and Cajun dishes loved by so many have been reduced in fat and calories. Fans of the first two *River Road Recipes* cookbooks will be delighted to see old favorites in a lighter light.

    $19.95   Retail Price
      $1.80   Tax LA residents
      $3.25   Shipping and handling

Make check payable to Junior League of Baton Rouge

River Road Recipes IV Warm Welcomes
Junior League of Baton Rouge, Inc.
9523 Fenway Avenue • Baton Rouge, LA 70809
225-924-0298

The creators of the nation's number one best-selling community cookbook series welcome you to celebrate life's ordinary and extraordinary occasions in 48 inspiring menus and over 300 new and innovative recipes from Baton Rouge, where our culinary history is legendary . . . we celebrate life through our cooking.

    $28.95   Retail price   Hardcover
      $2.60   Tax LA residents
      $6.95   Postage and handling

Make check payable to Junior League of Baton Rouge

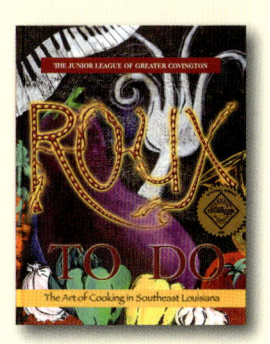

Roux To Do
The Art of Cooking in Southeast Louisiana
Junior League of Greater Covington
P. O. Box 2580 • Covington, LA 70434
985-898-3989 • Fax 985-898-3990
www.jlgc.net

Just as we appreciate beautiful art, South Louisianians also relish our food. Like any good artist, a southern cook uses instinct and heart to create a pièce de résistance. We invite you to share our love of art and food with our cookbook, *Roux To Do!*

    $28.95   Retail price includes postage and handling

Make check payable to Junior League of Greater Covington
ISBN 0-9740695-0-7 • 978-0-9740695-0-0

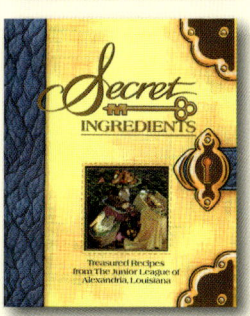

Secret Ingredients
Junior League of Alexandria, LA
P. O. Box 13086 • Alexandria, LA 71315
318-443-6975 • Fax 318-443-6927

In 207 pages and with over 230 recipes, the keys to our spicy cuisine and flavorful meals, as well as interesting cultural tidbits, are interspersed throughout the full color pages of this official cookbook of the city of Alexandria.

    $24.95   Retail price
      $5.00   Postage and handling

Make check payable to Junior League of Alexandria
ISBN 0-9675255-0-0

CONTRIBUTING COOKBOOKS

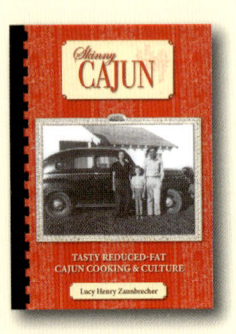

Skinny Cajun
by Lucy Henry Zaunbrecher
P. O. Box 3 • Jones, LA 71250
800-257-5829 • www.mslucy.com

Known far-and-wide for her rich heritage of Cajun cuisine, Lucy is now shedding a new "light" on her classic dishes. This time she is serving up proof that food can be healthful, delicious, and Cajun…all at the same time. 172 pages, hardbound, spiral-bound.

    $16.95   Retail price
      $1.19   Tax LA residents
      $3.50   Postage and handling

Make check payable to Skinny Cajun
ISBN 078-096407482-8

So Good…Make You Slap Your Mama!
by Marlyn Monette
165 Vidor Lane • Shreveport, LA 71105
318-868-5804 phone and fax • Marlynm4@comcast.net

A collage of classic recipes, both new and old, family memories, pictures, and anecdotes from a lifetime of entertaining. These books are a tribute to fine southern heritage. Volume I has 170 pages, 210 recipes.

    $16.95   Retail price
      $1.46   Tax LA residents
      $5.00   Postage and handling

ISBN 0-9673339-0-3

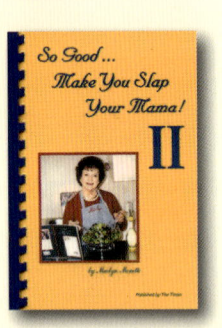

So Good…Make You Slap Your Mama! II
by Marlyn Monette
165 Vidor Lane • Shreveport, LA 71105
318-868-5804 phone and fax • Marlynm4@comcast.net

More classic recipes, both new and old, family memories, pictures, and anecdotes from a lifetime of entertaining. These books are a tribute to fine Southern heritage. Volume II has 263 pages, 335 recipes.

    $19.95   Retail price
      $1.72   Tax LA residents
      $5.00   Postage and handling

ISBN 0-9673339-1-1

Something to Talk About
Occasions We Celebrate in South Louisiana
Junior League of Lafayette
504 Richland Avenue • Lafayette, LA 70508
337-988-2739 • Fax 337-988-1079
JLL@juniorleagueoflafayette.com • www.juniorleagueoflafayette.com

This award-winning cookbook, the fourth in the TALK ABOUT GOOD! SERIES, includes 230 kitchen-tested recipes, color photographs, entertaining hints, informative sidebars, and 12 menus.

    $28.95   Retail price   VISA/MC
      $2.32   Tax LA residents
      $8.00   Postage and handling

Make check payable to Junior League of Lafayette
ISBN 0-9350-32-51-7

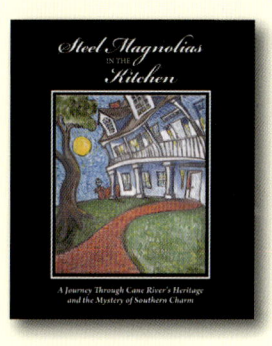

CONTRIBUTING COOKBOOKS

Steel Magnolias in the Kitchen
Service League of Natchitoches, Inc.
P. O. Box 2206 • Natchitoches, LA 71457 • 800-889-7462
s/cookbooks@cp-tel.net • www.service-league.net

Extraordinary women from along Louisiana's Cane River come alive in these 284 pages. With 895 classic and modern recipes influenced by French, Spanish, Native American, and Creole cultures, this cookbook will tantalize any appetite.

    $29.95   Retail price   Paypal, MC, VISA
     $2.70   Tax for LA residents
     $8.00   Postage and handling

Make check payable to Service League of Natchitoches
ISBN 978-0-9823893-0-0

A Streetcar Named Delicious
by Todd-Michael St. Pierre
www.LouisianaBoy.com

Why depend on the kindness of strangers, when you can cook New Orleans world-famous cuisine yourself? It's easy, Blanche! Timeless favorites like The Dubois Family Beignets and Burgundy Street Oyster Dressing! There's even a recipe for Stella and Stanley's Crawfish Étouffée! Need I say more? Bon Appetit, Y'all!

www.amazon.com/144212864X
   $12.95

Taste of Tremé
by Todd-Michael St. Pierre
www.LouisianaBoy.com

In Tremé, jazz is always in the air and something soulful is simmering on the stove . . . favorites like: Muffulettas, Chargrilled Oysters, Crawfish and Corn Beignets, Chicken and Andouille Gumbo, Creole Tomato Shrimp Jambalaya, Bananas Foster.

Includes fascinating cultural facts about the music, architecture and dining that make up Tremé. Let your taste buds tap to the beat of a big brass band.

www.amazon.com/161243097X
   $21.95

Tell Me More
Junior League of Lafayette
504 Richland Avenue • Lafayette, LA 70508
337-988-2739 • Fax 337-988-1079
JLL@juniorleagueoflafayette.com • www.juniorleagueoflafayette.com

With over 65,000 copies sold, *Tell Me More* is bursting with recipes and stories chronicling Cajun ways, past and present. Featuring art by the late Floyd Sonnier, the book won the 1994 Southern Regional Tabasco Community Cookbook Award.

    $18.95   Retail price
     $1.52   Tax LA residents
     $8.00   Postage and handling

Make check payable to Junior League of Lafayette
ISBN 13-988-0-935032-25-3

CONTRIBUTING COOKBOOKS

Thinner You with a Vampire
by Todd-Michael St. Pierre
www.LouisianaBoy.com
NEW ORLEANS IRRESISTIBLE CUISINE ON A DIET! Try the Jugular Juice, or O Negative Sangria! Enjoy Sookie's Cookies, Velvet La Rouge Cake, Fangtasia's Shrimp Creole, Bite Me Bread Pudding, No Pulse-No Problem Remoulade Sauce, and Bloodsucking Bloke's Blue Salad! Big Easy taste with fewer calories and less cholesterol!
www.amazon.com/1461122368
  $12.95

Variations & Improvisations
KEDM Public Radio
225 Stubbs Hall • University of Louisiana Monroe
Monroe, LA 71209 • 318-342-5556 • fax318-342-5570
www.kedm.org • Strode@ulm.edu
Variations and Improvisations is a cookbook like no other. In addition to over 400 fabulous recipes, this cookbook features literary quotations, wine suggestions, and music to cook or eat by.

  $19.95   Retail price
     $.80   Tax LA residents
   $3.50   Postage and handling
Make check payable to Friends of KEDM
ISBN 0-9673350-0-0

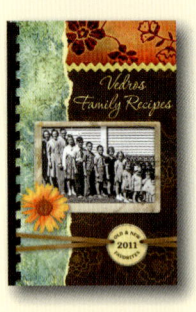

Vedros Family Recipes
by The Vedros Family
22157 Fem Street • Ponchatoula, LA 70454
rjlaurent@att.net
These 233 recipes were submitted by five generations of the Vedros family from all over the United States. The book is dedicated to deceased members.

  $10.00   Retail price
   $3.00   Postage and handling
Make check payable to Carolyn Vedros Laurent

Who Dat Cookin'
by Todd-Michael St. Pierre
www.LouisianaBoy.com
Score a touchdown with some famous and flavorful Bayou State favorites! From top-notch tailgating to celebratory cocktails! From game-night appetizers to Super Bowl party-pleasers! WHO DAT say dey gonna out-cook Louisiana? A cookbook with serious Yattitude! YEAH, YOU RIGHT!
www.amazon.com/1453845569
  $14.95   Retail price

Index of Recipes

A

Appetizers: *See also Dips*
  Alligator Balls 32
  Artichoke Toast 32
  Atchafalaya Cheese Straws 23
  Baked Brie 21
  Baked Cheese Petits Fours 24
  Cajun Hot Bites 27
  Cajun Stuffed Mushrooms 30
  Checkerboard Cheese 22
  Chocolate Chip Cream Cheese Ball 17
  Crawfish Saganaki 26
  Jalapeño Cheese Squares 20
  Lirette's Pesto 24
  Marlyn's Trash 33
  Muffuletta Croquettes 28
  Onion Soufflé 18
  Shrimp-Boursin Mousse Canapés with Fresh Thyme 25
  Spicy Catfish Puffs 31
  Spinach Cheese Squares 20
  Sweet Potato Cheese Pâté 18
Artichokes:
  Artichoke Toast 32
  Cream of Artichoke Soup with Bleu Cheese 61
  Green Beans and Artichokes Romano 90
  Shrimp and Grits with Artichokes 172
Asparagus:
  Make-Ahead Chicken Casserole 129
  Pasta Primavera 113

B

Bacon:
  Hot Bacon and Swiss Dip 13
  Old-Fashioned Wilted Salad 87
  Yellow Squash and Bacon 98
Bananas Foster Soufflé with Vanilla Ice Cream 247
Beans:
  Chicken and Black Bean Enchiladas 138
  Creole String Beans 90
  Green Beans and Artichokes Romano 90
  Red Bean Gumbo 70
Beef: *See also Meatloaf*
  Baked Cabbage Jambalaya 120
  Beef Bourguignon 144
  Beef Stew Crockpot 73
  Beef Vegetable Soup 64
  Cajun Pot Roast 150
  Deluxe Weekend Dish 142
  Easy Beef Brisket 147
  Eggplant Ritz Casserole 92
  Grilled Beef Tenderloin with Mushroom Stuffing 148
  Lasagna 115
  Leftover Roast Hash 154
  Meat-and-Spinach-Stuffed Pasta Shells 112
  Meatball Fricassée 154
  Mirliton Casserole 95
  New Orleans Grillades 149
  New Orleans Roast Beef 152
  Roast Beef Po-Boys 153
  Slow Cooker Brisket 147
  Smothered Steak 145
  Stuffed Bell Peppers 99
Beignets:
  Creole Beignets 46
  Faubourg Coconut Shrimp Beignets with Pepper Jelly Sauce 48
  Hot Beignets 47
Beverages:
  Almond Tea 10
  Café au Lait Punch 12
  Coffee KEDM 12
  Minted Ice Tea 10
  New Orleans Milk Punch 11
  NOLA Hot Buttered Rum 11
  Red Rooster 11
Biscuits:
  Captain John's Cathead Biscuits 43
  Creole Chicken & Biscuits 136
  Ollie's Biscuits 45
  Sausage Biscuit Bites 45
  Sweet Potato Biscuits 46
Bread: *See also Beignets, Biscuits, Pudding, Cornbread, Dressing, Sandwiches*
  Artichoke Toast 32
  Baked Cheese Petits Fours 24
  Confetti French Bread 40
  French Bread 40
  Hushpuppies 180
  Lost Bread 52
  Muffuletta 122
  Muffuletta Croquettes 28
  Pain Perdu 52
  Stuffed French Toast 52

INDEX OF RECIPES

Bread Pudding:
   Booyee 198
   Diet Bread Pudding 239
   Kind Stranger's Bread Pudding with
      Whiskey Sauce 237
   Pineapple Bread Pudding 238
   White Chocolate Blueberry Bread
      Pudding 240

Breakfast:
   Aunt Pitty Pat's Blintz Casserole 50
   Breakfast Rice 49
   Magnificent Morning Breakfast Pie 53
   Olive It! Muffuletta Frittata 42

Broccoli Soup 64

Brownies and Bar Cookies:
   Big Booty Brownies 220
   Bodacious Brownies 220
   Chocolate Graham Cracker Bars 217
   "Everything But the Kitchen Sink"
      Bar Cookies 220
   Lisa's Peanut Butter Squares 219
   Pecan Pie Surprise Bars 217
   Pumpkin Bars 218
   Seven Layer Cookies 219

c

Cakes: *See also Cheesecakes*
   Gahto ah la Booyee 198
   Grandmother Garrison's 14-Carat
      Cake 204
   Joie de Vivre Heavenly Hash Cake 196
   King Cake 193
   King Cake with Cream Cinnamon
      Filling 192
   Millionaire Cake 205
   Moist and Yummy Yam Cake 206
   Pineapple-Coconut Cake 201
   Praline Cake 194
   Pudding Cake 198
   Pumpkin Upside-Down Cake 200
   Regal Almond Cake 202
   Sour Cream Somersault Cake 199
   Tortuga Rum Cake 195

Candies:
   Almond Bark Candy 222
   Creole Pralines 223
   Mom's Peanut Butter Fudge 224
   Strawberry Fudge Balls 222
   Toasted Pecan Clusters 224

Carrots:
   Beef Vegetable Soup 64
   Grandmother Garrison's 14-Carat
      Cake 204

Catfish:
   Baked Catfish à la Melissa 181
   Catfish Courtbouillon 182
   Southern-Fried Catfish and
      Hushpuppies 180
   Spicy Catfish Puffs 31

Cheesecakes:
   Cheesecake 208
   Turtle Cheesecake Des Amis 209

Chicken:
   Bourbon Chicken 130
   Cajun Hot Bites 27
   Chicken and Black Bean
      Enchiladas 138
   Chicken and Sausage Gumbo 68
   Chicken and Waffle Sandwiches 135
   Chicken Cakes with Sherry Sauce 134
   Chicken Fricassée 128
   Chicken Sauce Piquante 132
   Chicken Tetrazzini 108
   Crawfish-Stuffed Chicken Breasts 133
   Creole Chicken & Biscuits 136
   Curried Chicken and Dried Cherry
      Salad 81
   Dirty Rice Dressing 117
   Make-Ahead Chicken Casserole 129
   Mitty Mitty's Chicken Breast 129
   Oriental Chicken Salad 81
   Paulie's Poulet Dijonaise 126
   Smothered Chicken 130

Chili, Deer 73

Chocolate: *See also White Chocolate*
   Big Booty Brownies 220
   Bodacious Brownies 220
   Chocolate Chip Cream Cheese Ball 17
   Chocolate Frosting 214
   Chocolate Graham Cracker Bars 217
   Coffee KEDM 12
   "Everything But the Kitchen Sink"
      Bar Cookies 220
   Joie de Vivre Heavenly Hash Cake 196
   Lisa's Peanut Butter Squares 219
   Millionaire Cake 205
   Seven Layer Cookies 219
   Strawberry Fudge Balls 222
   Toasted Pecan Clusters 224
   Turtle Cheesecake Des Amis 209
   White Chocolate Blueberry Bread
      Pudding 240
   White Chocolate/Macadamia Crème
      Brûlée 241

INDEX OF RECIPES

Cobblers:
    Blackberry Cobbler 234
    Champion Cobbler at Ruston Peach Festival 235

Coconut:
    Coconut Macaroons 212
    Faubourg Coconut Shrimp Beignets with Pepper Jelly Sauce 48
    Pineapple-Coconut Cake 201

Cookies: *See also Brownies and Bar Cookies*
    Gamoo's Almond Iced Tea Cakes 213
    McKenzie's Turtle Cookies 214
    Robert's Sand Tarts 216
    Shortbread Cookies 216
    Toffee Crunch Cookies 212

Corn:
    Corn Casserole 103
    Crawfish and Corn Soup 58
    Fresh Corn Soup 56
    Jalapeño Corn Soufflé 103
    Shoepeg Corn Salad 77
    Shrimp and Corn Soup 56

Cornbread:
    Crawfish Cornbread 36
    Trosclair's Cornbread and Andouille Sausage Stuffing 38
    Ursula's Cornbread Dressing 37

Crab:
    Crabmeat au Gratin 168
    Crabmeat Cheesecake 164
    Cup O' Crab Gumbo 71
    Louisiana Crab Cakes with Sauce Ravigotte 166
    She-Crab Soup 60
    Spinach & Lump Crabmeat Quiche 121

Crawfish:
    Angel Hair Pasta with Crawfish Tails 110
    Breaux Bridge Crawfish Stew 72
    Crawfish and Corn Soup 58
    Crawfish Cornbread 36
    Crawfish Rice 117
    Crawfish Saganaki 26
    Crawfish-Stuffed Chicken Breasts 133
    Easy Crawfish Casserole 178
    Oliver's Crawfish Boulettes 179
    Stella and Stanley's Crawfish Etouffée 178
    Stuffed Crawfish Heads 59
    Vedros Family's Crawfish Bisque 59

Cucumber Dip, Cool As a 15

D

Deer:
    Deer Chili 73
    Deer Roast 152

Desserts: *See also specific dessert*
    Bouillie 245
    Old-Fashioned Custard 245
    Strawberry 'n Cream Shortcakes 242
    White Chocolate/Macadamia Crème Brûlée 241

Dips:
    Andouille Cheese Dip 13
    Cool As a Cucumber Dip 15
    Holiday Pecan Dip 17
    Hot Bacon and Swiss Dip 13
    Hot Spinach and Oyster Dip 14
    Rosalie's Tangy Shrimp Dip 16
    Shrimp Dip 15

Dressing:
    All Saints Day Oyster Dressing 39
    Dirty Rice Dressing 117
    Trosclair's Cornbread and Andouille Sausage Stuffing 38
    Ursula's Cornbread Dressing 37

E

Eggplant:
    Eggplant Casserole 93
    Eggplant Ritz Casserole 92

F

Fish: *See also Catfish, Trout*
    Andouille-Crusted Fish with Cayenne Butter Sauce 184
    Barbecued Redfish 185

Fruit: *See also specific fruit*
    Blackberry Cobbler 234
    Curried Chicken and Dried Cherry Salad 81
    Grape Salad 77
    Raspberry-Peach Trifle 244
    White Chocolate Blueberry Bread Pudding 240

G

Grits:
    Cheese Grits 172, 176
    Garlic Cheese Grits 149
    Sautéed Shrimp and Peppers over Cheese Grits 176
    Shrimp and Grits with Artichokes 172

INDEX OF RECIPES

Gumbo:
  Basic Roux 65
  Chicken and Sausage Gumbo 68
  Cup O' Crab Gumbo 71
  Red Bean Gumbo 70
  Tail of the Turkey Gumbo 67

H
Ham, Okra, and Tomatoes 99

I
Ice Cream:
  Bananas Foster Soufflé with Vanilla Ice Cream 247
  Café au Lait Punch 12
  Cajun Amaretto Freeze 245

J
Jambalaya:
  Baked Cabbage Jambalaya 120
  C'est Bon Jambalaya 118
  Pork Chop Jambalaya 118

L
Lasagna:
  Lasagna 115
  Shrimp and Scallop Lasagna 114
Lemon Sherbet 246

M
Meatloaf:
  Italian Meatloaf 143
  Mitty Mitty's Meatloaf 143
Mirlitons:
  Mirliton Casserole 95
  Shrimp-Stuffed Mirliton 94
Muffuletta:
  Muffuletta 122
  Muffuletta Croquettes 28
  Olive It! Muffuletta Frittata 42
Mushrooms:
  Cajun Stuffed Mushrooms 30
  Grilled Beef Tenderloin with Mushroom Stuffing 148

N
Nuts: *See also Pecans*
  Marlyn's Trash 33
  Sugared Almonds 78

O
Okra:
  Chicken and Sausage Gumbo 68
  Cup O' Crab Gumbo 71
  Fried Okra 102
  Ham, Okra, and Tomatoes 99
  Pickled Okra 102
Olives:
  Olive It! Muffuletta Frittata 42
  Olive Salad 122
Onions:
  Onion Soufflé 18
  Orange and Onion Salad 80
Orange:
  Duck Breasts with Wine and Marmalade Sauce 139
  Orange and Onion Salad 80
Oysters:
  All Saints Day Oyster Dressing 39
  Hot Spinach and Oyster Dip 14
  Oyster Po-Boys 186
  Oysters Larose 187

P
Pasta: *See also Lasagna*
  Angel Hair Pasta with Crawfish Tails 110
  Bow Tie Pasta Salad with Pesto 86
  Chicken Tetrazzini 108
  Meat-and-Spinach-Stuffed Pasta Shells 112
  Orzo and Shrimp Salad 85
  Pasta Primavera 113
  Peggy's Shrimp Fettuccine 109
  Shrimp and Pasta Boscolli Salad 82
  Southern Baked Macaroni and Cheese 116
Peaches:
  Champion Cobbler at Ruston Peach Festival 235
  Raspberry-Peach Trifle 244
Peanut Butter:
  "Everything But the Kitchen Sink" Bar Cookies 220
  Fluffy Peanut Butter Pie 232
  Lisa's Peanut Butter Squares 219
  Mom's Peanut Butter Fudge 224
Pecans: *See also Praline*
  Holiday Pecan Dip 17
  McKenzie's Turtle Cookies 214
  Mystery Pecan Pie 230
  Pecan Pie Surprise Bars 217
  Southern Pecan Pie 230
  Squash Pecan 98
  Toasted Pecan Clusters 224
  Trout Pecan 183
  Yam Pecan Pie in Gingersnap Crust 229

INDEX OF RECIPES

Pesto:
  Bow Tie Pasta Salad with Pesto 86
  Lirette's Pesto 24
  Shrimp and Pasta Boscolli Salad 82
Pies:
  Fluffy Peanut Butter Pie 232
  Grand Finale Pie 233
  Magnificent Morning Breakfast Pie 53
  Magnolia (Buttermilk) Pie 232
  Mystery Pecan Pie 230
  Southern Pecan Pie 230
  Strawberry Pie 234
  Sweet Potato Pie 228
  Yam Pecan Pie in Gingersnap Crust 229
Pineapple:
  Pineapple Bread Pudding 238
  Pineapple-Coconut Cake 201
Pork: *See also Bacon, Ham, Sausage*
  Alma's Pork Tenderloin in a Bed 157
  Barbecued Spareribs 156
  Breaded Pork Chops 161
  Meatball Fricassée 154
  Pork Chop Jambalaya 118
  Pork Medallions in Creole Mustard Sauce 158
  Pork Roast 155
  Stuffed Pork Chops 160
  Ted's Cochon de Lait 161
Potatoes: *See also Sweet Potatoes*
  Beef Vegetable Soup 64
  Ollie's Hot Potato Salad 87
Poultry: *See also Chicken, Turkey*
  Duck Breasts with Wine and Marmalade Sauce 139
Praline:
  Creole Pralines 223
  Pat's Pralines 223
  Praline Cake 194
  Praline Icing 194
Pumpkin:
  Pumpkin Bars 218
  Pumpkin Upside-Down Cake 200

R

Rice:
  Baked Cabbage Jambalaya 120
  Beef Vegetable Soup 64
  Breakfast Rice 49
  Catfish Courtbouillon 182
  C'est Bon Jambalaya 118
  Chicken and Sausage Gumbo 68
  Chicken Sauce Piquante 132
  Crawfish Rice 117
  Cup O' Crab Gumbo 71
  Dirty Rice Dressing 117
  Easy Crawfish Casserole 178
  Pork Chop Jambalaya 118
  Red Bean Gumbo 70
  Rice–Fluff Method 116
  Stuffed Bell Peppers 99
  Tail of the Turkey Gumbo, The 67
Roux, Basic 65

S

Salads:
  Bow Tie Pasta Salad with Pesto 86
  Curried Chicken and Dried Cherry Salad 81
  Eunice and Steve's Strawberry Festival Salad 78
  Grape Salad 77
  Green Shrimp Salad 82
  Mixed Greens with Green Goddess Dressing 76
  Old-Fashioned Wilted Salad 87
  Ollie's Hot Potato Salad 87
  Orange and Onion Salad 80
  Oriental Chicken Salad 81
  Orzo and Shrimp Salad 85
  Shoepeg Corn Salad 77
  Shrimp and Pasta Boscolli Salad 82
Sandwiches:
  Chicken and Waffle Sandwiches 135
  Muffuletta 122
  Oyster Po-Boys 186
  Roast Beef Po-Boys 153
Sausage:
  Andouille Cheese Dip 13
  Andouille-Crusted Fish with Cayenne Butter Sauce 184
  Baked Cabbage Jambalaya 120
  Breakfast Rice 49
  Cajun Stuffed Mushrooms 30
  C'est Bon Jambalaya 118
  Chicken and Sausage Gumbo 68
  Chicken Sauce Piquante 132
  Red Bean Gumbo 70
  Sausage Biscuit Bites 45
  Trosclair's Cornbread and Andouille Sausage Stuffing 38
Seafood: *See Crab, Crawfish, Fish, Oysters, Shrimp*
Sherbet:
  Lemon Sherbet 246
  Louisiana Strawberry Sherbet 246

INDEX OF RECIPES

Shrimp:
Barbecue Shrimp 170
Dot's New Year's Eve Shrimp 173
Faubourg Coconut Shrimp Beignets with Pepper Jelly Sauce 48
Green Shrimp Salad 82
Grilled Garlic Shrimp Fajitas 175
Magnificent Morning Breakfast Pie 53
Orzo and Shrimp Salad 85
Peggy's Shrimp Fettuccine 109
Perfect Boiled Shrimp 169
Ron's Bar-B-Que Shrimp 171
Rosalie's Tangy Shrimp Dip 16
Sautéed Shrimp and Peppers over Cheese Grits 176
Shrimp and Corn Soup 56
Shrimp and Grits with Artichokes 172
Shrimp and Pasta Boscolli Salad 82
Shrimp and Scallop Lasagna 114
Shrimp-Boursin Mousse Canapés with Fresh Thyme 25
Shrimp Dip 15
Shrimp Luncheon Dish 168
Shrimp Rémoulade 171
Shrimp-Stuffed Mirliton 94
Soups: *See also Chili, Gumbo, Stews*
Beef Vegetable Soup 64
Broccoli Soup 64
Crawfish and Corn Soup 58
Cream of Artichoke Soup with Bleu Cheese 61
Fresh Corn Soup 56
She-Crab Soup 60
Shrimp and Corn Soup 56
Turtle Soup 62
Vedros Family's Crawfish Bisque 59
Spinach:
Hot Spinach and Oyster Dip 14
Meat-and-Spinach-Stuffed Pasta Shells 112
Spinach Casserole 105
Spinach Cheese Squares 20
Spinach & Lump Crabmeat Quiche 121
Spinach Madeleine 104

Squash: *See also Mirlitons*
Aline's Squash Casserole 97
Angel Hair Pasta with Crawfish Tails 110
Squash Fritters 97
Squash Pecan 98
Yellow Squash and Bacon 98
Stews:
Beef Stew Crockpot 73
Breaux Bridge Crawfish Stew 72
Strawberries:
Eunice and Steve's Strawberry Festival Salad 78
Louisiana Strawberry Sherbet 246
Strawberry Fudge Balls 222
Strawberry 'n Cream Shortcakes 242
Strawberry Pie 234
Stuffing: *See Dressing*
Sweet Potatoes:
Mardi Gras Sweet Potatoes 100
Moist and Yummy Yam Cake 206
Sweet Potato Biscuits 46
Sweet Potato Cheese Pâté 18
Sweet Potato Pie 228
Yam Pecan Pie in Gingersnap Crust 229

T

Tomatoes, Ham, Okra, and 99
Trout:
Trout Meunière 183
Trout Pecan 183
Turkey:
Meat-and-Spinach-Stuffed Pasta Shells 112
The Tail of the Turkey Gumbo 67
Turnips, Nonnon Yeagley's 105
Turtle Soup 62

V

Vegetables: *See also specific vegetable*
Baked Cabbage Jambalaya 120
Nonnon Yeagley's Turnips 105

Y

Yams: *See Sweet Potatoes*

The Quest for the Best

The story of how two ladies,
Gwen McKee and Barbara Moseley,
went out to find America's best recipes,
and in the process, created the
BEST OF THE BEST STATE COOKBOOK SERIES

The process began in the early 1980s. After being involved in the development and publication of numerous cookbooks, Gwen McKee and Barbara Moseley were frequently asked what were their favorite cookbooks and recipes. From their own cookbook collections, they had highlighted recipes they thought were special. From this, the idea was born, "Why not collect all those highlighted recipes from different cookbooks into one cookbook?" They quickly realized that this ambitious undertaking could best be accomplished on a state-by-state basis. The BEST OF THE BEST STATE COOKBOOK SERIES had begun!

From the very beginning, Gwen and Barbara established goals. They would search for cookbooks that showcased recipes that captured local flavor. They would insist on kitchen-friendly recipes that anybody anywhere could cook and enjoy. They would make the books user friendly, and edit for utmost clarity.

The criteria for including a recipe was that it have three distinguishing features: *great taste, great taste,* and *great taste!*

THE QUEST FOR THE BEST

In 1982, *Best of the Best from Mississippi: Selected Recipes from Mississippi's Favorite Cookbooks* was published. It was an immediate success and prompted going next door to Louisiana, Gwen's native state. The Louisiana edition, published in 1984, has been reprinted twenty-five times and is the best seller of all the states.

The two editors then took on Texas—four trips were required just to cover the territory! But cover it they did, selecting ninety-four cookbooks from all over Texas to contribute their most popular recipes to *Best of the Best from Texas Cookbook*. Texas is still one of the best-selling cookbooks in the Series.

With three states under their belts, Gwen and Barbara now had a mission and a motto: *Preserving America's Food Heritage*. The editors committed themselves to tracking down those classic family recipes that have been refined and perfected over generations. It had become an interesting, sometimes fascinating, often exhilarating process . . . and they knew they were hooked on wanting to explore each state and taste their cuisine.

Talking to townfolk was always fun and informative. Gwen and Barbara would usually be directed to someone else if that person couldn't help them— "Go see Sarah at the drugstore; she has lots of cookbooks."

Over the next four years, Gwen and Barbara concentrated on those neighboring states that were convenient to get to. In the early days before the Internet, their normal method of finding local cookbooks was to travel throughout the state. Gwen usually did the driving, and Barbara—with map in lap—the navigating. They stopped at bookstores, gift and kitchen shops, chamber of commerce offices, tourist bureaus, and any other place that might offer the possibility of discovering a popular local cookbook. Without fail, in every state, the best thing was the people they met and the information they so proudly shared.

. . . We're covering the South! 1986–1990

Throughout the '90s, Gwen and Barbara continued to search with renewed dedication to finding and preserving those little recipe gems that might be tucked away in a modest church cookbook published in a small community. Junior League cookbooks, because they are developed by local members and contain recipes from their city and community, have been a particularly valuable contributor to the series.

In addition to the over 400 wonderful recipes that each BEST cookbook con-

THE QUEST FOR THE BEST

Tasting the local fare is one of the best bonuses of a trip through any region in search of great recipes. In Hurricane Mills, Tennessee, Gwen and Barbara visited Loretta Lynn's Kitchen and found tasty local vittles and recipes.

each state. These are fun and informative, and help to convey the unique features of the state.

Each cookbook contains photographs and illustrations that capture some of the visual highlights of each state.

In the late '90s, the editors finished the Midwest and set their sites on the "big" states of the West. These states with their vast areas provided major challenges to locating those local cookbooks that might contain that special recipe.

In the Southwest, the *Arizona* and *New Mexico* editions became instant favorites. The popularity of the Mexican influence on the cuisine of this region, abundantly represented in these

tains, Gwen and Barbara have added other features that make the cookbooks more useful and enjoyable.

"Editor's Extras" have occasionally been added to the original recipes to ensure complete understanding, suggest an alternate ingredient if the original was not available, or offer an embellishment or variation the editors particularly liked and wanted to share.

Sprinkled throughout each BEST cookbook is a series of short "quips" that provide interesting facts about

. . . We're halfway there!
1991–1996

Hot Cheese in a Jar

2 pounds Velveeta cheese, melted
1 medium onion, grated
1 (5.33-ounce) can evaporated milk
1 pint Miracle Whip salad dressing
1 (8-ounce) can seeded, deveined
   jalapeño peppers, chopped fine
   (cut off stems)

Melt cheese in top of double boiler. Add onion, milk, Miracle Whip, and peppers to melted cheese, and mix well. Pour into 6 (8-ounce) jelly jars. Cool, screw on caps, and refrigerate.

This recipe was often made before road trips and a supply taken along. Many times the editors relied on this treat to make it through some long days of travel. The recipe was contributed by Cowtown Cuisine *and is included in* Best of the Best from Texas Cookbook *(page 23). It is truly a classic.*

THE QUEST FOR THE BEST

cookbooks, surely contributed to their appeal.

The *California* edition, like *Texas* and *New England*, required more pages to accommodate the large number of contributing cookbooks. The great variety of recipes selected makes these cookbooks particularly interesting and enjoyable to use.

Gwen and Barbara knew from the beginning that they did not want the BEST OF THE BEST cookbooks to be hardbound, oversized, expensive books that would stay on the coffee table and not be allowed to go in the kitchen. They preferred a ringbound format that would allow for convenient lay-flat usage.

In 2000, after nearly two decades, Gwen and Barbara were still going strong. They had completed thirty-six states, had met many delightful people, had seen a great portion of their beautiful country, and were even more committed to their goal of **Preserving America's Food Heritage.**

... We're almost there!
1997–2000

Seattle's Pike Place Market was an exciting experience. The great variety of vegetables, fruits, and fish on display challenged the editors to find recipes that could fully exploit such an abundance of fresh ingredients. They feel they have met the challenge with Best of the Best from Washington Cookbook.

Gwen and Barbara greeted the new millennium with continued enthusiasm and dedication. They completed the remaining five states in the east, three of which (New Jersey, Delaware, and Maryland) were combined in the *Best of the Best from Mid-Atlantic* edition.

Now it was time to gear-up for the final push. They knew they would be a long way from home as they pursued recipes in the Northwest, Alaska, and Hawaii.

Oregon's fruit-growing district, "The Fruit Loop," offered many fresh fruit treats that inspired recipes like Boysenberry Swirl Cheesecake with Hazelnut Crust (*Best of the Best from Oregon Cookbook*, page 212).

The state fair in Palmer, Alaska, was another unique occasion to taste some local fare. The exhibit at the fair contained remarkable blue-ribbon winning fruits and vegetables.

THE QUEST FOR THE BEST

In beautiful Hawaii, the editors encountered many helpful people, particularly Faith in Kauai who allowed the editors to review her own extensive cookbook collection, many of which were of a vintage nature. As with other states, the cookbook distributors were most helpful in bringing many local cookbooks to the attention of the editors. This was particularly true with Booklines in Hawaii and Todd Communications in Alaska.

Utah and Nevada, the final two states, offered an opportunity for the editors to experience not only the tasteful cuisine but also the unique beauty of the desert, quite different from their lush, green, southern landscapes.

When the final states were completed in 2005, and copies of *Best of the Best from Utah* and *Best of the Best from Nevada* cookbooks arrived from the printer, there was a great celebration at the Quail Ridge Press offices.

Now that the SERIES has been completed, what next? Gwen and Barbara, both grandmothers many times over, are not ready to retire. "There are still cookbooks to be discovered and tasteful recipes to be preserved," says Barbara, ". . . we might just start over."

"Regardless of what we do in the future," Gwen adds, "we set out to collect, and celebrate the food of America on a state-by-state basis, and that mission has been accomplished."

We did it!

On the road again . . .

Gwen and Barbara have not retired, but have continued their pursuit of those treasured recipes that are hidden away in locally produced cookbooks. They have published a second edition in Texas, second and third editions in Louisiana and Virginia, and revised editions in twelve other states. With the publication of revised full-color editions for Alaska, Virginia, and Louisiana, they have entered a new era. They continue their search for the most popular recipes from selected cookbooks within a given state. But now they enhance the presentation with full-color food photographs, adding additional material that captures the unique history and culture of each state, which is a popular feature.

The following page offers a special discount offer for anyone who may wish to collect copies of the BEST OF THE BEST STATE COOKBOOK SERIES.

Special Collect the Series Discount!
BEST OF THE BEST STATE COOKBOOK SERIES

Over 3.5 million copies sold! Cookbook collectors love this series! The BEST OF THE BEST STATE COOKBOOKS, covering all 50 states, contain the most popular local and regional recipes collected from the leading cookbooks from all over the United States.

To assist individuals who have purchased copies of the BEST OF THE BEST STATE COOKBOOKS and wish to collect the entire series, we are offering a special **Collect the Series Discount.** You get:

"Come join us."

- 25% discount off the retail price per copy: $16.95 minus 25% = $12.70; *Alaska* and *Virginia*: $17.95 minus 25% = $13.45; *Louisiana III*: $18.95 minus 25% = $14.20

- With a single order of five copies, you receive a sixth copy free. A single order of ten cookbooks gets two free copies, etc.

- Only $5.00 shipping for any number of books ordered (within contiguous United States).

- Order the entire 42-book series* for $395.00 plus $25.00 shipping. This represents a 45% discount off the retail price.
   (*Some of the cookbooks cover multiple states.)

To order by credit card, call toll-free **1-800-343-1583**, or use the form below. Be sure to mention the special **Collect the Series** discount. Visit **www.quailridge.com**, for a complete listing of all our cookbooks.

Order Form

Send check, money order, or credit card info to:
QUAIL RIDGE PRESS • P. O. Box 123 • Brandon, MS 39043

Name _____

Address _____

City _____

State/Zip _____

Phone # _____

Email _____
❏ Check enclosed
Charge to: ❏ Visa   ❏ MC   ❏ AmEx   ❏ Disc

Card # _____

Expiration Date_____

Signature _____

Qty.	Title of Book (or State) (or Set)	Total
	Subtotal	
Mississippi residents add 7% sales tax	
Postage (any number of books)	+$5.00
Total	

QUAIL RIDGE PRESS
P. O. Box 123 • Brandon, MS 39043 • 1-800-343-1583
info@quailridge.com • www.quailridge.com
www.facebook.com/cookbookladies